The School Practitioner's Concise Companion to Mental Health

The School Practitioner's Concise Companion to Mental Health

Edited by

Cynthia Franklin
Mary Beth Harris
Paula Allen-Meares

OXFORD
UNIVERSITY PRESS

2008

OXFORD
UNIVERSITY PRESS

Oxford University Press, Inc., publishes works that further
Oxford University's objective of excellence
in research, scholarship, and education.

Oxford New York
Auckland Cape Town Dar es Salaam Hong Kong Karachi
Kuala Lumpur Madrid Melbourne Mexico City Nairobi
New Delhi Shanghai Taipei Toronto

With offices in
Argentina Austria Brazil Chile Czech Republic France Greece
Guatemala Hungary Italy Japan Poland Portugal Singapore
South Korea Switzerland Thailand Turkey Ukraine Vietnam

Copyright © 2008 by Oxford University Press, Inc.

Published by Oxford University Press, Inc.
198 Madison Avenue, New York, New York 10016

www.oup.com

Oxford is a registered trademark of Oxford University Press

Library of Congress Cataloging-in-Publication Data

The school practitioner's concise companion to mental health / edited by
Cynthia Franklin, Mary Beth Harris, and Paula Allen-Meares.
p. cm.
Includes bibliographical references and index.
ISBN 978-0-19-537058-4
1. School children—Mental health services.   2. Students—Mental health services.
3. School children—Mental health.   4. Crisis intervention (Mental health services)
5. School health services. I. Franklin, Cynthia. II. Harris, Mary Beth.
III. Allen-Meares, Paula, 1948-
RC451.4.S7S36 2009
371.7'13—dc22   2008018233

Preface

School-based practitioners are frequently called upon to address mental health problems in children and adolescents. Many school systems in our society have become the de facto institution for mental health treatment. This mental health role of schools is especially apparent for students from low income and ethnic minority backgrounds that may lack access to other services and resources from the private sector. We currently live in a society where school-based professionals are confronted with students who have serious mental health issues and the need for effective practice approaches is growing. As issues such as autism, bipolar disorder, and anxiety disorders are frequently encountered and appear to be on the rise, it raises the awareness of schools that additional resources for mental health are needed but are too often overlooked. Effective practices are especially needed to assist vulnerable and high-risk populations of students that may be predisposed to mental health–related problems through both their genetic history and social experiences. Practitioners are asking, "What are the nuts and bolts of research-based information for addressing various mental health challenges?" *The School Practitioner's Concise Companion to Mental Health* is a book designed to provide knowledge on timely issues and practices for assisting students with mental health disorders.

Contents of this Book

The School Practitioner's Concise Companion to Mental Health was developed with the practicing school professional in mind. This companion book offers targeted content on how to address the mental health problems of students through identifying promising programs and practices. Contents of this book provide easy-to-read practice information, including, case studies and practice guidelines to use when intervening with students, families, and school systems. This book covers several mental disorders that are in the *Diagnostic and Statistical Manual for Mental Disorders (DSM-TR)* and that may also qualify for special educational services under the condition of "other related health impairment". Individuals with mental disorders are often considered a challenge to educate within school systems. Chapters in this book offer timely reviews of effective interventions for important mental health issues such as conduct and oppositional disorders, attention deficit hyperactivity (ADHD), anxiety disorders (obsessive compulsive disorder and separation anxiety disorder), mood disorders (unipolar and bipolar depression), schizophrenia, autism spectrum disorders, and suicidal ideation and behavior. In addition, chapters cover important interventions for those challenging situations where multiple diagnoses exist, including those cases where substance abuse and one or more mental disorders occur.

Finally, this book summarizes current and potentially effective psychopharmacological interventions for a variety of childhood mental disorders including a discussion of the risks and side effects associated with the use of these medications. To add to the usefulness of the content of this book, each chapter follows a practice-friendly outline that includes the headings: *Getting started; What We Know; What We Can Do; Tools and Practice Examples; and Points to Remember*—thus providing a quick reference guide to the mental health information.

The School Practitioner's Concise Companion to Mental Health is one of four companion books that were created to equip school professionals to effectively take action on social and health issues, and mental health problems that are confronting schools. All four books in this series offer a quick and easy guide to information and solutions for today's pressing school problems. Content for the companion books was developed using chapters from Oxford's popular resource volume, *The School Services Sourcebook*. In contrast to the exhaustive and comprehensive *Sourcebook*, the briefer companion books were designed to provide succinct information for those who want to address a particular topic.

Objectives of the Companion Books

When planning the concise companion books, we had three main objectives in mind. First, our objective was to provide a series of affordable books whose content covered important and timely topics for school-based practitioners. We wanted the companion books to be like a search command on a computer where a quick search using a key word or phrase can selectively lead you to the information you need. Each companion book contains updated knowledge, tools, and resources that can help practitioners to quickly access information to address a specific problem area or concern. The second objective was for these books to communicate evidenced-based knowledge from research to practice and to do so in a way that practitioners could easily consume this knowledge. As editors, we wanted each chapter to be application based, providing practice examples and tools that can be used in day-to-day practice within a school.

A third objective was to create a series of practical books that school practitioners could use daily to guide their practices, prepare their presentations, and to answer questions asked to them by teachers, parents, and administrators. For this reason, each chapter in this concise companion book on mental health is replete with quick reference tables, outlines, practice examples, and Internet resources to consult.

How the Topics Were Selected

There are many important concerns that today's schools face and you may be wondering why we chose to address these particular mental health issues instead of a dozen other problem areas. School professionals who helped us create the timely topics addressed in this companion book provided selected topics. The original chapter topics in this book were identified through feedback from school social workers in six regions of the country. Social workers in California, Georgia, Michigan, New Mexico, Oregon, and Texas communicated with us through an e-mail questionnaire, individual interviews, and focus groups. We asked about the overall challenges of working in a school setting. We asked for the most urgent and frequent problems school social workers and other practitioners encounter with students and families. School practitioners told us, for example, that their practice requires knowledge and skills for a variety of mental health and behavioral problems. A primary aspect of their work is direct services to individuals (school staff as well as students), to groups, and to families. Practitioners further told us that they need information on how to work with school professionals to interpret educational policies and design effective interventions that will positively impact students with mental health disorders.

Acknowledgments

First and foremost we want to thank the Oxford University Press for supporting this work. Our deepest gratitude goes to Joan H. Bossert and Maura Roessner for their help and guidance in developing the companion books. In addition, we are thankful to Dr. Albert Roberts who gave us inspiration and support to develop resource books for practitioners. We would further like to thank all from the team of professionals that worked on *The School Services Sourcebook*—Melissa Wiersema, Tricia Cody, Katy Shepard, and Wes Baker and our editorial board. Finally, we give credit to all the school social workers and school mental health professionals who participated in our survey and all those who informally gave us feedback on what topics to cover.

Cynthia Franklin, PhD
The University of Texas at Austin

Mary Beth Harris, PhD
Central Florida University

Paula Allen-Meares, PhD
The University of Michigan

Contents

Contents

Contributors

Michelle S. Ballan, PhD
Assistant Professor
School of Social Work
Columbia University

Kia J. Bentley, PhD
Professor
School of Social Work
Virginia Commonwealth University/
    University of Pittsburgh

Marilyn Camacho
Department of Child Psychiatry
Columbia University

Kathleen A. Casey
Graduate Student
School of Social Work
University of Texas, Austin

Kathryn S. Collins, PhD
Assistant Professor
School of Social Work
University of Pittsburgh

Jacqueline Corcoran, PhD
Associate Professor
School of Social Work
Virginia Commonwealth University

Diana M. DiNitto, PhD
Cullen Trust Centennial Professor in
    Alcohol Studies and Education and
    Distinguished Teaching Professor
School of Social Work
University of Texas, Austin

Jane Hanvey-Phillips
School of Social Work
University of Texas, Arlington

Karen S. Hoban
Speech Language Pathologist
Cerebral Palsy of New Jersey

Lisa Hunter, PhD
Assistant Professor
Department of Child Psychiatry
Columbia University

Johnny S. Kim
Graduate Student
School of Social Work
University of Texas, Austin

Tammy Linseisen, LCSW, ACSW
Clinical Assistant Professor
School of Social Work
University of Texas, Austin

Courtney J. Lynch, MSSW
Graduate Research Assistant
School of Social Work
University of Texas, Austin

Albert R. Roberts, PhD
Professor of Criminal Justice
Faculty of Arts and Sciences
Rutgers University

David W. Springer, PhD
Associate Dean
School of Social Work
University of Texas, Austin

Susan Stone, JD, MD
President
Susan Stone & Associates
Austin, Texas

Martell Teasley, PhD
College of Social Work
Florida State University

Meghan Tomb
Department of Child Psychiatry
Columbia University

Stephen J. Tripodi, MSSW
Graduate Research Assistant
School of Social Work
University of Texas, Austin

The School Practitioner's Concise Companion
to Mental Health

Effective Interventions for Students With Conduct Disorder

David W. Springer
Courtney J. Lynch

Getting Started

School-aged children and adolescents with externalizing disorders are a challenging, yet rewarding, population to help. Many school-based practitioners, teachers, and administrators may be all too familiar with the behaviors associated with a diagnosis of conduct disorder (CD), such as aggressive behavior toward others, using a weapon, setting fire, cruelty to animals or persons, vandalism, lying, truancy, running away, and theft (American Psychiatric Association, 2000). The *DSM-IV-TR* allows for coding a client with one of two subtypes of CD: childhood-onset type (at least one criterion characteristic occurs prior to age 10) and adolescent-onset type (absence of any criteria prior to age 10). A youth must be engaged in a pattern of behavior over an extended period of time (at least 6 months) that consistently violates the rights of others and societal norms.

According to findings from the Dunedin Multidisciplinary Health Study, the prevalence of adolescent-onset type of CD (24%) is higher than that of childhood-onset type (7%) (Moffitt, Caspi, Dickson, Silva, & Stanton, 1996). This is good news, as the prognosis for childhood-onset type is poorer than it is for adolescent-onset type. While the focus of this chapter is on students with a diagnosis of conduct disorder, there is some indication that disruptive behavior disorders in general are on the rise (Loeber, Farrington, & Waschbusch, 1998) and that the prevalence of school-based conduct disturbance, such as bullying or fighting, is also high.

Part of what makes helping school-aged youth with CD so challenging is the multifaceted nature of their problems. Indeed, students with CD are often viewed by their teachers as experiencing a wide range of additional types of school adjustment difficulties (comorbidity) (Pullis, 1991). Fortunately, in recent years, significant advances in psychosocial treatments have been made to treat children and adolescents with disruptive behavior disorders. Unfortunately, some states operate with policies that exclude conduct-disordered students from eligibility for services in schools. Nevertheless, in keeping with a recent U.S. surgeon general's report (U.S. Department of Health and Human Services,

2001), this chapter is grounded in the assumption that conduct-disordered youth can be helped using innovative and research-based interventions. Some of these evidence-based practices are applied to the following case example of Alex. For purposes here, Rosen and Proctor's (2002) definition of evidence-based practice (EBP) has been adopted, whereby "practitioners will select interventions on the basis of their empirically demonstrated links to the desired outcomes" (p. 743).

What We Know

Classroom-based interventions of conduct problems have not received as much attention as interventions for conduct problems in the home (Fonagy & Kurtz, 2002). Little and Hudson (1998) reviewed classroom interventions, concluding that these interventions are diverse, lack empirical support, and are often not consistent with home-based interventions. Nevertheless, there are some general factors that are associated with lower levels of problem behaviors in schools, including strong positive leadership; high pupil expectations; close monitoring of pupils; good opportunities to engage in school life and take on responsibility; well-functioning incentive, reward, and punishment systems; high levels of parental involvement; an academic emphasis; and a focus on learning (Mortimore, 1995; Reynolds, Sammons, Stoll, Barber, & Hillman, 1996; cited in Fonagy & Kurtz, 2002). All of these factors have an overall positive influence on youth development, learning, and behavior management, and are explored in more detail in subsequent chapters of this book.

What We Can Do

Among the effective interventions for children with conduct problems, two were found to be well-established, according to the Division 12 (Clinical Psychology) Task Force on Promotion and Dissemination of Psychological Procedures (Brestan & Eyberg, 1998). One of these is the Incredible Years: Parents, Teachers, and Children Training series developed by Webster-Stratton and based on a trained leader using videotape modeling to trigger group discussion. Supporting randomized control group studies using the program as a treatment program for parents of children aged 3 to 8 years with conduct problems and as a prevention program for high-risk families include those by Reid, Webster-Stratton, and Baydar (2004); Reid, Webster-Stratton, and Hammond (2003); Spaccarelli, Cotler, and Penman (1992); Webster-Stratton (1984, 1990, 1994, 1998); Webster-Stratton, Kolpacoff, and Hollinsworth (1988); and Webster-Stratton, Reid, and Hammond (2001a). The second well-established approach is parent training programs based on Patterson and Gullion's (1968) manual *Living With Children* (Alexander & Parsons, 1973; Bernal, Klinnert, & Schultz, 1980; Wiltz &

Table 1.1 Well-Established Treatments and Supporting Studies

Best-Supported (Well-Established) Treatments	Supporting Studies
Videotape Modeling Parent Training	Reid, Webster-Stratton, & Hammond (2003); Spaccarelli, Cotler, & Penman (1992); Webster-Stratton (1984, 1990, 1994, 1998); Webster-Stratton, Kolpacoff, & Hollinsworth (1988); Webster-Stratton, Reid, & Hammond (2001b)
Parent Training Based on Living With Children	Alexander & Parsons (1973); Bernal, Klinnert, & Schultz (1980); Wiltz & Patterson (1974)

Patterson, 1974). See Table 1.1 for supporting studies. In short, parent management training (PMT) is the only intervention that is considered well established for the treatment of conduct disorder.

Several treatments for children with conduct problems were found to be probably efficacious, according to the same criteria (Brestan & Eyberg, 1998). Probably efficacious treatments for preschool-age children include parent–child interaction therapy, time-out plus signal seat treatment, delinquency prevention program, and parent training program. Two treatments meeting the probably efficacious criteria designed for use with school-age children are problem-solving skills training (PSST) and anger coping therapy. Finally, four treatments for adolescents with conduct problems were found to be probably efficacious: multisystemic therapy, assertiveness training, rational–emotive therapy, and anger-control training with stress inoculation. See Table 1.2 for supporting studies.

Parent Management Training

PMT is a summary term that describes a therapeutic strategy in which parents are trained to use skills for managing their child's problem behavior (Kazdin, 2004), such as effective command giving, setting up reinforcement systems, and using punishment, including taking away privileges and assigning extra chores. While PMT programs may differ in focus and therapeutic strategies used, they all share the common goal of enhancing parental control over children's behavior (Barkley, 1987; Cavell, 2000; Eyberg, 1988; Forehand & McMahon, 1981; Patterson, Reid, Jones, & Conger, 1975; Webster-Stratton, 1998).

While PMT approaches are typically used for parents with younger children (Serketich & Dumas, 1996), they have been successfully adapted for parents with adolescents (Bank, Marlowe, Reid, Patterson, & Weinrott, 1991;

Table 1.2 Probably Efficacious Treatments and Supporting Studies

Promising (Probably Efficacious) Treatments	Supporting Studies
For Preschool-Aged Children	
Parent–Child Interaction Therapy	Eyberg, Boggs, & Algina (1995); McNeil, Eyberg, Eisenstadt, Newcomb, & Funderburk (1991); Zangwill (1983)
Time-Out Plus Signal Seat Treatment	Hamilton & MacQuiddy (1984)
Delinquency Prevention Program	Tremblay, Pagani-Kurtz, Masse, Vitaro, & Phil (1995); Vitaro & Tremblay (1994)
For School-Aged Children	
Parent Training Program for School-Aged Children	Peed, Roberts, & Forehand (1977); Wells & Egan (1988)
Problem-Solving Skills Training	Kazdin, Esveldt-Dawson, French, & Unis (1987a, 1987b); Kazdin, Siegel, & Bass (1992)
Anger-Coping Therapy	Lochman, Burch, Curry, & Lampron (1984); Lochman, Lampron, Gemmer, & Harris (1989)
For Adolescents	
Multisystemic Therapy	Borduin, Mann, Cone, Henggeler, Fucci, Blaske, & Williams (1995); Henggeler, Melton, & Smith (1992); Henggeler, Rodick, Bourdin, Hanson, Watson, & Urey (1986)
Assertiveness Training	Huey & Rank (1984)
Rational-Emotive Therapy	Block (1978)
Anger Control Training With Stress Inoculation	Feindler, Marriott, & Iwata (1984); Schlichter & Horan (1981)

Source: This table was compiled by synthesizing information from the following: Brestan, E. V., & Eyberg, S. M. (1998). Effective psychosocial treatments of conduct-disordered children and adolescents: 29 years, 82 studies, and 5,272 kids. *Journal of Clinical Child Psychology*, 27(2), 180–189; www.effectivechildtherapy.com.

Barkley, Edwards, Laneri, Fletcher, & Metevia, 2001; Barkley, Guevremont, Anastopoulos, & Fletcher, 1992). The effectiveness of parent training is well documented and, in many respects, impressive. Still, school practitioners should be aware that studies examining the effectiveness of PMT with adolescents are equivocal, with some studies suggesting that adolescents respond less well to

PMT than do their younger counterparts (Dishion & Patterson, 1992; Kazdin, 2002). In much of the outcome research, PMT has been administered to individual families in clinic settings, while group administration has been facilitated primarily through videotaped materials. PMT has been effective in reducing conduct problems and increasing positive parenting behaviors when implemented on a large scale as part of early school intervention (Head Start) programs (Webster-Stratton, 1998; cited in Kazdin, 2004).

Problem-Solving Skills Training
PSST is a cognitively based intervention that has been used to treat aggressive and antisocial youth (Kazdin, 1994). The problem-solving process involves helping clients learn how to produce a variety of potentially effective responses when faced with problem situations (D'Zurilla & Nezu, 2001). Regardless of the specific problem-solving model used, the primary focus is on addressing the thought process to help adolescents address deficiencies and distortions in their approach to interpersonal situations (Kazdin, 1994). A variety of techniques are used, including didactic teaching, practice, modeling, role-playing, feedback, social reinforcement, and therapeutic games (Kronenberger & Meyer, 2001).

The problem-solving approach includes five steps for the practitioner and client to address: (1) defining the problem; (2) brainstorming; (3) evaluating the alternatives; (4) choosing and implementing an alternative; and (5) evaluating the implemented option. Several randomized clinical trials (Type 1 and 2 studies) have demonstrated the effectiveness of PSST with impulsive, aggressive, and conduct-disordered children and adolescents (cf. Baer & Nietzel, 1991; Durlak, Fuhrman, & Lampman, 1991; Kazdin, 2000; cited in Kazdin, 2002). Webster-Stratton and colleagues have developed a small-group treatment program that teaches problem solving, anger management, and social skills for children aged 4 to 8 years, and two randomized control group studies demonstrate the efficacy of this treatment program (Webster-Stratton & Hammond, 1997; Webster-Stratton & Reid, 2003a; Webster-Stratton, Reid, & Hammond, 2001b; Webster-Stratton, Reid, & Hammond, 2004). Problem-solving training produces significant reductions in conduct disorder symptoms and improvements in prosocial behavior among antisocial youth.

Videotape Modeling Parent Program
Webster-Stratton's Videotape Modeling Parent Program, part of the Incredible Years training series, was developed to address parent, family, child, and school risk factors related to childhood conduct disorders. The series is a result of Webster-Stratton's own research, which suggested that comprehensive videotape training methods are effective treatments for early-onset oppositional defiant disorder ODD/CD. The training series includes the Incredible Years Parent Interventions, the Incredible Years Teacher Training Intervention, and the

Incredible Years Child Training Intervention, each of which relies on performance training methods, including videotape modeling, role play, practice activities, and live therapist feedback (Webster-Stratton & Reid, 2003b).

The parent component aims to promote competencies and strengthen families by increasing positive parenting skills, teaching positive discipline strategies, improving problem solving, and increasing family supports and collaboration, to name a few. The teacher component of the training series aims to promote teacher competencies and strengthen home–school relationships by increasing effective classroom management skills, increasing teachers' use of effective discipline and collaboration with parents, and increasing teachers' abilities in the areas of social skills, anger management, and problem solving. The child component aims to strengthen children's social and play skills, increase effective problem-solving strategies and emotional awareness, boost academic success, reduce defiance and aggression, and increase self-esteem.

Webster-Stratton and Reid (2003b) assert that the most proactive and powerful approach to the problem of escalating aggression in young children is to offer their programs using a school-based prevention/early intervention model designed to strengthen *all* children's social and emotional competence. Their reasons are threefold: (1) Offering interventions in schools makes programs more accessible to families and eliminates some of the barriers (i.e., transportation) typically encountered with services offered in traditional mental health settings; (2) offering interventions in schools integrates programs before children's common behavior problems escalate to the point of needing intense clinical intervention; and (3) offering a social and emotional curriculum such as the Dinosaur School program to an entire class is less stigmatizing than a "pullout" group and is more likely to produce sustained effects across settings and time.

For more information about the Incredible Years: Parent, Teacher, and Child Programs, the reader is encouraged to visit the Web site http://www.incredibleyears.com.

Tools and Practice Example

Practice Example

Alex is a 12-year-old White male who was recently arrested at school for stealing several items from his teacher, including a cell phone, $200, a watch, a lighter, and some pocket-sized school supplies. At the time of the arrest, Alex was found to be in possession of marijuana. For these offenses, Alex was placed on probation and ordered to receive mental health counseling for the length of his probation. Alex has always had minor behavior problems, but over the last year his behavior problems have escalated considerably. He lives with his parents and three siblings in a rural farming community. Though it was never confirmed,

Alex's parents suspect that he was responsible for setting a small grass fire in a field behind their home last month. Alex frequently returns home from school with items that do not belong to him, and he engages in physical fights on the school bus at least once a week. Witnesses to these altercations report that Alex instigates fights with no apparent provocation. Although he tests above grade level in most subjects and his IQ falls within the normal range, Alex's teachers report that he is in danger of failing the sixth grade because he does not complete class or homework assignments. When his parents gave a blank check to his sibling for a school project, Alex stole the check, forged his parent's signature, and attempted to cash the check for $50. At home, his siblings complain that Alex steals things from them, bullies them into doing things his way, and breaks their belongings. Last month, he denied carving his initials into the bathroom wall and breaking his bedroom window with a baseball.

Among the various interventions available for use with Alex and his family, his school social worker chose to use interventions that had a solid evidence base in an effort to maximize the possibility for a successful outcome. As the first active phase of treatment, a thorough assessment is the cornerstone of a solid treatment plan (Springer, 2002). During their initial session together, the school social worker conducted a complete biopsychosocial assessment with Alex and his parents, which resulted in the following diagnoses:

Axis I	312.81: Conduct disorder, childhood-onset type, moderate
Axis II	V71.09: No diagnosis
Axis III	None
Axis IV	V61.8: Sibling relational problem
	V62.3: Academic problem
	V61.20: Parent–child relational problem
	Involvement with juvenile justice system
Axis V	GAF = 45

In light of Alex's diagnosis, his age (12 years), the evidence supporting the use of PMT and PSST as probably efficacious approaches, and the availability of Alex's parents to participate in his treatment, the school social worker chose to utilize PMT and PSST with Alex and his parents. Using a combination of PMT and PSST together tends to be more effective than using either treatment alone (Kazdin, 2003). Both treatments are manualized and have core sets of themes and skills domains for treatment sessions (see Tables 1.3 and 1.4).

PMT With Alex

One core session of PMT teaches parents to use positive reinforcement to change behavior (see step 3 in Table 1.3). Alex's social worker first spent some

Table 1.3 Parent Management Training Sessions: Overview
of the Core Sessions

1. *Introduction and overview.* This session provides the parents with an overview
   of the program and outlines the demands placed on them and the focus of the
   intervention.

2. *Defining and observing.* This session trains parents to pinpoint, define, and
   observe behavior. The parents and trainer define specific problems that can
   be observed and develop a specific plan to begin observations.

3. *Positive reinforcement (point chart and praise).* This session focuses on learning
   the concept of positive reinforcement, factors that contribute to the effective
   application, and rehearsal of applications in relation to the target child. Specific
   programs are outlined where praise and points are to be provided for the
   behaviors observed during the week. An incentive (token/point) chart is
   devised, and the delivery praise of the parent is developed through modeling,
   prompting, feedback, and praise by the therapist.

4. *Time-out form reinforcement.* Parents learn about time out and the factors
   related to its effective application. Delivery of time out is extensively role
   played and practiced. The use of time out is planned for the next week for
   specific behaviors.

5. *Attending and ignoring.* In this session, parents learn about attending and
   ignoring and choose an undesirable behavior that they will ignore and a
   positive behavior to which they will attend. These procedures are practiced
   within the session. Attention and praise for positive behaviors are key
   components of this session and are practiced.

6. *Shaping and school intervention.* Parents are trained to develop behaviors by
   reinforcement of successive approximations and to use prompts and fading of
   prompts to develop terminal behaviors. Also, in this session, plans are made to
   implement a home-based reinforcement program to develop school-related
   behaviors. These behaviors include individually targeted academic domains,
   classroom deportment, and other tasks (e.g., homework completion). Prior
   to the session, the therapist identifies domains of functioning, specific goals,
   and concrete opportunities to implement procedures at school. The specific
   behaviors are incorporated into the home-based reinforcement program.
   After this session, the school-based program continues to be developed and
   monitored over the course of treatment, with changes in foci as needed in
   discussion with the teachers and parents.

7. *Review of the program.* Observations of the previous week as well as
   application of the reinforcement program are reviewed. Details about the
   administration of praise, points, and back-up reinforcers are discussed and
   enacted so the therapist can identify how to improve parent performance.

(continued)

Table 1.3 (*Continued*)

Changes are made in the program as needed. The parent practices designing programs for a set of hypothetical problems. The purpose is to develop skills that extend beyond implementing programs devised with the therapist.

8. *Family meeting.* At this meeting, the child and parent(s) are bought into the session. The programs are discussed along with any problems. Revisions are made as needed to correct misunderstandings or to alter facets that may not be implemented in a way that is likely to be effective. The programs are practiced (role played) to see how they are implemented and to make refinements.

9–10. *Negotiating, contracting, and compromising.* The child and parent meet together to negotiate new behavioral programs and to place these in contractual form. In the first of these sessions, negotiating and contracting are introduced, and the parent and child practice with each other on a problem/issue in the home and develop a contract that will be used as part of the program. Over the course of the sessions, the therapist shapes negotiating skills in the parent and child, reinforces compromise, and provides less and less guidance (e.g., prompts) as more difficult situations are presented.

11. *Reprimands and consequences for low-rate behaviors.* Parents are trained in effective use of reprimands and how to deal with low-rate behaviors, such as setting fires, stealing, or truancy. Specific punishment programs (usually chores) are planned and presented to the child, as needed, for low-rate behaviors.

12–13. *Review, problem solving, and practice.* Material from other sessions is reviewed in theory and practice. Special emphasis is given to role playing the application of individual principles as they are enacted with the trainer. Parents practice designing new programs, revising ailing programs, and responding to a complex array of situations in which principles and practices discussed in prior sessions are reviewed.

Source: From Kazdin, A. E. (2003). Problem-solving skills training and parent management training for conduct disorder. In A. E. Kazdin & J. R. Weisz (Eds.), *Evidence-based psychotherapies for children and adolescents* (pp. 241–262). New York: Guilford. Copyright 2003 by Guilford Press. Reprinted with permission.

time training his parents to pinpoint, define, and observe problematic behavior in new ways, focusing on careful inspection of the problems. She then worked with the family to develop a token system to be implemented in their home, which would provide them a structured, consistent way to reinforce Alex's behavior. Rather than creating an exhaustive list of behaviors that would likely be difficult to track, Alex's parents began with three target behaviors/goals that

Table 1.4 Problem-Solving Skills Training: Overview of the Core Sessions

1. *Introduction and learning the steps.* The purpose of this initial session is to establish rapport with the child, to teach the problem-solving steps, and to explain the procedures of the cognitively based treatment program. The child is acquainted with the use of tokens (chips), reward menus for exchange of the chips, and response-cost contingencies. The child is trained to use the problem-solving steps in a game-like fashion in which the therapist and child take turns learning the individual steps and placing them together in a sequence.

2–3. *Applying the steps.* The second session reviews and continues to teach the steps as needed. The child is taught to employ the problem-solving steps to complete a relatively simple game. The child applies the steps to simple problem situations presented in a board-game fashion in which the therapist and child alternate turns. During the session, the therapist demonstrates how to use the problem-solving steps in decision making, how to provide self-reinforcement for successful performance, and how to cope with mistakes and failure. One of the goals of this session is to illustrate how the self-statements can be used to help "stop and think" rather than respond impulsively when confronted with a problem. The third session includes another game that leads to selection of hypothetical situations to which the child applies the steps. The therapist and child take turns, and further practice is provided using prompts, modeling, shaping, and reinforcement to help the child be facile and fluid in applying the steps. The therapist fades prompts and assistance to shape proficient use and application of the steps. A series of "supersolvers" (homework assignments) begins at this point, in which the child is asked to identify when the steps could be used, then to use the steps in increasingly more difficult and clinically relevant situations as treatment continues.

4. *Applying the steps and role playing.* The child applies the steps to real-life situations. The steps are applied to the situation to identify solutions and consequences. Then, the preferred solution, based on the likely consequences, is selected and then enacted through repeated role plays. Practice and role play are continued to develop the child's application of the steps. Multiple situations are presented and practiced in this way.

5. *Parent–child contact.* The parent(s), therapist, and child are all present in the session. The child enacts the steps to solve problems. The parents learn more about the steps and are trained to provide attention and contingent praise for the child's use of the steps and selecting and enacting prosocial solutions. The primary goal is to develop the repertoire in the parent to encourage (prompt) use of the steps and to praise applications in a way that will influence child behavior (i.e., contingent, enthusiastic, continuous, verbal, and nonverbal praise). Further contacts with the parents at the end of later sessions continue this aspect of treatment as needed.

(continued)

Table 1.4 (*Continued*)

6-11. *Continued applications to real-life situations.* In these sessions, the child uses the problem-solving steps to generate prosocial solutions to provocative interpersonal problems or situations. Each session concentrates on a different category of social interaction that the child might realistically encounter (peers, parents, siblings, teachers, etc.). Real-life situations, generated by the child or parent or from contacts with teachers and others, are enacted; hypothetical situations are also presented to elaborate themes and problem areas of the child (e.g., responding to provocation, fighting, being excluded socially, and being encouraged by peers to engage in antisocial behavior). The child's supersolvers also become a more integral part of each session; they are reenacted with the therapist beginning in session in order to better evaluate how the child is transferring skills to the daily environment.

12. *Wrap-up and role reversal.* This wrap-up session is included (1) to help the therapist generally assess what the child has learned in the session, (2) to clear up any remaining confusions the child may have concerning use of the steps, and (3) to provide a final summary for the child of what has been covered in the meetings. The final session is based on role reversal in which the child plays the role of the therapist and the therapist plays the role of the child learning and applying the steps. The purpose of this session is to have the child teach and benefit from the learning that teaching provides, to allow for any unfinished business of the treatment ("spending" remaining chips, completing final supersolvers), and to provide closure for the therapy.

13. *Optional sessions.* During the course of therapy, additional sessions are provided to the child as needed, if the child has special difficulty in grasping any features of the problem-solving steps or their application. For example, the child may have difficulty in applying the steps, learning to state them covertly, and so on. An additional session may be applied to repeat material of a previous session, so that the child has a solid grasp of the approach. Optional sessions may be implemented at any point that the child's progress lags behind the level appropriate to the session that has been completed. For example, if a facet of treatment has not been learned (e.g., memorization of steps and fading of steps), which is associated with the particular session that has been completed, an optional session may be implemented. Also, if there is a problem or issue of the child's or parent's participation in supersolvers, a session will be scheduled with the parent and child to shape the requisite behaviors in the session and to make assignments to ensure that this aspect of treatment is carried out.

Source: From Kazdin, A. E. (2003). Problem-solving skills training and parent management training for conduct disorder. In A. E. Kazdin & J. R. Weisz (Eds.), *Evidence-based psychotherapies for children and adolescents* (pp. 241–262). New York: Guilford. Copyright 2003 by Guilford Press. Reprinted with permission.

they believed would be easier to manage and accomplish: respecting others' property and belongings, completing and turning in homework, and riding the school bus without fighting. In reviewing Alex's behavior, his father realized that Alex experienced very few behavior problems when he worked on outdoor projects with him. Spending time outdoors with his father, extra recreation/ video game time, and an extra trip to the corner store to spend his money were the main incentives integrated into the token system. The tokens, paired with praise, were contingent on Alex's behavior specific to the targeted behaviors/ goals. The social worker spent the bulk of this treatment session modeling and role-playing the implementation of this token system, developing the parents' proficiency in prompting, praising behavior, and delivering consequences. The social worker reviewed the previous week's events in each subsequent session, reenacting and rehearsing problems or difficulties as needed.

The following exchange among Alex, his family, and his social worker illustrates positive reinforcement and developing effective discipline strategies:

Social worker [to parents]: You've stated that Alex's fighting is a big problem that seems to remain no matter what you do. You said that you tried time out, but that did not work. What reward do you give Alex when he does not get into fights?

Mother: I don't want to give him toys or money because it's too expensive and usually just starts more fights with his brother and sisters.

Social worker: Your husband said that Alex behaves well when he works outside with him. Is that something you would consider giving him for a reward?

Alex: I'd rather be with Dad than at home with people who pick on me and accuse me of stealing their stuff anyway!

Mother [following social worker's earlier suggestion to avoid "proving" Alex's misbehavior]: Absolutely, and if he can make it through one dinner without a fight, he can go with his father to do the evening chores outside.

The dialogue continued in this vein until the family agreed on two more problems, rewards, and consequences. The social worker met with Alex's parents to review the purpose and effective use of time out as an intervention. The last time he was in time out, Alex threw a baseball through his bedroom window. They discussed finding a safer time-out area in the house where Alex could be directly monitored and removing possibly dangerous items from his bedroom. The social worker cautioned Alex's parents that his behaviors might escalate as they begin to implement these new interventions. She encouraged them to have back-up plans in the event that their first attempt to intervene did not work. Together, they role-played some possible scenarios and practiced back-up plans, alternating roles to develop proficiency. See Sells (1998) for step-by-step and detailed descriptions on developing creative and proactive interventions with parents who have challenging adolescents.

PSST With Alex

Since Alex's parents were actively participating in his treatment, the first few sessions with Alex were spent not only introducing steps in problem solving, but also discussing the token system and how consequences (positive or negative) were contingent on his behavior (see steps 1–4 in Table 1.4). Alex was initially very confident in his ability but anticipated that his siblings would sabotage his efforts with their constant provocations and false accusations of stealing. Hearing this, the social worker introduced the following self-statements in problem solving in order to guide Alex's behavior and lead to developing effective solutions (Kazdin, 2003):

1. What am I supposed to do?
2. I have to look at all my possibilities.
3. I'd better concentrate and focus in.
4. I need to make a choice.
5. I did a good job (or) Oh, I made a mistake.

Alex reported that he often fought with his siblings because they provoked him, so the social worker engaged Alex in multiple role plays, repeatedly practicing how he might respond to perceived provocation. The social worker effusively praised Alex's quick recall of the self-statements and his efforts to use a "stop and think" technique that she modeled and prompted. Additionally, they practiced how to respond to mistakes and failures without exploding at others or destroying property. Alex's parents were instructed to praise and reward his efforts to avoid conflicts and employ the problem-solving steps in everyday situations at home. Subsequent treatment sessions would require Alex to use the steps in increasingly more difficult and clinically relevant, real-life situations (Kazdin, 2003).

It is important to note that medication management was not part of Alex's treatment plan. While there is survey evidence for the significant use of polypharmacy in the treatment of children with CD in the United States, "medication cannot be justified as the first line of treatment for conduct problems. A diagnosis-based approach, which defines primary or comorbid psychiatric disorders associated with aggression, should guide the pharmacological treatment of CD" (Fonagy & Kurtz, 2002, p. 192).

Had Alex been younger (ages 4 to 8 years), the social worker could have selected from the range of interventions available under the Incredible Years Training Series developed by Webster-Stratton and colleagues at the University of Washington's Parenting Clinic (see Table 1.5). One of the appealing qualities of this approach is that it has been tailored for work with youth in school settings.

Table 1.5 Program Recommendations for Webster-Stratton Programs Depending on Degree of Risk, Treatment, or Prevention Focus

Population and Intended Use	Minimum Core Program	Recommended Supplemental Programs for Special Populations
Prevention programs for selected populations (i.e., high-risk populations without overt behavior or conduct problems) Settings: preschool, day care, Head Start, schools (grades K–3), public health centers	BASIC (12–14, 2-hour weekly sessions)	• ADVANCE Parent Program for highly stressed families • SCHOOL Parent Program for children kindergarten to grade 3 • Child Dinossaur Program if child's problems are pervasive at home and school • TEACHER classroom management program if teachers have high numbers of students with behavior problems or if teachers have not received this training previously
Treatment programs for indicated populations (i.e., children exhibiting behavior problems or diagnosed with conduct disorders) Settings: mental health centers, pediatric clinics, HMOs	BASIC and ADVANCE (22–24, 2-hour weekly sessions)	• Child Dinosaur Program if child's problems are pervasive at home and at school • TEACHER Program if child's problems are pervasive at home and at school • SCHOOL Program for parents if child has academic problems

Source: From Webster-Stratton, C., & Reid, M. J. (2003b). The incredible years parents, teachers, and children training series: A multifaceted treatment approach for young children with conduct problems. In A. E. Kazdin & J. R. Weisz (Eds.), *Evidence-based psychotherapies for children and adolescents* (pp. 224–240). New York: Guilford. Copyright 2003 by Guilford Press. Reprinted with permission.

Key Points to Remember

Some of the key points from this chapter are as follows:

- Conduct-disordered youth in schools can be effectively treated.
- There are two well-established and a range of probably efficacious treatment approaches from which to select when working with conduct-disordered youth.

- Using a combination of PMT and PSST together tends to be more effective than using either treatment alone (Kazdin, 2003). Both treatments are manualized and have core sets of themes and skills domains for treatment sessions.
- Medication cannot be justified as the first line of treatment for conduct problems.
- One of the well-established approaches, Webster-Stratton's videotape modeling parent program, the Incredible Years Training Series, was developed to address parent, family, child, and school risk factors related to childhood conduct disorders.
- The most proactive and powerful approach to the problem of escalating aggression in young children is to offer their programs using a school-based prevention/early intervention model designed to strengthen all children's social and emotional competence.

Despite the promising treatment effects produced by the interventions reviewed above, existing treatments need to be refined and new ones developed. We cannot yet determine the short- and long-term impact of evidence-based treatments on conduct-disordered youths, and it is sometimes unclear what part of the therapeutic process produces change. A child's eventual outcome is most likely dependent on the interrelationship among child, parent, teacher, and peer risk factors; accordingly, the most effective interventions should be those that assess these risk factors and determine which programs are needed for a particular family and child (Webster-Stratton & Reid, 2003b).

The focus in this chapter has been geared toward school social workers and other mental health practitioners working with individual students in school settings. We cannot emphasize enough that contextual issues should not be ignored. Equally important in sustaining therapeutic change with conduct-disordered youth are issues surrounding classroom management and strategies that promote positive behavior through schoolwide interventions. Accordingly, practitioners must work collaboratively with parents, teachers, peers, and school administrators to sustain change across settings. For a detailed exposition on best practice models for schoolwide interventions, the reader is referred to Bloomquist and Schnell (2002), which is an excellent source.

Resources

Barkley, R. A. (1987). *Defiant children: A clinician's manual for parent training.* New York: Guilford.

Bloomquist, M. L., & Schnell, S. V. (2002). *Helping children with aggression and conduct problems: Best practices for intervention.* New York: Guilford.

Blueprints. Developed by the Center for the Study and Prevention of Violence at the University of Colorado at Boulder: http://www.colorado.edu/cspv/blueprints.

Cavell, T. A. (2000). *Working with parents of aggressive children: A practitioner's guide.* Washington, DC: American Psychological Association.

Centers for Disease Control and Prevention: http://www.cdc.gov.

Evidence-Based Treatment for Children and Adolescents: http://www.effectivechildtherapy.com.

Fonagy, P., & Kurtz, A. (2002). Disturbance of conduct. In P. Fonagy, M. Target, D. Cottrell, J. Phillips, & Z. Kurtz (Eds.), *What works for whom? A critical review of treatments for children and adolescents* (pp. 106–192). New York: Guilford.

Forehand, R. L., & McMahon, R. J. (1981). *Helping the noncompliant child: A clinician's guide to parent training.* New York: Guilford.

Henggeler, S. W., Schoenwald, S. K., Rowland, M. D., & Cunningham, P. B. (2002). *Serious emotional disturbance in children and adolescents: Multisystemic therapy.* New York: Guilford.

Incredible Years Parent, Teacher, and Child Programs: http://www.incredibleyears.com.

Lochman, J. E., Barry, T. D., & Pardini, D. A. (2003). Anger control training for aggressive youth. In A. E. Kazdin & J. R. Weisz (Eds.), *Evidence-based psychotherapies for children and adolescents* (pp. 263–281). New York: Guilford.

National Institute of Mental Health: http://nimh.gov.

Parenting Clinic, University of Washington: http://www.son.washington.edu/centers/parenting-clinic/bibligraphy.asp.

Sells, S. P. (1998). *Treating the tough adolescent: A family-based, step-by-step guide.* New York: Guilford.

Substance Abuse and Mental Health Services Administration: http://www.mentalhealth.samhsa.gov.

UCLA School Mental Health Project, Center for Mental Health in Schools: http://smhp.psych.ucla.edu.

U.S. Department of Health and Human Services, Administration for Children and Families: http://www.acf.dhhs.gov.

2

Effective Interventions for Students With ADHD

Martell Teasley

Getting Started

This chapter provides an overview of evidence-based practice methods for school social workers and other school counselors in the assessment and treatment of attention-deficit/hyperactivity disorder (ADHD) (DuPaul & Eckert, 1997; DuPaul, Eckert, & McGoey, 1997; Erk, 1995, 2000; Hoagwood, Kelleher, Feil, & Comer, 2000; Jensen, 2000; Jensen et al., 1999; McGoey, Eckert, & DuPaul, 2002; Olfson, Gameroff, Marcus, & Jensen, 2003; Perrin et al., 2001; Richters et al., 1995; Thomas & Corcoran, 2000). Step-by-step procedures and guidelines for assessment and treatment interventions are discussed. Resources that will assist school social workers with specific intervention procedures and methods are cited. These resources contain in-depth information supported by evidence-based research and intervention methods that are cited in the reference list for this chapter. Some examples and one case scenario that will assist school social workers with the development of a framework for understanding how to develop an intervention plan for school children diagnosed with ADHD are provided.

What We Know

ADHD is a complicated neurobiological disorder caused by malfunctioning neurotransmitters within the central nervous system (Litner, 2003). It is usually an inherited disorder "typically beginning in childhood and continuing throughout the lifespan…it has been estimated that nearly 70% of children diagnosed with ADHD continue [to experience] ongoing problems as adolescents" (Litner, 2003, p. 138). Individuals with ADHD experience a host of psychological, behavioral, and cognitive problems that present them with specific challenges in their activities of daily living and interactions with their families, peers, and communities. Complications include inconsistency in sustaining attention, poor organization and planning, lack of forethought, low energy, mood swings, poor memory, overactive behavior, and impulsivity (DuPaul, Eckert, & McGoey, 1997; Erk, 2000). While coexisting learning disorders, such as conduct or oppositional disorder, are common in children diagnosed with ADHD, prevalence rates vary in research findings (Richters et al., 1995).

ADHD has multiple consequences in the school setting and presents a host of challenges for students, their families, educators, and related school services personnel. Many students diagnosed with ADHD exhibit higher than average rates of interrupting classroom activities, calling out answers or asking questions without raising their hand, getting out of an assigned seat without permission, and failing to complete assigned tasks in the classroom as well as at home. For the ADHD student, a great deal of energy and behavior in the classroom is often aimed at avoiding the completion of tasks (DuPaul et al., 1997). As a result, there is an association between individuals with ADHD and academic under-achievement, school suspension, dropping out, peer rejection, development of antisocial patterns, low self-esteem, and depression (DuPaul et al., 1997). School disciplinary problems, such as suspension and expulsion, are more characteristic of those diagnosed as hyperactive (Richters et al., 1995). Moreover, students with ADHD often do not develop the academic skills necessary for college.

What We Can Do

Assessment and Diagnosis of ADHD in Children
The *Diagnostic and Statistical Manual of Mental Disorders* (*DSM-IV-TR*) defines ADHD as a multidimensional disorder identified by subtypes: "Diagnosis is based on a collaborative process that involves children and adolescent psychiatrists or other physicians, the child, and the child's family, and school-based or other health care professionals as appropriate" (American Psychiatric Association, 2000, p. 1). School social workers and other mental health counselors should become familiar with the diagnostic criteria for ADHD as stated in the *DSM-IV-TR*. There are several psychometric instruments with which school social workers should become knowledgeable (Table 2.1) that are frequently used in the diagnosis of ADHD. Greater information on clinical practice guidelines and the evaluation of ADHD in children (Perrin et al., 2001) can be found on the American Academy of Pediatrics Web site: www.help4adhd.org.

Research in Support of Treatment Interventions
Nationwide estimates of the prevalence of ADHD suggest that between 3% and 9% of children are afflicted (Richters et al., 1995). However, it is estimated that 3.4% of children aged 3 to 18 receive treatment for ADHD (Erk, 2000). There is also a high comorbidity with other mental disorders, such as conduct disorder, depression, and anxiety disorders. Although ADHD is arguably one of the most common mental health disorders challenging schools, it is also the most amenable to treatment. The most successful interventions for ADHD in school settings have been with the use of the multimodal approach consisting of pharmaceutical intervention, cognitive-behavioral training, parent training,

Table 2.1 Instrumentation Used in the Assessment and Diagnosis of ADHD

1. *Child Attention Profile* (DuPaul, 1990). A 12-item scale taken from Child Behavior Checklist Teacher Report that measures rate and severity of undesirable behaviors	Ages 6–16
2. *Child Behavior Checklist* (CBCL). Used to measure behavioral problems in children and adolescents. It relies on parent and caregiver reports and provides a total problem score in the assessment of depression, social problems, attention problems, and withdrawn, delinquent, and aggressive behavior	Ages 3 years and older
3. *Conners's Teacher Rating Scale.* A 28-item questionnaire designed to measure various types of clinical and research applications with children. It contains four indexes including for assessment of hyperactivity and for assessment of inattention	Ages 2–18
4. *Caregiver–Teacher Report Form.* Adapted from items in the CBCL, it replaces problems more likely observed at home with those more likely observed in daycare and preschool settings	Ages 2–5
5. *Teacher Report Form.* Contains many of the problem items found in the CBCL but substitutes the assessment of home-specific items with school-specific behaviors and provides a standardized description of problem behaviors, academic functioning, and adaptive behaviors	Ages 5–18
6. *Youth Self-Report for Age.* Contains specific components of the CBCL as they relate to adolescents and many items that youth may not report about themselves. Using this instrument in an interview may be the best method	Ages 11–18
7. *ADHD Rating Scale* (DuPaul, 1990). This is a scale using 14 items from the *DSM-III-R* on ADHD	Ages 5–18

and teacher training in classroom management techniques and special education methods. This was confirmed in separate investigations of evidence-based best practice research findings from the National Institute of Mental Health's (NIMH) Collaborative Multisite Multimodal Treatment Study of Children with ADHD and the American Academy of Pediatrics Committee on Quality Improvement's Subcommittee on ADHD (Perrin et al., 2001). Intervention strategies suggested in this chapter are consistent with research findings from these investigations.

Approximately 70%–80% of children with ADHD are treated with pharmacological intervention. In general, stimulants assist in the connection of neurotransmissions, which may help to diminish motor activity and impulsive behaviors characteristic of those diagnosed with ADHD. The clinical use of stimulant drugs has demonstrated short-term efficacy in the reduction of a range of core symptoms of ADHD, such as fidgetiness, finger tapping, fine motor movement, and classroom disturbances (Richters et al., 1995). "Stimulants have been found to enhance the sustained attention, impulse control, interpersonal behavior, and academic productivity of 70% to 80% of children with ADHD" (DuPaul & Eckert, 1997, p. 5). Additionally, stimulants have been shown to have positive effects on problem solving with peers, parent–child interactions, and a variety of controlled laboratory tasks, such as auditory and reading comprehension, spelling recall, continuous performance tasks, cue and free recall, and arithmetic computation (Richters et al., 1995). For discussion of the common medication used, see Bentley and Collins (in press).

Compliance with prescription medication protocols in the treatment of ADHD varies because of the possibility of complications from side effects (e.g., appetite reduction, insomnia, nervousness, etc.), possible addiction, or differences in environmental (home, school, or control settings) treatment reinforcement (DuPaul & Eckert, 1997). Comprehensive research studies have found that among the estimated 90% of children and adolescents with ADHD who receive prescription medication to treat ADHD, only 12%–25% regularly take their medication (Smith, Waschbusch, Willoughby, & Evans, 2000). However, research on samples of children using pharmaceutical interventions in the treatment of ADHD (DuPaul & Eckert, 1997; Jensen et al., 1999; Richters et al., 1995) suggest that side effects of medication treatments may be unpleasant in the short run but are usually reversible and often dose dependent (Smith et al., 2000).

Unfortunately, previous studies are often inconsistent regarding the efficacy of pharmacological intervention in differential settings (e.g., home, school, and peer groups). The use of stimulants has demonstrated greater success in the treatment of hyperactivity than in curbing challenges with academic achievement and inattention. There is also evidence that the magnitude of stimulant benefits is not consistent across age groups. Likewise, the impact of comorbidity diagnoses in individuals with ADHD may produce differential effectiveness in the use of stimulants. Research studies have demonstrated that stabilization of treatment through pharmaceutical intervention takes approximately 14 months for school-aged children (Perrin et al., 2001). Medication regimens should be monitored closely for possible side effects (Table 2.3). Most medication side effects occur early during treatment, tend to be mild, and are short-lived. Conversely, for some children, side effects from medication have a greater effect than the reduction of problem behaviors or an increase in cognitive performance. Although rare, with high doses, some children experience mood disturbances, psychotic reactions, or hallucinations. Medication adjustments (lowering dosage or switching medication) may curb side effects. Many clinicians and physicians recommend "drug holidays"—no prescription ADHD medication on the weekends during the school year and/or during the entire summer—as a way of reducing the impact of side effects and potential long-term medical complications (Perrin et al., 2001). Overall, the use of stimulants for the treatment of ADHD may have minimal benefits in some clients, become contraindicated in others, and may be expected to yield gains beyond reduction of inattention and impulsivity in others (Richters et al., 1995).

An essential component of behavior management for school children diagnosed with ADHD is home-based treatment, with parental involvement that is coordinated with school-based interventions. Parent training in behavior modification techniques and stress management has shown improvement in school behavior and home behavior for hyperactive children and has demonstrated improvements in parent, child, and family relations (see Thomas & Corcoran, 2000, for a review of literature on family-centered approaches to ADHD). Cognitive-behavioral interventions, such as the use of token reinforcement as a reward for desired classroom behaviors, have demonstrated positive results. Successful use of behavioral therapy in the classroom must include teacher training in classroom management techniques and individualized strategies to combat behavioral maladaptation. Techniques that encourage and accommodate students with ADHD should be at the core of a teacher's class management interventions.

On the basis of subgroup differences in comorbidity, age, cognitive ability, and the varied impact of pharmaceutical interventions, researchers have become increasingly interested in combined forms of treatment, or multimodal treatment strategies. *Multimodal treatment strategies* are those that tailor specific pharmaceutical and behavioral interventions to suit a client's particular needs in a given setting (e.g., home, school, and social). Treatment interventions outlined below are consistent with the multimodal approach.

Treatment Interventions

Figure 2.1 contains an evidence-based treatment algorithm developed by the American Academy of Pediatrics for children diagnosed with ADHD. Primary care clinicians should establish a management program that recognizes ADHD as a chronic condition. Prior to engaging in treatment intervention, social workers must determine the source of the ADHD diagnosis and review all accessible documentation, including those completed by psychologists, psychiatrists, and parents and teachers' evaluations of the student's classroom behavior and grades. Evidence-based treatment intervention guidelines identified from a review of the literature are outlined below.

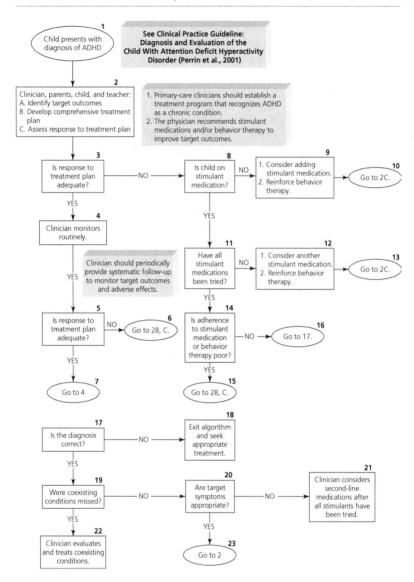

Figure 2.1. Algorithm for the Treatment of School-Aged Children With Attention Deficit/Hyperactivity Disorder.

Source: Reproduced with permission from *Pediatrics, 108*, 1033–1044. Copyright 2001.

Development of Intervention Plan
- Determine target outcomes. Desired results may include the following:
  - decrease in disruptive behaviors
  - improvements in relationships with parents, siblings, teachers, and peers
  - improved academic performance, particularly in completion of work, volume of work, efficiency, and accuracy
  - increased independence and self-direction
  - enhanced safety in the community, such as riding a bicycle or crossing the street without incident
  - improved self-esteem
- Treatment plan must include the following:
  - collaboration with other school-based professionals (e.g., school psychologists, counselors, nurses) for special education services
  - coordination of services exterior to the school system (e.g., primary care, psychological, support groups)
  - parental and home-based intervention
  - specific cognitive-behavioral interventions
  - educational services (teachers and other faculty)
  - ongoing and outcome evaluation

Collaborative Practice
- "Collaboration between service providers and teachers is an important tool for optimizing ADHD treatment intervention" (LeFever, Villers, Morrow, & Vaughn, 2002, p. 68). An individualized approach to treatment intervention is necessary.
- Discuss findings from psychometric instrumentation used in assessment and diagnosis with the treatment team.
- Assist treatment team in the development of a functional behavioral assessment. Assist teachers with the development of a classroom individualized education program (IEP).

Medication
School social workers and mental health counselors should have a working knowledge of the most commonly used medications in the treatment of ADHD. The NIMH has developed a list of stimulants for the treatment of ADHD approved by the federal Food and Drug Administration (Table 2.2). The most common potential side effects of these medications are listed in Table 2.3; however, for more detailed information see nlm.nih.gov/medlineplus. Also, see Chapter 12 in this book for a discussion of side effects and other issues in the prescription of stimulant drugs such as Ritalin.
- Monitor medication compliance: Is the individual taking medication as prescribed by physician/psychiatrist?

Table 2.2 List of Medications for the Treatment of Children With ADHD

Medication	Approved Age
Adderall (amphetamine)	3 and older
Concerta (methylphenidate)	6 and older
Cylert (pemoline)	6 and older
Dexedrine (dextroamphetamine)	3 and older
Dextrostat (dextroamphetamine)	3 and older
Focalin (dexmethylphenidate)	6 and older
Metadate ER (Methylphenidate, extended release)	6 and older
Metadate CD (Methylphenidate, extended release)	6 and older
Ritalin (methylphenidate, extended release)	6 and older
Ritalin SR (Methylphenidate, extended release)	6 and older
Ritalin LA (methylphenidate, extended release)	6 and older

- Monitor bodily movement pre- and postmedication interventions.
- Determine when medication is most beneficial (e.g., time of day, duration of effects, differences in body movement).
- Monitor side effects of medication.
- Assess parents' knowledge of medication and attitude toward use of medications.
- If necessary, provide information to parents:
  - See Medline at www.ncbi.nlm.nih.gov.
  - Provide handouts, videotapes, Internet Web sites, and support group information.

Behavioral Therapy
- Set specific goals: Develop and set clear goals; set small, reachable goals; and make certain that the child understands the goals. For example, require the child to stay focused on homework for a specified period of time or to share a toy while playing with a friend.
- Provide rewards and consequences:
  - Positive reinforcement: Provide privileges and rewards as responses to desired behavior. Instruct parents to give their child rewards when

Table 2.3 Common Side Effects of Medications Prescribed for Children With ADHD

Generic Names	Possible Side Effects
Amphetamine	Restlessness or tremors, anxiety, nervousness, headaches, dizziness, insomnia, diarrhea, constipation, dryness of the mouth, unpleasant taste in the mouth
Dexmethylphenidate	Stomach pain, fever, loss of appetite, upset stomach, vomiting, difficulty falling asleep or staying asleep, dizziness, nervousness, weight loss, skin rash, headache
Dextramphetamine	Nervousness, restlessness, difficulty falling or staying asleep, false feeling of well-being, feeling of unpleasantness, dizziness, tremor, difficulty coordinating movements, headache, dry mouth, diarrhea, constipation, loss of appetite, weight loss, bad taste in mouth
Methylphenidate	Nervousness, difficulty falling asleep or staying asleep, dizziness, drowsiness, upset stomach, vomiting, headache, loss of appetite
Pemoline	Loss of appetite, trouble sleeping, weight loss, dizziness, drowsiness, headache, increased irritability, mental depression, stomach ache

desired behavior is demonstrated or request that teachers give points for appropriate behavior in the classroom. For example, after the completion of homework, a parent might provide free time for a desired activity, such as bike riding or playing computer games.

- Time out: Remove access to desired activities when undesirable behavior occurs. For example, a teacher might decrease recess time for inappropriate classroom behavior, or a parent might require the child to sit in the corner of a room for hitting a sibling.
- Response cost: Withdraw privileges or rewards in case of undesirable behavior, for example, the loss of free time or other desired activities because homework has not been completed.
- Token economy: Combine rewards and consequences based on type of behavior, in which the child is given a reward for desired behavior and loses privileges and rewards for unwanted behavior: (1) A teacher might give points for not daydreaming and take points away for missing assignments. (2) A teacher might give points for turning in

completed assignments but deduct points if the child gets out of an assigned seat at an inappropriate time.

- The child cashes in the sum total of points daily and weekly for assessment of behavior and a possible prize if set goals are attained.
- Maintain rewards and consequences: The benefit of constant, long-term use of rewards and consequences is the eventual shaping of the child's behavior.

Intervention With Parents

Assist parents in monitoring school assignments and require that they

- create a routine environment in the home:
  - Organize home: Provide specific and logical places to place the child's schoolwork and supplies.
  - Make a daily/weekly schedule.
  - Insist that the child prepare for school each evening.
  - Help the child stay on task: Make use of charts and checklists to track progress in school and with chores in the home.
  - Place items for school in highly visible areas.
  - Reduce distractions during homework and meal times, such as loud music, television, and computer games, as such distractions can over-stimulate children with ADHD.
  - Engage in daily/weekly discussion of schoolwork and behavior:
    - Discuss ways to improve problem behaviors.
    - Role-play and demonstrate desired behaviors and require the child to role-play problem behaviors as well as desired behaviors.
    - If multiple problems persist, partialize role-playing sessions.
    - Do not use time for behavior training as a punitive measure.
- give the child praise for completion of tasks.
- do not overemphasize failures.

Assist parents in the development of positive reinforcement measures and ensure that they obtain support and seek counseling if necessary.

Interventions With Teachers

- Assist teachers with the development of classroom management techniques:
  - Require the student to sit in the front of the classroom near the teacher.
  - Make sure that the student is away from other students who may provoke him or her.
  - Give the student classroom tasks, such as collecting books or homework.

- Develop a plan for the student to release energy (e.g., stretching, classroom activities, educational games that require movement).
- Determine the student's ability to take notes and assist as necessary with classroom note-taking strategies.
- Assist teachers in setting up behavioral monitoring mechanisms in the classroom, including positive reinforcement measures, token economy, and time outs.
- If possible, the student should receive a copy of notes prior to class.
- Review and outline all lesson plans.
- Provide the student with written and oral instructions on homework assignments.
- Break down homework instructions into simple components.
- If available, make use of study carrel for assignment completion.
- Assist the student in the development of organizational skills.
  - Provide positive reinforcement for organizational milestones (e.g., not forgetting homework for one week, completion of all homework assignments, neatness of work, preparation for class).
  - Make checklist of school supplies and review with child.
- Give short but frequent assignments rather than one large assignment.
- Prepare daily or weekly report cards for home discussion.
- Assist with test taking:
  - Provide clear instructions on materials to be covered during the test.
  - Allow for additional time.
  - Consider giving verbal tests if there is no success with written tests.
  - Provide retesting on the same materials until student scores well.
  - Communicate with parents about upcoming tests.
- When possible, make use of word processors, recorded books, calculators, videotapes, and cassette recorders.
- It is important to emphasize to teachers that behavioral intervention techniques should be sustained over time.
- Schedule regular meetings with teachers.

Homework Assignments

- Make sure homework assignments are given verbally as well as in writing.
- If possible, have the student repeat and acknowledge understanding of homework assignments.
- If possible, have pre- and postclassroom group sessions in which assignments are reviewed:
  - Closely monitor students in group dynamics.

- Anticipate problems with group dynamics, and implement changes as necessary.
- Pair the student with another student who is more patient or younger.
- Assist the student in the development of a homework log book. Parents and teachers should review the homework log with the student weekly.
- Assist parents in establishing a consistent homework protocol. Parents should personally check and verify completion of homework.

Assess Response to Treatment Plan

Develop routine monitoring to evaluate the following:

- Individual and combined effects of medication and behavioral therapy
- Effectiveness of behavioral interventions and any necessary revisions
- Adequacy of treatment plan toward accomplishing set goals:
  - Determine cause-and-effect relationship between treatment plan and specific goals.
  - Revise treatment plan as necessary.

Base the assessment on collaborative findings using information from the IEP.

Tools and Practice Example

Case Scenario: ADHD, Predominantly Inattentive Type

Michelle is a 9-year-old girl who just started the fourth grade. Her teacher has referred her to social work services because she believes that Michelle needs special education testing. Michelle's teacher has based this request on several behavioral patterns that she has noticed during the first month of the school year. First, although homework assignments are printed on the blackboard daily, Michelle often forgets to write them down, as instructed. Second, Michelle has had poor scores on all of her tests and fails to complete her reading assignments. The teacher states that she has to call Michelle several times before getting a response. "It often appears as if she is daydreaming or mentally somewhere else," she states. During recess, the teacher also has noticed that Michelle does not play with her fourth-grade classmates but with children from the second grade instead.

In your discussion with Michelle, you record the following: She says that she does not like her sisters because they are always teasing her and that her mother treats her like a baby. When asked about her reading and her homework, Michelle states that she does not like reading because it takes too long. She states that she forgets to do her homework sometimes, and on other occasions, she gets sleepy while doing it and does not finish.

In your interview with Michelle's mother, she informs you of the following: "Michelle reminds me of my brother. He was always tripping over things, and he got into fights at school because the other kids called him goofy." Michelle's mother only lets her ride her bicycle in the backyard because Michelle was almost struck by a car twice. "Both times, Michelle stated that she thought that she could beat the car going across the street," her mother says. Michelle is also very untidy around the house: "She really makes a mess in the bathroom, so I tend to supervise her in order to avoid extra cleaning, but I don't always have time to do this." Because she makes such a mess, neither of her siblings wants to go in the bathroom after her. This sometimes starts arguments and confrontations in the mornings, when the family is preparing for the day. Her sisters, Elizabeth (age 12) and Kelly (age 8), complain that Michelle has poor cleaning habits in their room. When asked about Michelle's homework routine, her mother remarks, "It's the strangest thing. Sometimes Michelle completes her homework and forgets to take it to school or forgets that she has taken it with her and does not turn it in. I have scolded her several times for this, but nothing I do has really done much good." Sometimes, she plays too much and starts her homework late, then falls asleep; she also claims that her stomach hurts when it is time to do homework.

Assessment and Diagnosis

You suspect that Michelle is exhibiting signs of ADHD, predominantly inattentive. Follow the protocol as suggested by the American Academy of Pediatrics:

- Verify the appropriate social work protocols specific to your particular school system.
- Suggest that parents refer the ADHD child to a primary care physician for a standard history and physical.
- Coordinate school-based services in assessing a child's behavior.
- Gather evidence and make use of assessment tools.
- Document individual observations, including report cards and written comments from teachers.
- Document specific elements of behavior, including age of onset, duration of symptoms, multiple settings, and degree of functional impairment.
- Conduct a family assessment.
- Develop an individual treatment program (ITP) with the assistance of other school-based professionals (e.g., schoolteacher, counselor, psychologist, nurse).

Numerous resources exist to help school social workers and other school counselors work with youth with ADHD. Internet Web sites that are useful in the understanding and treatment of ADHD can be found in Table 2.4.

Table 2.4 Internet Resources on ADHD

Resource	Description	Web Site
Pediatrics	Clinical guidelines for evaluation and treatment of ADHD	www.help4adhd.org
National Resource Center on ADHD, Children and Adults With ADHD (CHADD)	Major advocate for those with ADHD; contains frequently asked questions, educational resources, newsletters, conference information, membership opportunity, prescription discount card, employment information, and evidence-based research information	www.chadd.org
National Institute of Mental Health	ADHD publication: a detailed booklet that contains information on signs and symptoms of ADHD, causes, coexisting disorders, family treatment strategies, diagnostic and treatment information, behavioral, therapy, and information on help with coping	www.nimh.nih.gov/publicat/adhd 800-237-4513
MEDLINE's PubMed	Contains the latest research publication on ADHD funded by the National Institutes of Health	www.ncbi.nlm.nih.gov
Medline Plus	Contains information on pharmaceutical medications	www.nlm.nih.gov/medlineplus
ADD Kids Area, Friends and Me and ADD	Internet Web sites that contain information on explaining ADHD to children	www.helpforadd.com/talk add.org/content/kid1& add.org/content/kids/friends

(*continued*)

Table 2.4 (*Continued*)

Resource	Description	Web Site
PSEP Technical Assistance Center on Positive Behavioral Interventions & Supports	Contains information on behavioral interventions for unwanted behavior in the school, home, and community	www.pbis.org
American Academy of Pediatrics	Contains information on ADHD resources, symptoms and behaviors common to ADHD, diagnosis, common coexisting conditions, treatment plan, treatment with medication, unproven treatment, and evaluation methods	www.aap.org
Attention Deficit Disorder Association (ADDA)	Advocacy and support organization for individuals diagnosed with ADHD	www.ADDA.org
ADHD: A Complete and Authoritative Guide by the American Academy of Pediatrics	A guidebook for families affected by ADHD. Based on evidence-based clinical treatment guidelines, answers the most frequently asked questions; contains the latest research on coexisting conditions and behavior therapy	www.aap.org
ADHA Support Company	Contains information on ADHD concerning teachers, parents, clients, medical treatment, nurses, family coping, and relationships	www.adhdsupportcompany.com

Key Points to Remember

- The diagnosis of ADHD should be made only after reliable diagnostic interviewing methods.
- Diagnosis is based on history and observable behaviors in multiple settings (e.g., home, school, play).
- Therapists should develop a comprehensive treatment plan through collaborative efforts with other school-based professionals and community service providers.
- The most successful treatment of ADHD for the context of the school setting has been with the use of the multimodal approach, consisting of pharmaceutical intervention, cognitive-behavioral training, parent training, and teacher training in classroom management techniques and special education methods.
- Provide teacher and parental support, and develop a supportive network for the client.
- Provide ongoing assessment, reassessment, and evaluation of treatment regimen.
- Follow the treatment algorithm as stated in Figure 2.1.

Acknowledgment

I would like to thank Angela Moore for her excellent work in editing this chapter.

Effective Interventions for Youth With Oppositional Defiant Disorder

Tammy Linseisen

Getting Started

"Disruptive," "mad all the time," "can't handle frustration," "touchy," "annoying," "driving me crazy," "emotionally disturbed," "passive-aggressive," "blames everyone for everything," "never takes responsibility," "doesn't listen," "noncompliant," "rude," "pushy," "oppositional," "defiant"—do any of these words or descriptions sound familiar? These are some of the terms and phrases used when parents and professionals are describing their observations of and reactions to children and adolescents who exhibit symptoms consistent with the diagnosis of oppositional defiant disorder (ODD). The prevalence of children with symptoms and/or actual diagnoses of ODD has been documented in a number of publications (Eamon & Altshuler, 2004; Freeman, Franklin, Fong, Shaffer, & Timberlake, 1998; Markward & Bride, 2001; Sprague & Thyer, 2002). In fact, in the early school years, more than one half and maybe as many as two-thirds of referrals made for clinical purposes are for behaviors consistent with this diagnosis (Fisher & Fagot, 1996). This diagnosis is not relegated to young children alone. The following are facts about this disorder as listed in the *Diagnostic and Statistical Manual of Mental Disorders* (*DSM-IV-TR*) (American Psychiatric Association, 2000) (see Box 3.1):

- Evidence of the disorder is usually shown before the child is 8 years old.
- Evidence of the disorder will usually be shown by early adolescence.
- It is more common in families where marital difficulties exist.
- It appears more in families where at least one parent has a history of one of the following psychiatric diagnoses: mood disorder, ODD, conduct disorder, attention deficit/hyperactivity disorder, antisocial personality disorder, or a substance-related disorder.
- Amount of oppositional symptoms seems to increase with age.
- ODD is found more often in males than in females until puberty.
- After puberty, ODD is found in both males and females at equal rates.

A critical responsibility of the school mental health professional is to accurately assess a youth's level of functioning in the school setting, although the provision of a diagnosis is not always helpful or necessary. For the orderly classification of symptoms, though, it is beneficial to work from one set of criteria. Not only are these behaviors disruptive to learning and the school setting in general,

Box 3.1.

According to the *DSM-IV-TR* (2000), a youth can be diagnosed with ODD if he or she shows "a pattern of negativistic, hostile, and defiant behavior lasting at least 6 months, during which four (or more) of the following are present:

1. often loses temper;
2. often argues with adults;
3. often actively defies or refuses to comply with adults' requests or rules;
4. often deliberately annoys people;
5. often blames others for his or her mistakes or misbehavior;
6. is often touchy or easily annoyed by others;
7. is often angry and resentful;
8. is often spiteful or vindictive" (p. 102).

Source: Reprinted with permission from the Diagnostic and Statistical Manual of Mental Disorders, Copyright 2000, American Psychiatric Association.

but the literature indicates that children with these kinds of behaviors are more prone to dropping out of school, substance use, peer rejection, adolescent-onset psyciatric disorders, and later antisocial behavior (Coie, Kupersmidt & Coie, 1990; Kupersmidt & Patterson, 1991; Lochman, Terry, & Hyman, 1992; Loeber, 1990). *DSM-IV-TR* (2000) further states that significant impairment in social, academic, or occupational functioning must be caused by these behavioral disturbances. ODD should not be considered to be an accurate diagnosis if the criteria for the diagnosis of conduct disorder are met, and the same holds true if the individual is 18 years of age or older and the criteria for antisocial personality disorder are met. Even though conduct disorder and ODD are considered to be distinct, they do appear to exist on a spectrum of related disruptive behavior disorders. For this reason, the effective treatments of the two are similar, as can be seen from comparing this chapter to Chapter 1 on conduct disorders.

What We Know

A literature review of evidence-based interventions for ODD has revealed minimal results for individual practice but more promising results for group methods. Also, parent-training interventions have shown some promise, but no pharmacological treatment has been shown to be successful for the treatment of ODD in current studies. Practice wisdom as well as resiliency theory have informed the examples provided in this chapter, and information highlighting the resources not addressed in detail are located at the chapter's end.

If evidence-based programs or interventions discussed in the literature targeted youth with aggressive behaviors only, the information is not included here because the defining difference between ODD and conduct disorder, according to the *DSM-IV-TR* (2000), is that disruptive behaviors of individuals with ODD do not ordinarily involve aggression toward animals or people or the destruction of property.

The language used in research-based literature is variable when discussing behavioral problems of youth. Phrases like "disruptive school behavior," "conduct problems," "bullying and/or violent behaviors," "attachment disorders," and "emotional and/or behavioral disorders" are common when evidence-based interventions are being mentioned. This offers a challenge to determine which of the studies is speaking to treatment of ODD specifically. Additionally, few studies have been conducted that involve youth who meet only the criteria for ODD without symptoms of other disorders or related conditions (Sprague & Thyer, 2002). This confounds the ability to define effective treatments for specified disorders, such as ODD by itself.

Certain evidence-based specifics might prove helpful to school social workers and mental health workers in their attempts to affect students via multiple systems. The following information might be useful when planning and facilitating groups with youth who meet the diagnostic criteria for ODD; when consulting with teachers who are managing students with ODD in their classrooms; or when attempting to provide effective interventions with an individual youth displaying oppositional and/or defiant behavior.

- Interventions that succeed in helping students to comply with adult directives usually lead to a decrease in disruptive behaviors (Musser, Bray, Kehle, & Jenson, 2001).
- Training parents and teachers to give commands and provide consequences effectively has been shown to improve compliance with adult requests (Musser et al., 2001).
- Delivery of requests for compliance in a firm but quiet tone of voice and also in statement form increased one program's effectiveness (O'Leary, Kaufman, Kass, & Drabman, 1970).
- Requests for compliance are more effective if specific and delivered within approximately 3 feet from the student (Van Houten, Nau, MacKenzie-Keating, Sameoto, & Colavecchia, 1982) and eye contact is established only once (Hamlet, Axelrod, & Kuerschner, 1984).

- Improving rates of students' compliance with adult requests can be achieved by obvious posting of four or five positively and behaviorally stated rules (Osenton & Chang, 1999; Rosenberg, 1986).
- Teacher movement in the classroom provides more supervision, earlier detection of potential problem situations, and increased opportunity to reward positive and prosocial behaviors (Rhode, Jenson, & Reavis, 1993).
- The use of mystery motivators can promote requests for compliance (Rhode et al., 1993). Mystery motivators are positive reinforcers that are not made known to the child, and they have been shown to help with the improvement of inappropriate behaviors (Kehle, Madaus, Baratta, & Bray, 1998).

What We Can Do

Assessment
In order to use evidence-based interventions most effectively, an accurate assessment must be conducted to ensure that the youth meets the diagnostic criteria for ODD. Eamon and Altshuler (2004) highlighted the "multilayered and reciprocal nature of child, family, peer, neighborhood, and school factors in development" (p. 24). For this reason, it can be beneficial to observe children in different settings within school during a school day or week, obtain data from others in the school environment, read and review school files and referral materials, obtain data from parents regarding the youth's behavior in the home environment, as well as conduct individual interviews with the youth. The Eyberg Child Behavior Inventory (ECBI) and the Sutter-Eyberg Student Behavior Inventory (SESBI) are two of the instruments outlined in the literature that might offer some information regarding the child's behavioral functioning in the schools (Burns & Patterson, 2001). The Achenbach Child Behavior Checklist is another assessment tool utilized for home and school data, although the evidence base is not strong regarding its accuracy for diagnosis of ODD (Abolt & Thyer, 2002).

Individual Interventions
Currently, no individual interventions have been shown to be effective in producing clinically significant changes in children or adolescents who meet the criteria of ODD (Hemphill & Littlefield, 2001).

Relational and attachment theories subscribe to the notion that change can occur based on the healing power of the relationship, and although more evidence is likely in the future regarding the effectiveness of relationship to the treatment of ODD, currently there is only practice wisdom and the theory of resilience that suggest that these approaches might have a positive outcome on engaging students in a change process. In school settings, relational approaches may be integrated with evidence-based practices, such as problem-solving skills training, anger-control training, and cognitive-behavioral therapies.

Resiliency

Garbarino (1999) identifies certain characteristics and conditions as directly relevant to making an impact on boys with behavioral disorders and their futures. Some of these are particularly relevant to the school environment: a stable positive emotional relationship with at least one person; actively coping with stress by finding meaning in it or making something positive out of it; an intelligence quotient (IQ) in the average range (but IQ scores can be misleading; a child's emotional intelligence is not scored on standard IQ measures); awareness of the student's own strengths and possession of a real concept of self; and positive social support from persons or institutions outside of the family (p. 168). Garbarino (1999) goes on to say that there are a number of "psychological anchors of resilience" that "are important in generating ideas for programs to save boys before they become troubled and violent" (p. 170). He defines social anchors as "the characteristics of a healthy community that holds and protects boys as they grow" (p. 170). Some of these social anchors are particularly relevant to schools and their communities:

1. Youth need some level of predictability and routine in their lives, and they thrive when this stability is present for them (the concept of stability).
2. All children need to be affirmed, which means "receiving messages of one's value and worth" (p. 171).
3. An environment that provides a sense of security allows for active exploration of the environment without fear of abandonment or danger.
4. Adults need to invest time and be physically and psychologically present with the youth.

Schools can create environments that will act as social anchors for the students, enhancing their resiliency and making a systemic impact on their overall functioning in constructive ways.

Relationship-Based Interventions

Although no efficacious individual interventions are presently documented, skilled practitioners discuss the positive effects of relational, cognitive-behavioral, and supportive individual work with children and adolescents who meet the criteria for the diagnosis of ODD. So often, these youth are disliked or disregarded by adults, and this is understandable in schools, given the challenges they can present in a classroom and with authority. Relationships with these youngsters, identified in the system as "problematic" or "defiant," can sometimes take time and require great patience from the school mental health worker or social worker. It is likely that the older the youth, the more challenging the relationship is to develop. The worker must meet the youth where he is, without pushing him to make changes in his behavior or to connect with the worker faster or more intimately than the youth can manage. By working with the youth at his own pace, the worker can gain trust and promote security and stability in the relationship. Once a relationship is established, infusion of problem-solving skill curricula or social skills training can occur, although modeling of prosocial behaviors is occurring all along within the relationship-building process. As part of the modeling process, games that emphasize turn taking, promote problem solving, and de-emphasize competition can be played with the youth.

Play Therapy

For children of age 12 and below, individual, child-centered play therapy is supported by practice wisdom to be an effective option, although adequate evaluative research does not exist to support this model. Briefly, then, the basic skills of child-centered play therapy lend themselves to creating an atmosphere that encourages the development of "necessary coping skills within safe boundaries" (Mader, 2000, p. 57). Play therapy is based on the premise that children express themselves via play, as opposed to adults who express themselves via talking. Mader (2000) suggests "a framework within which one can work with the principal, teaching colleagues, and parents to develop an action plan that includes play counseling as a viable approach to changing behavior in disruptive students" (p. 56).

Group Interventions

Problem-Solving and Social Skills Training in Groups

Problem-solving training and social skills training have evidence bases in the literature for affecting younger children who show symptoms of ODD (Bierman, Miller, & Stabb, 1987; Kazdin, 1997). Dodge and Price (1994) relate that children who accurately perceive and effectively solve interpersonal problems use a five-stage, sequential, problem-solving decision-making process. See Chapter 1 on conduct disorder for an additional review of problem-solving skills interventions. Group settings are ideal for teaching and practicing social problem-solving skills in the school setting. One problem-solving method using these highlighted steps is Second Step, "a violence-prevention curriculum created with the dual goals of reducing development of social, emotional, and behavioral problems and promoting the development of core competencies" (Frey, Hirschstein, & Guzzo, 2000, p. 103).

Using the group process, students practice this problem-solving model with hypothetical situations. Providing role-plays and dramatic and comedic scenes for the youth to practice sometimes offers emotional distance when skills teaching and practicing begins in the group. Video clips are also useful for this purpose. Shorter role-plays, scenes, and video clips might be utilized with younger children, and puppets or doll play might also benefit this age-group.

Meichenbaum (1977) discusses the use of verbal mediation, or "self-talk," as a strategy, in this case, for youth to remember to manage impulses and to think about consequences of behavior or solutions. Self-talk can also be used to reward the children and adolescents for their own positive or successful behaviors. The third step of the problem-solving process is particularly important because it "establishes four basic values or norms for behavior: safety, fairness, people's feelings, and effectiveness" (Frey, Hirschstein, & Guzzo, 2000, p. 105) (see Box 3.2). Values clarification is considered relevant when teaching children to problem solve, as children's problem-solving skills are improved once they are able to establish their own positive norms (Lochman, Coie, Underwood, & Terry, 1993).

Anger Control and Stress Inoculation Training

Because the peer group is such an important part of adolescent development and because schools tend to have limited resources to provide mental health services to greater numbers of students in need, group treatment can be an effective modality for the youth and for the school. Anger-control groups have been shown to be efficacious in treating ODD youngsters (Sprague & Thyer, 2002).

The following steps might be helpful to make the group work:

Preparation

- Review the files and referral materials of those youth indicated to be showing symptoms of ODD.
- Complete assessments of the youth by interviewing them individually and speaking with their various teachers directly about their behaviors.
- Using the written materials and the interviews, determine if the referred youth meet the criteria for ODD as indicated by the *DSM-IV-TR*.

Box 3.2. Problem-Solving Method

1. Identify the problem.
2. Brainstorm solutions.
3. Evaluate solutions by asking, "Is it safe? Is it fair? How might people feel? Will it work?"
4. Select, plan, and try the solution.
5. Evaluate if the solution worked and what to do next. (Frey, Hirschstein, & Guzzo, 2002, p. 105)

- Consider limiting the group to no more than six to eight members if the facilitator's group experience with this type of adolescent is minimal or if the acuity of the collective behaviors is intense. The group can be limited to as few as four students, but it can be quite small then when students are absent or unable to attend.
- In this age-group, it is suggested that same-sex membership might be more effective in order to minimize the heterosexual peer issues inherent in early adolescence.
- A cofacilitator is a helpful resource when working with youth who require a higher level of supervision and subsequent intervention. With cofacilitation, though, much work must be done to ensure active and open communication between facilitators in order to minimize splitting by the group members and other potential downfalls.
- Determine a plan for effective evaluation of the group treatment intervention. One might use disciplinary referrals to the office, teacher reports of in-class behavioral problems/consequences, and in-school suspensions to evaluate pre- and posttreatment outcomes. A pretest can be administered to the group members as well, determining their own views of their behaviors or their responses to conflictual situations.
- The group meets two times per week for 5 weeks, and it would consist of 10 50-minute training sessions. This might be modified to a 9-week session of one group session per week if necessary.
- Individual meetings occur again with the group members chosen for the group, and relationship development begins between the facilitator and the student. The facilitator begins to learn more about the student and his view of the world.

Group Process

- Group one establishes a group contract about participation and rules for the group. The group leader will discuss behavioral rewards for participation and homework completion. Some programs use snacks and soft drinks as rewards. Others use a point system that can accumulate into rewards at the end of a session. With this age group, using rewards more quickly can provide the short-term reinforcement necessary to promote compliance and participation. Group 1 should engage group members to keep their interests and to whet their appetites for future groups. At the end of the first group session, it might be beneficial to review with the group the goals that might be accomplished in this group. If there is resistance, this question can wait until later or be asked individually of group members in separate sessions between the group meetings (see Box 3.3).

Box 3.3. Idea for Group One

Show video clips of popular movies where characters are exhibiting both negative and positive behaviors. Group discussions can occur after these video clips with specific questions offered, such as "What set the character off?" "What did you see happen?" "What were the consequences?"

Often, ODD youth do not see all of the consequences of their actions, particularly the consequences that involve their peer relationships and issues of respect or trust. This is an opportunity to point these things out without stepping on anyone's toes personally in the first meeting.

- It is critical that the group leader uses skills to prevent power struggles from occurring with these group members. Other than issues of safety, few reasons exist that warrant a struggle with the youth over power.
- Put a structure into place in the group that offers clear and direct guidelines and expectations for behavior. Determine what will happen if a group member is not following directions or is violating any other group rule.
- Find ways to reward group members for following the rules but also for the prosocial behavior of helping their peers to follow the rules.
- Use group process to help in sticky situations. For example: "What do you think we need to do about Joey's behavior, guys?" "What do you think our choices are?" "If Joey continues to break Rule #2, our group can't [pick something positive that is planned or a group reward that could be given]. I'm wondering how the group can help?" Give verbal praise to the suggestions that are beneficial, while trying to ignore or minimize the negative or threatening comments.
- It is sometimes helpful to use humor to defuse negative comments as well. "Well, Freddy, punching Joey in the face is an option. However, then, you would be in even more trouble with the group than Joey is. Great idea?"
- Group Two would teach the group about the cycle of provocation, which includes how to identify one's own cues of anger and one's own aggressive or inappropriate responses and then the consequences of

these types of events. Movie clips can again be shown to demonstrate this cycle, and group members can use these to understand the way the cycle works with others. Depending on the group's willingness at this point, role-plays can begin to demonstrate either predetermined situations provided on index cards to the players, or if the group is engaging more readily, they can provide their own scenarios. Inside-the-group reinforcements happen when certain students are shown how to work and commandeer the video player or they are chosen as the director of a scene (Sprague & Thyer, 2002).

- Future groups can focus on common self-control strategies as well as assertiveness versus aggression. Specific microskills must be defined for each strategy in order to teach it in a step-by-step way. Videotaping role-plays of the youth engaging in a problematic situation can be extremely helpful. The group can review the tape together, with individual input from group members about what details led to the problems in the situation. They might identify details such as voice tones, facial expressions, hand gestures, defensiveness, hostile posturing, and angry eye contact. The scenes can be rehearsed then, using different types of coping and self-control strategies, and videotapes can be reviewed again during the course of the group. Voice tone, eye contact, the broken-record technique, problem solving, choosing battles, taking time outs, and other forms of relaxation for de-escalation are all suitable for the self-control strategy curricula.

- Rehearsal is a critical component of this type of program. Practice! Practice! Practice! Have different kids role-play alternative responses for other kids. Practice the new skills as much as possible, and provide homework to the youth to try these new skills in other situations. Have them write about their experiences and bring this information back to the group. Reward them for completing assignments and bringing them back to the group.

Termination

- Begin preparing the group for termination several sessions prior to the last one. Remind them of the number of group meetings left. Anticipate that the group members might regress some or even miss a group or two while they begin the process of preparing for termination. Youth with ODD sometimes have issues with attachment and intimacy, and termination might trigger these issues. Encourage the group members to talk about termination and how endings have happened for them in the past. If the group is unable to do this as a whole, provide one more individual session to each student and discuss his progress in the group, strengths, and areas for growth. Offer the opportunity for more discussion about termination in this one-to-one meeting.

- Provide an ending to remember! Offer certificates for completion of the training, and it might even be worthwhile to frame them so that the youth are less likely to throw them away or misplace them. Provide a letter to the youth outlining the things discussed at the individual meetings, particularly the issues where growth has taken place and where strengths have been shown. If possible, this ending session might even involve a party where teachers and others are invited to celebrate the program's completion. This will depend on resources as well as the group's functioning and state of cohesion at the time of termination. Have the group members talk to each other about what they learned from each other specifically and ask what they will take with them from the group.

- Conduct a posttest to review the students' evaluation of their behaviors now that the group intervention has taken place. Review the posttreatment data to determine if changes have occurred in the students' school behavior and problem-solving abilities.

Group Assertiveness Training

Huey and Rank (1984) provided group assertiveness training to African American boys who were identified as demonstrating aggression in the classroom. The following definitions were provided to distinguish assertive, passive, or aggressive responses:

"A response that was forthright and honest without being threatening or abusive was considered an assertive response" (Sprague & Thyer, 2002, p. 68). A passive response was one that showed unwillingness for the student to stand up for his rights (Sprague & Thyer, 2002). An aggressive response was when the student "used sarcasm, insults, threats, and tried to reach his goals in an abusive way" (Sprague & Thyer, 2002, p. 68). The boys receiving assertiveness training showed significant improvement posttreatment with their aggressiveness and anger in the classroom, more so than those assigned to group discussion only or to no treatment at all (Sprague & Thyer, 2002). This provides another intervention option, then, using the group formation and implementation suggestions above.

Rational-Emotive Therapy

Finally, Block (1978) reviewed a mental health program utilized with African American and Latino youth in the 11th and 12th grades. These youth were "prone to misconduct" and were also at risk of school failure. The program was one of rational-emotive therapy (RET), which is based on cognitive theory and which was made famous by Albert Ellis, a psychologist. Barker (1999) writes that the therapy is one in which the "client is encouraged to make distinctions between what is objective fact in the environment and the inaccurate, negative, and self-limiting interpretations made of one's own behavior and life" (p. 400). The group leaders used a task-oriented approach, and they maintained a more directive stance in the group. The process used much role-play, small-group directed discussion, and homework assignments. Exercises involved direct confrontations and taking risks, and the youth were asked to discuss openly their feelings and reactions to the homework and the assignments in the group (Sprague & Thyer, 2002). With more information about the RET method and more study about the processes underlying this model, group interventions could be developed in schools that utilize this evidence-based approach (see Box 3.4).

School mental health professionals starting groups should consider this important caution. Although particular cognitive-behavioral interventions have shown some promise with improving problematic behavior in adolescents, it is always a challenging practice to bring together a group of youth, especially of adolescent age, who demonstrate the same types of ego limitations or

---

Box 3.4. Four Methods to Teach Alternative Responses to Conflict or Provocation

1. Self-Instruction: This is also called self-talk. The student might remind himself to keep cool or to ignore a situation.
2. Covert Modification of the Participant's Understanding of the Aggression-Causing Conditions: This is the "you're just jealous" reaction. The student uses self-talk to reframe the reason for the person's provocative behavior.
3. Self-Evaluation of Behavior During a Conflict and of Efficient Goal Accomplishment: This is a technique that asks the student to evaluate his own reactions as they are happening: "How am I doing here?" or "How did I handle that?"
4. Cognitive Control Technique of Thinking Ahead: This method focuses on changing faulty thinking skills inherent in many troubled youth.

Sources: Feindler, Marriott, & Iwata, 1984; Sprague & Thyer, 2002.

acting-out defenses. Ideally, prosocial and cognitive restructuring opportunities might happen in a group carefully selected with a balance of personality types and varied strengths. Who decided to put all the kids with behavior problems in the same class anyway, expecting them to be educated? Balancing a group with students who have various issues or varying degrees of symptoms could be beneficial for all involved.

Parent Training

Parent–child interaction therapy (PCIT) is a family therapy approach to the treatment of psychological problems of preschool children that integrates both traditional and behavioral methods (Brinkmeyer & Eyberg, 2003). Treatment is conducted in two phases, labeled child-directed interaction (CDI) and parent-directed interaction (PDI). In CDI, the parents are taught to allow their child to lead the play activity. Parents are taught to describe, imitate, and praise the child's appropriate behavior, and they are also taught not to criticize the child. In PDI, the parents are taught how to direct and redirect their child's activity. Parents are taught to use clear and positive statements and direct commands as well as consistent consequences, both positive and negative, for behavior. Quite a bit of evidence base exists for the use of parent training models with oppositional defiant children.

Pharmacological Interventions

No one type of medication is usually prescribed for ODD because no particular medication or class of medication has been shown to be beneficial. There is no evidence base for effective use of psychotropic medications to treat ODD (Hoagwood, Burns, Kiser, Ringeisen, & Schoenwald, 2001). This finding highlights the importance of accurate assessment of the child diagnosed with ODD, as there can be co-occurring disorders that might respond to pharmacological treatment (e.g., depression). It is the ethical responsibility of the school social worker or mental health worker to refer the student for psychiatric consultation, should any information from the youth's assessment indicate the need for further medical intervention.

Tools and Practice Examples

Practice Example

A 13-year-old, Latino male student (Rico) was referred to a 27-year-old, Caucasian female social work intern (Polly) because of his school-based acting-out behavior, which included angry outbursts in the classroom and truancy. Rico told Polly that he did not have any problems, and when she asked specifically about why he thought he might have been referred to her, he replied,

"I don't know, Miss." Polly established a consistent date and time to see Rico, and she met with him in the same office for several sessions, even though both of these issues were very difficult to achieve in her schedule and in this school setting. His attention span was reported to be short, so Polly started sessions at 30 minutes each.

Polly played cards with Rico and engaged him in discussions about things that he liked, disliked, enjoyed, and did not enjoy (his favorite movies, favorite foods, favorite sports, important people in his life, people he admired, people he did not, and so on). Polly raised questions about this in her supervision, questioning her effectiveness and purpose if this were the extent of her intervention with this young male. If Rico were absent on a day when a session was supposed to occur, Polly would call his home and leave a message and follow up on a subsequent day to see him in the school environment. She would not offer him a full session, but instead, she would notice his absence from their session and express her hope that he would be there for the next one.

Polly challenged Rico to think before he answered and to use different words to express himself, rather than "I don't know." She countered his potential resistance to engaging in the intervention by saying, "This probably won't work, or you might choose not to do it, but it might be interesting to see what happens." Rico eventually began to stop himself from answering with "I don't know" without any prompting, but Polly had to wait for him to do this in his own time frame. There were days that he did not seem interested, most often due to a problem he had in school prior to the session or to a health issue, and Polly did not pressure Rico to perform. Any outside pressure can regress the relationship to an earlier stage or push the child to cope ineffectively, as in previous times.

Polly walked around the school track and played basketball with Rico during some sessions. She worked with Rico's teachers, assisting them to manage their own impatience regarding his change process. Work with teachers is critical for the youth's success, as the youth often experiences negativity from school professionals about the rate of his progress. This allows the teachers to express their frustrations appropriately to the worker, while also gaining wisdom about the youth's progress. Providing support to teachers can infuse energy into their work as well, and this might be demonstrated via more patience with the youth or by employing alternative techniques, such as humor or planned ignoring, to manage behavioral difficulties.

Polly implemented more one-on-one problem-solving skills training. She and Rico practiced the skills and videotaped the role-plays, showing all types of responses. Polly brought professional movie clips into her sessions with Rico also and discussed what worked and what did not work for the characters in the movies. At year's end, Rico tolerated 50-minute sessions. Truancy was no longer a problem, and his classroom behavior showed significant improvement.

Resources

The following list offers resources to locate further information as needed about other relevant research.

Social Skills Training Program for Peer-Rejected Boys
Bierman, K. L., Miller, C. M., & Stabb, S. (1987). Improving the social behavior and peer acceptance of rejected boys: Effects of social skill training with instructions and prohibitions. *Journal of Consulting and Clinical Psychology, 55,* 194–200.

Webster-Stratton, C., & Reid, M. (2003). *The incredible years parents, teachers, and children training series: A multifaceted treatment approach for young children with conduct problems.* http://www.incredibleyears.com.

Community-Based Collaboration With School Professionals
Multisystemic Therapy: http://www.mstservices.com. (This evidence-based approach requires interventions outside of school with professionals trained specifically in this area. Schools will often collaborate with this type of treatment as part of a team. This treatment is appropriate for adolescent youth who engage in severe willful misconduct that places them at risk for out-of-home placement.)

Anger Management Curriculum for 8- to 12-Year-Olds
Larson, J., & Lochman, J. (2002). *Helping schoolchildren cope with anger: A cognitive-behavioral intervention.* New York: Guilford. (The Anger Coping Program, an empirically supported group intervention for 8- to 12-year-olds with anger and aggression problems, is offered in this manual. This program is supported by research to reduce teacher- and parent-directed aggression; improve on-task behavior in the classroom; and improve participants' verbal assertiveness and compromise skills, social competence, and academic achievement.)

Mystery Motivators
Rhode, G., Jenson, W., & Reavis, H. (1993). *The tough kid book: Practical classroom management strategies.* Longmont, CO: Sopris West. (This book offers further information about mystery motivators, mentioned above.)

Classroom Behavior Management
Harris, V. W., & Sherman, J. A. (1973). Use and analysis of the "good behavior game" to reduce disruptive classroom behavior. *Journal of Applied Behavior Analysis, 6,* 405–417. (The good behavior game is a school-based prevention program that has an evidence base for reducing problem behaviors in children.)

Key Points to Remember

Given the prevalence of ODD in children and adolescents, it is somewhat surprising that a limited number of evidence-based treatments are documented to be effective with this population. Within a school setting, particular group interventions and parent-training modules have been shown to be effective in treating ODD, but presently no pharmacological or individual interventions have shown clinical effectiveness. Practice wisdom gains support from the concept of resiliency, suggesting that certain relational therapies can be effective in ameliorating the symptoms of ODD in youth, even though no current research demonstrates evidence-based effectiveness. Clearly, further research is necessary to expand the list of what works with these youth, and it is hoped that this research can focus specifically on the symptoms of ODD, rather than grouping it together with other disorders and, consequently, creating confounds about what really works with ODD youth.

Within the school setting, though, a number of the evidence-based interventions are appropriate for implementation. Groups targeting social skills training, problem solving, assertiveness, and anger management can be offered in the schools, and consultation regarding these issues can be provided to educators by school social workers and mental health workers. Individual relationship building seems relevant in order to model prosocial behaviors as well as build resiliency in the youth. Parent training is another possibility. From a systems perspective, a model of intervention for youth with ODD that targets multiple layers of the system is likely to offer the most chances for youth to gain the skills necessary for optimum functioning within the school environment.

Effective Interventions for Students With Separation Anxiety Disorder

Marilyn Camacho
Lisa Hunter

Getting Started

Children experiencing separation anxiety display signs of distress when separated from their parents or primary caregivers. Separation anxiety is a normal phase of development typically evident between 10 and 18 months, and symptoms tend to dissipate by the time the child reaches the age of 2 or 3 years (Carruth, 2000). Separation anxiety becomes a disorder when "the expected developmental levels are exceeded, resulting in significant distress and impairment at home, school, and in social contexts" (Albano & Kendall, 2002, p. 130). The detrimental effects of separation anxiety disorder (SAD) are particularly noticeable in schools, given that they form the setting where children are separated from their parents for the longest period of time. As such, school-based practitioners are in the unique position to identify and treat SAD. Their access to students, parents, and school staff facilitates the identification of the disorder and the implementation of appropriate interventions. In this chapter, we will briefly review the diagnostic criteria and epidemiology of SAD, describe the Coping Cat program (Kendall, 2000a), the intervention of choice for this disorder, and discuss how it can be implemented in a school setting.

What We Know

Diagnosis and Prevalence of Separation Anxiety Disorder

According to the American Psychiatric Association's *Diagnostic and Statistical Manual of Mental Disorders (DSM-IV-TR)*, SAD in children and young adolescents is marked by "developmentally inappropriate and excessive anxiety concerning separation from the home or from those to whom the person is attached" (American Psychiatric Association, 2000, p. 125). The *DSM-IV-TR* diagnostic criteria for SAD are listed in Table 4.1.

The prevalence rate for SAD is 4% (American Psychiatric Association, 2000). Children with SAD typically range in age from 8 to 12 years (Compton, Nelson, & March 2000) with age of onset being 9 years in clinical samples (Tonge, 1994). SAD is more common in children from lower socioeconomic backgrounds (Saavedra & Silverman, 2002) and is more prevalent in girls than boys (Last,

Table 4.1 DSM-IV-TR Diagnostic Criteria for Separation Anxiety Disorder

Criterion A: Developmentally inappropriate and excessive anxiety concerning separation from home or from those to whom the individual is attached, as shown by at least three of the following:
  • Recurrent excessive distress when separation from home or major attachment figures occurs or is anticipated
  • Persistent and excessive worry about losing, or about possible harm befalling, major attachment figures
  • Persistent and excessive worry that an untoward event will lead to separation from a major attachment figure
  • Persistent reluctance or refusal to go to school or elsewhere because of fear of separation
  • Persistently and excessively fearful or reluctant to be alone or without major attachment figures at home or without significant adults in other settings
  • Persistent reluctance or refusal to go to sleep without being near a major attachment figure or to sleep away from home
  • Repeated nightmares involving the theme of separation
  • Repeated complaints of physical symptoms (such as headaches, stomachaches, nausea, or vomiting) when separation from major attachment figures occurs or is anticipated

Criterion B: Duration of disturbance is at least 4 weeks

Criterion C: Age of onset is before 18 years (specify if early onset occurs before age 6 years)

Criterion D: Disturbance causes clinically significant distress or impairment in social, academic (occupational), or other important areas of functioning

Criterion E: Disturbance does not occur exclusively during the course of a pervasive developmental disorder, or other psychotic disorder and, in adolescents, is not better accounted for by panic disorder with agoraphobia

Source: Reprinted with permission from the *Diagnostic and Statistical Manual of Mental Disorders,* Copyright 2000, American Psychiatric Association.

Hersen, Kazdin, Finkelstein, & Strauss, 1987). Overall, there is no evidence that SAD is more prevalent in any particular culture (Albano & Kendall, 2002).

Children with SAD often have other psychiatric disorders as well. Disorders that most commonly occur with SAD include generalized anxiety disorder (GAD) and social phobia (SoP) (Velting, Setzer, & Albano, 2004). There is also evidence of comorbidity between SAD and depression, obsessive-compulsive disorder, and gender identity disorder (Silverman & Dick-Niederhauser, 2004).

What Does SAD Look Like?

There are some developmental variations in the presentation of SAD among children. Younger children tend to report more symptoms than their older counterparts (Francis, Last, & Strauss, 1987). In addition, the presentation of SAD in younger children has been described as "amorphous" while older children present more explicit concerns relating to separation (Perwien & Berstein, 2004).

Young children may express SAD by closely shadowing their parents throughout the day and checking on their whereabouts for fear that the parents may become harmed (Fischer, Himle, & Thyer, 1999). In a school-aged child, symptoms associated with school refusal are most evident (Fischer et al., 1999). Some of these symptoms may include somatic complaints accompanied by frequent visits to the school nurse (Walkup & Ginsburg, 2002), tantrums, terror outbursts, attempts to leave the school to go home (Fischer et al., 1999), and high rates of school absence (Walkup & Ginsburg, 2002). It is important to note that although school refusal is a common symptom of SAD, it is not unique to the disorder and can be attributed to other disorders, such as specific phobia, social phobia, mood disorder, disruptive behavior disorder, or family conflict (Silverman & Dick-Niederhauser, 2004). Additional symptoms associated with SAD among school-aged children include frequent nightmares depicting threats to or separation from parents (Francis et al., 1987), refusal to participate in social activities that involve separation from parents, and a tendency to sleep with parents (Fischer et al., 1999).

Importance of Treating SAD in Schools

School personnel may not view SAD as a problem in need of immediate attention since externalizing disorders are so much more disruptive. This lack of attention may contribute to the underrecognition of SAD, leaving children suffering from the disorder significantly impaired and never referred for treatment. Left untreated, SAD may contribute to limited academic achievement, substance abuse, development of additional psychiatric disorders, and minimal social supports (Velting et al., 2004). In addition, there may be a relationship between SAD in childhood and panic disorder in adulthood (Gittelman & Klein, 1984). Given these possibilities, it is imperative that school staff, particularly teachers, learn how to identify children with SAD. School-based practitioners can provide teachers with informational sessions on how to identify SAD behaviors and guidance on when and how to make referrals to the school-based mental health clinic.

What We Can Do

Assessing Separation Anxiety Disorder

Clinical judgment is necessary to distinguish "developmentally appropriate levels of separation anxiety from the clinically significant concerns about separation seen in SAD" (American Psychiatric Association, 2000, p. 124). Diagnostic interviews have been developed to augment clinical judgment by providing systematic means of establishing the primary diagnosis and aid in the differential diagnosis of comorbid disorders (Langley, Bergman, & Piacentini, 2002). This is especially helpful in diagnosing anxiety disorders given the high incidence of comorbidity associated with these disorders. In addition, the use of self-report scales for anxiety disorders has proven to be useful in collecting information on patients' symptomology through multiple informants (Albano, 2003). These assessment measures may be administered in the beginning, middle, and termination phases of treatment in order to track changes in symptoms.

Clinical Interviews

There are two types of clinical interviews—structured and unstructured—that can be used to assess anxiety disorders in children. The structured interview can be used flexibly and by clinicians with "limited clinical judgment" (Albano, 2003). Semistructured interviews "provide guidelines for adapting inquiries to the age or developmental level of the child, and also allow for some flexibility in probing for clarification and further information" (Albano, 2003, p. 134). Although there are no diagnostic interviews designed exclusively to assess SAD, there are several interviews with an SAD subscale. Some examples of clinical interviews with specific subscales for assessing SAD include the Anxiety Disorders Interview Schedule for *DSM-IV* (ADIS; Silverman & Nelles, 1988), the Diagnostic Interview Schedule for Children (DISC-IV; Shaffer, Fisher, Lucas, Dulcan, & Schwab-Stone, 2000), the Diagnostic Interview for Children and Adolescents (DICA; Reich, 2000), the Child and Adolescent Psychiatric Assessment (CAPA; Angold & Costello, 2000), and the Children's Interview for Psychiatric Symptoms (ChIPS; Weller, Weller, Fristad, Rooney, & Schecter, 2000). Table 4.2 provides brief descriptions of these instruments.

Although clinical interviews such as those listed in Table 4.2 are useful tools for assessing SAD, they are most frequently used in research settings, can be time consuming to administer (2–3 hours), and may require clinician training. As such, they may not be practical for use in a school setting. The school-based practitioner, however, may find it useful to review these interviews to learn how to ask questions about SAD. Table 4.3 provides some sample questions that school-based clinicians can use when assessing for SAD.

Self-Report Measures

A number of self-report anxiety rating scales can be completed by children, as well as by parents. Although there is no established self-report measure for SAD, there are several assessment measures with items relevant to SAD that can be used to assess the disorder. These include the Multidimensional Anxiety Scale for Children (MASC; March, Parker, Sullivan, Stallings, & Conners, 1997), Screen for Child Anxiety Related Emotional Disorders (SCARED; Birmaher et al., 1997),

Table 4.2 Clinical Interviews With Separation Anxiety Disorder Subscales

Clinical Interview: Diagnostic Interview Schedule for Children (DISC-IV; Shaffer et al., 2000)
Characteristic Features of Interview:
  Age (years): 6–17
  Informant: Child and parent
  Format: Highly structured
  Administration: 90–120 minutes
  Source:
    DISC Development Group
    Division of Child Psychiatry
    1051 Riverside Drive, Box 78
    New York, NY 10032
    888-814-3472,
    disc@worldnet.att.net
    http://www.c-disc.com

Clinical Interview: Diagnostic Interview for Children and Adolescents (DICA; Reich, 2000)
Characteristic Features of Interview:
  Age (years): 6–17
  Informant: Child, parent
  Format: Structured and semi-structured
  Administration: 60 minutes
  Source:
    Wendy Reich, PhD
    Division of Child Psychiatry
    Washington Univertsity
    660 S. Euclid, Box 8134
    St. Louis, MO 63110
    314-286-2263
    Wendyr@twins.wustl.edu

Clinical Interview: Child and Adolescent Psychiatric Assessment (CAPA; Angold & Costello, 2000)
Characteristic Features of Interview:
  Age (years): 9–17
  Informant: Child & Parent
  Format: Structured
  Administration: 60–150 minutes
  Source:
    Adrian Angold, MD
    Department of Psychiatry & Behavioral Sciences
    Duke University Center,

(continued)

Table 4.2 (*Continued*)

Box 3454
Durham, NC 277710
919-687-4686
Adrian.angold@duke.edu

Clinical Interview: Anxiety Disorders Interview Scale for DSM-IV (ADIS; Silverman &
Nelles, 1988)
Characteristic Features of Interview:
Age *(years):* 6–17
Informant: Child & Parent
Format: Semi-structured
Administration: 60 minutes
Source:
Wendy Silverman, PhD
Department of Psychology
Florida International University
University Park Miami, FL 33199
305-348-2064
Wendy.Silverman@fiu.edu

Clinical Interview: Children's Interview for Psychiatric Symptoms (ChIPS; Weller
et al., 2000)
Characteristic Features of Interview:
Age *(years):* 6–18
Informant: Child and parent
Format: Highly structured
Administration: 40 minutes
Source:
Elizabeth Weller, M.D.
Department of Child Psychiatry
The Children's Hospital of Philadelphia
34th Street & Civic Boulevard
Philadelphia, PA 19104
212-590-7555
Weller@email.chop.edu

and Spence Children's Anxiety Scale (SCAS; Spence, 1997). Table 4.4 describes
the above-mentioned self-report measures. In addition, the School Refusal
Assessment Scale (SRAS; Kearney & Silverman, 1993) may be particularly useful
for SAD in order to establish whether symptoms of school refusal are indeed a
feature of SAD and not of other disorders, such as school phobia. These measures are particularly useful in school settings given that they require little time
to administer (10–15 minutes), do not require special equipment, and are of
minimal cost (James, Reynolds, & Dunbar, 1994).

Table 4.3 Sample Questions for Assessing Separation Anxiety Disorder in School-Aged Children [a]

- Are there times when you don't want to be in places without your mother like school or at a relative's house?
- Sometimes you may know ahead of time if you are going to a place without your mother. Do you ever start feeling sick when thinking about not being with your mother?
- Do you ever feel sick (e.g., headaches or stomachaches) when you are someplace without your mother?
- Do you worry that something bad will happen to your mother? What do you worry may happen to her?
- Has your mother ever been very sick, or hurt by someone, or been in a bad situation, like a car accident or robbery?
- Does your mother complain that you follow her around too much?
- Does your mother get upset with you when you worry about being away from her?
- Do you know anyone in your family or any of your friends who is very ill?
- Do you remember a time that you were not with your mother for a long time? When was that time and why were you not with her?
- At bedtime, do you sleep by yourself or with your mother?
- Does your mother ever ask you to sleep by yourself? How often does she ask you to sleep on your own?
- Do you ever have nightmares about someone in your family getting sick, or that you get lost, or even about something happening that stops you from being with your family? How often do you have these dreams?
- Do you like sleeping over at a friend's or relative's home? How did you feel the last time you slept over at someone's home?
- Do you have trouble getting to school in the morning?
- How often are you absent from school?
- How often do you visit the school nurse's office?
- Do you often want to leave school during the day and go home to be with your mother?
- Do you think about your mother often during the day while you are in school?
- Does thinking about your mother make it difficult for you to concentrate on your schoolwork?
- When you are at home, do you get dressed or shower by yourself?
- When you are at home without your mother, who takes care of you? Do you like spending time with him or her when your mother is away?

[a] The term "mother" should be replaced with "father" or "caregiver" as indicated.

Table 4.4 Self-Report Measures With Separation Anxiety Disorder Subscales

Interview: Multidimensional Anxiety Scale for Children (MASC; March et al., 1997)
Characteristic Features of Interview:
  Age: 8–19
  Informant: Child
  Length: 39 items
  Assessment: Four subscales: physical anxiety; harm avoidance; social anxiety; and separation anxiety
  Source:
    John S. March, MD
    Duke University Medical Center
    Department of Psychiatry, Box 3527
    Durham, NC 27710
    919-416-2404
    jsmarch@acpub.duke.edu

Interview: Screen for Anxiety and Related Emotional Disorders (SCARED; Birmaher et al., 1997)
Characteristic Features of Interview:
  Age: 8–18
  Informant: Child & Parent
  Length: 41 items
  Assessment: Five subscales: separation anxiety; school phobia; panic/somatic symptoms, generalized anxiety; social phobia
  Source:
    Boris Birmaher, MD
    Western Psychiatric Institute & Clinic
    Department of Child Psychology
    3811 O'Hara Street
    Pittsburgh, PA 15213
    412-246-5788
    birmaherb@upmc.edu

Interview: Spence Children's Anxiety Scale (SCAS; Spence, 1997)
Characteristic Features of Interview:
  Age: 8–12
  Informant: Child
  Length: 44 items
  Assessment: Six scales: separation anxiety; social phobia; obsessive-compulsive disorder; panic/agoraphobia; generalized anxiety
  Source:
    Susan H. Spence, PhD
    University of Queensland
    Department of Psychology
    Brisbane, QLD 4072
    61-7-3365-6220
    sues@psy.uq.edu.au

Teacher Reports

In addition to parents, teachers are also valuable informants in the assessment of SAD symptoms. Teachers are often the first to witness SAD, particularly when school refusal is one of the more prominent features. They can report on the frequency of a child's absences, presentation of symptoms, and degree to which symptoms are manifested. Although there are currently no SAD-specific teacher report measures, the Teacher Report Form (TRF; Achenbach, 1991) has been recommended when working with SAD (Perwien & Berstein, 2004).

Interventions

Once SAD has been assessed and diagnosed, the school-based practitioner has sufficient information to decide what intervention will best meet the child's needs. When selecting a treatment, practitioners should consider life stressors (e.g., death in family), time constraints (e.g., school setting), level of family involvement, and the child's level of functioning. In the following section, we will present a cognitive-behavioral approach for treating SAD and its applicability in the school setting.

The Coping Cat Program: A Cognitive-Behavioral Approach for Treating SAD

Cognitive-behavioral therapy (CBT) for the treatment of anxiety involves both working with the child's external environment through the use of behavioral techniques such as practice and exposure tasks, and working with the child's internal environment through the mastery of cognitive techniques such as positive self-talk and problem solving (Kendall, 2000b).

Although there have been no randomized clinical trials exclusively for SAD (Silverman & Dick-Niederhauser, 2004), the efficacy of using cognitive-behavioral methods for the treatment of SAD has been well documented in case studies (Hagopian & Slifer, 1993; Ollendick, Hagopian, & Huntzinger, 1991; Thyer & Sowers-Hoag, 1988). Some efficacy has been demonstrated for the use of CBT in conjunction with medication (Walkup, Labellarte, & Ginsburg, 2002). However, it is important to note that the pharmacological evidence for treating SAD is limited (Kearney & Silverman, 1998). As such, medication is not recommended as a "front-line intervention" but rather should be used with patients who experience severe SAD symptoms (Silverman & Dick-Niederhauser, 2004, p. 179).

The Coping Cat treatment program developed by Kendall, Kane, Howard, & Siqueland (1990) is the only treatment specifically designed to treat children with SAD in addition to related anxiety disorders (Kendall, Aschenbrand, & Hudson, 2003). Coping Cat is an individual, short-term, manualized treatment for children and young adolescents ranging in age from 7 to 13 years with a principal diagnosis of SAD, GAD, or SoP (Kendall et al., 2003). The program uses a combination of behavioral strategies to achieve the following treatment goals (Kendall & Southam-Gerow, 1995):

- Identifying anxious feelings and the body's response to the anxiety
- Understanding the role that self-talk plays in worsening the anxiety
- Increasing the capability to deal with anxiety by utilizing problem-solving and coping techniques
- Evaluating one's use of coping strategies and provision of appropriate rewards

Empirical Support for Coping Cat

The effectiveness of the Coping Cat program has been well documented in the literature (Kendall, 1994; Kendall et al., 1997; Kendall & Southam-Gerow, 1996). It is identified as the "most widely disseminated CBT protocol for childhood anxiety" (Velting et al., 2004, p. 48) and has been used with success in the United States (Kendall, 1994), Australia (Barrett, Dadds, & Rapee, 1996), and Canada (Mendlowitz et al., 1999). Coping Cat is highly adaptable and has proven effective when used in a group format (Barrett, 1998; Cobham, Dadds, & Spence 1998; Flannery-Schroeder & Kendall, 2000; Silverman et al., 1999) and in conjunction with family anxiety management (Barrett, Dadds, & Rapee, 1996). In addition, the Coping Cat program is efficacious across different ethnic groups and genders (Treadwell, Flannery-Schroeder, & Kendall, 1995).

Implementing the Coping Cat Program

Detailed guidelines for implementing the Coping Cat program are found in *Cognitive-Behavioral Therapy for Anxious Children: Therapist Manual* (Kendall, 2000a). Information about purchasing this manual is available at www.workbookpublishing.com. In addition to the *Therapist Manual*, a *Coping Cat Workbook* (Kendall, 1992) is available for children to use throughout treatment. The workbook facilitates the implementation of the treatment manual by providing child-friendly tasks that help the child to understand and apply treatment concepts more easily. The accompanying notebook allows the child to record homework assignments (Show-That-I-Can (STIC) tasks) that reinforce strategies learned during the session. In the next section, we will describe the Coping Cat program for anxious youth aged between 7 and 13. A version for older adolescents also exists: the C.A.T. program (Kendall, Choudhury, Hudson, & Webb, 2002a, 2002b).

Training and Supervision

Coping Cat requires proper training and supervision for successful program implementation. Although there is no set protocol for training clinicians in the use of Coping Cat, training in a manualized treatment generally involves introduction to the manual, reading and learning the manual through seminars and/or workshops, and group or individual supervision (Miller & Binder, 2002). Supervision addresses the extent to which session goals were met by the clinician and the degree to which the treatment meets individual patient needs while maintaining the integrity of the protocol (Kendall & Southam-Gerow, 1995). As mentioned previously, this chapter will provide an overview of the Coping Cat program and offer specific suggestions for using it in a school setting for the treatment of SAD. This chapter is not meant to replace the treatment manual or appropriate training and supervision from a clinician knowledgeable in the Coping Cat program. It is highly recommended that school-based practitioners interested in using the Coping Cat program with their clients read the manual and receive proper supervision before doing so.

Flexibility With the Manual
Research indicates that flexible application of the Coping Cat manual does not lead to poor treatment outcomes (Kendall & Chu, 2000). It is likely that school-based practitioners will have to make modifications to the manual in order to use it effectively in a school setting. For example, practitioners may need to cover less material in a given session in order to fit sessions into a school schedule. This type of flexibility is acceptable and encouraged.

Role of the Family in Implementation
Family involvement is essential when implementing the Coping Cat program. It is important that the family be involved in the assessment, planning, and execution of treatment goals. This is especially the case for children with SAD given that their fears are directly related to separation from their parents. Parents are involved during the assessment phase of treatment by providing valuable information on the manifestation of symptoms and history through verbal reports and completion of parent assessment scales. In some cases, the assessment phase may be the first interaction with the family and serves as an opportunity to establish rapport with the family (Kendall & Gosch, 1994). Parent sessions are integrated into the course of treatment in order to provide additional opportunities for open dialogue between therapist and family, to allow therapists to get feedback from parents and track the progress of treatment, and to coach parents on how to help their child cope with anxiety (Kendall & Gosch, 1994).

Role of Teachers in Implementation
Not only can teachers play an active role in the identification of SAD behaviors, but they can also provide valuable information on the course of SAD symptoms and aid in the implementation of treatment. Given their everyday contact with the child, they are the most likely to notice fluctuations in behavior throughout treatment and should be encouraged to share these observations with the school-based practitioner. In addition, teachers can facilitate treatment by participating in exposure exercises when appropriate, monitoring a child's visits

to the school-based medical clinic in response to somatic symptoms associated with SAD, limiting these visits, and restricting the child's contact with parents throughout the school day (Perwien & Berstein, 2004).

The Coping Cat Program: Sequence and Content of Child Sessions

The main goal of the Coping Cat program is to teach children and young adolescents how to "recognize signs of unwanted anxious arousal and to let these signs serve as cues for the use of the strategies the child has learned" (Kendall et al., 2003, p. 84). The treatment involves 14–18 sessions completed over the course of 12–16 weeks. However, the program may need to be adapted to a shorter number of sessions in order to fit into the academic calendar. In addition, the length of each session may need to be shortened to 40–45 minutes in order to better fit the scheduling demands of school settings.

Scheduling treatment sessions during school hours may prove to be challenging. Teachers may be reluctant to allow the child to leave the classroom to meet with the therapist during class time. As such, it is recommended that sessions be scheduled flexibly around school periods that involve elective classes (e.g., gym, music) or any free periods (e.g., study hall). It also may be difficult to schedule parent sessions during school hours. In some cases, it may be necessary for school practitioners to involve parents in treatment through telephone rather than face-to-face sessions.

Treatment includes a training phase and a practice phase. During the training phase (sessions 1–8), the child learns different techniques to cope with anxiety-provoking situations. In the practice phase, the child begins to practice coping techniques learned within the session or in vivo (sessions 9–18) (Kendall, 2000a). STIC homework tasks are introduced during each session. STIC tasks give the child an opportunity to recap what is learned in the session and apply it in the form of an at-home assignment. Each session begins with a review of the assignment and positive reinforcement from the therapist for completed tasks. The following section summarizes the Coping Cat sessions while highlighting the key tasks for each. The session summaries are not meant to replace the manual but to introduce the session content to school-based practitioners.

The Coping Cat Training Phase (Sessions 1–8)

During the training phase, ideas and tasks are introduced to the child in the order from simplest to more complex. The segment begins with the child's awareness of how the body reacts to anxious situations and learning to use these reactions as internal cues that anxiety is present. These concepts are presented in a child-friendly four-step plan with the acronym FEAR (*Feeling Frightened? Expecting bad things to happen? Attitudes and Actions that will help? Results and Rewards?*).

Session 1: Program Orientation   The training phase begins with the therapist establishing rapport with the child. The therapist assumes the role of a "coach" as she works together with the child throughout the Coping Cat program. In this first session, the therapist provides the child with an overview of what treatment entails while at the same time collecting information about what situations make the child anxious. Together, the therapist and child identify those situations that trigger the child's anxious reactions (e.g., when child is dropped off at school; when parent goes to bed and leaves child alone in bedroom; when parent goes away on vacation). Treatment goals as well as the utility of the *Coping Cat Workbook* and *Coping Cat Notebook* in meeting these goals are introduced.

Session 2: Identifying Anxious Feelings   The second session focuses on the link between anxious feelings and how different feelings manifest themselves in physical expressions. One of the goals of this session is to normalize the experience of fears and explain that the program is to help cope with these feelings. The therapist models the experience of anxiety-provoking situations and overcoming them. In addition, role-playing ("feelings charades") is used to facilitate the child's understanding that different feelings have different physical expressions. A "feelings dictionary" is then created to help the child identify the associated feelings.

As the child identifies the somatic feelings he experiences when feeling anxious, he begins to construct a fear hierarchy that ranks these feelings from the least to the most anxiety provoking. The fear hierarchy is developed over time, beginning with the identification of low-level anxiety-provoking situations during the first sessions and then medium and high-level anxiety-provoking situations in subsequent sessions. For the SAD child, a low-anxiety situation may involve the mother cooking in the kitchen while the child is watching television in the living room. A medium-level anxiety-provoking situation may be staying home with a babysitter for a few hours while a high-anxiety situation may involve the mother leaving the home for business travel.

In the case of the school refuser, it is important to assess whether refusal is due to a phobia or to separation. Other low-stress situations that are not necessarily related to school or separation from parents are explored. Showing empathy is particularly important at this stage, given that children with SAD often experience a lot of anger from parents and teachers about missing school. Specific strategies, like making a "survival pack" (e.g., stickers, helpful positive thoughts, or coping strategies that can be brought to school), are implemented to remind the child of the coping strategies learned. In addition, an in-school reward, such as making contact with a favorite teacher or counselor, is recommended.

Session 3: Recognizing Somatic Responses to Anxiety   Here, the child learns about the different somatic responses that are felt when in anxiety-provoking situations and how these responses serve as internal cues that anxiety is present. During this session, the first step of the coping plan—"F" (Feeling Frightened?)—is introduced. The therapist and child review specific somatic reactions to anxiety (e.g., stomach pains, nausea, headaches) and the differences between low and high anxiety. Imagery, modeling, and role-playing strategies are used to help the child verbalize somatic feelings during an identified low-anxiety situation. Although the therapist will often take the lead in initiating these exercises, the child is encouraged to "tag along" by adding his feelings to the role-playing. Throughout the session, the child practices using his somatic responses as cues with higher-anxiety situations (via modeling and role-playing exercises). The coping concept of "freeze frame" is introduced to allow the child to stop the anxiety-provoking situation, take a deep breath, and regroup.

Parent Session 1: Engaging the Parent   The primary purpose of the first parent session is to encourage parental cooperation in treatment. During this session, the therapist provides the parent with information about the treatment and discusses the child's progress in treatment. The parent is encouraged to ask questions regarding the treatment and to provide additional information about the child's anxiety (i.e., identify troublesome situations and somatic/cognitive reactions).

Parents often need to be reminded that the beginning sessions are only training sessions and that reductions in symptoms will not be seen until later when the skills learned during the training are applied and practiced. During the first parent session, the therapist should also discuss with parents the active role they will be required to take in treatment (e.g., practice the relaxation techniques to be learned in session 4 at home with their child, help their child with STIC tasks).

When working with SAD children who refuse to go to school, it is important to assess stressors in the home or community that may potentially interfere with the course of treatment. The therapist should explore whether the parent is facilitating the behavior through their fears or inability to cope with disruptive behaviors (e.g., tantrums, crying). It is also important to address parental concerns and to provide strategies the parents can use to cope with their child's illness. Also, parents should be strongly encouraged to reward any attempts by the child to go to school as a means of reinforcing the behavior.

Session 4: Relaxation Training   During the fourth session, the therapist teaches the child relaxation techniques that can be used to alleviate symptoms of anxiety. Here, the child identifies the connection between anxiety and muscle tension. The therapist introduces the concept of relaxation by differentiating between how the body feels when relaxed and when tense (e.g., have child lift shoulders as high as possible and then release) and by introducing relaxation procedures, such as deep breathing, visualization, and deep muscle tension and relaxation. (This exercise takes approximately 15 minutes.) Together, the therapist and child tape-record a relaxation script and practice using relaxation, coping modeling, and role-playing in anxious situations.

Session 5: Identifying Anxious Self-Talk   As the child becomes aware of his bodily responses, he is also taught to become aware of his thoughts during anxiety-provoking situations. In the fifth session, the child begins to identify his self-talk during anxiety-provoking situations with the goal of reducing anxiety-provoking self-talk and using more coping self-talk. Here, the "E" step (Expecting bad things to happen?) is introduced to help the child identify thoughts associated with anxiety and the differences between anxious thoughts and coping thoughts. The child can use cartoon bubbles to identify thoughts that reduce stress and thoughts that might induce stress (see workbook). Through modeling and role-playing, the child practices coping self-talk, detecting possible thinking traps, and coping in more anxiety-provoking situations.

Session 6: Identifying Coping Thoughts and Actions   During this session, the child is taught how to cope in an anxiety-provoking situation. The therapist introduces the "A" step (Attitudes and Actions that will help?). In this sixth session, problem solving is introduced and an action plan is developed to help the child cope in anxious situations. Both the therapist and the child practice problem solving with low- and moderate-stress situations and then practice with increasingly higher-anxiety situations.

Session 7: Self-Evaluation and Rewards   In the seventh session, self-rating and rewards are introduced as the final step ("R": Results and Rewards) of the coping plan. Here, the child learns how to evaluate his own work and reward successes. The child uses a "feelings barometer" to rate his performance and is encouraged to practice self-rating and -rewarding in stressful situations (e.g., how well did I handle the situation?).

Session 8: FEAR Plan Review   By the eighth session, the child has already learned the main anxiety coping skills covered in the Coping Cat program. To help facilitate recall of these strategies, they are conceptualized in a child-friendly four-step plan called the FEAR plan. During this session, the child creates a FEAR plan poster to illustrate the strategies learned. In addition, a wallet-sized FEAR card is created for the child to help remember the strategies learned and to use as an anchor during anxiety-provoking situations. The FEAR plan is practiced (via modeling/role-playing) during the session beginning with nonstressful situations and continuing with increasingly anxious situations.

The Coping Cat Practice Phase (Sessions 9–16)
The second half of treatment is the practice phase. During this phase, the child applies the skills learned during the training phase to situations that elicit anxiety. The child is exposed to anxiety-provoking situations gradually, moving along a continuum from low-grade anxiety to higher grades of anxiety. The practice phase of treatment begins with a parent session.

Parent Session 2: Introduction to Practice Phase of Treatment   A second parent meeting is planned to introduce the parent to the practice phase of treatment. The therapist explains to the parent that the child will begin to practice the learned coping skills, and this will most probably make him appear to be more anxious. The exposure and practice goals of treatment are reviewed with the parent, as well as the ways in which the parent can support the child in what has been learned and continue to encourage the child's efforts.

Sessions 9 and 10: Exposure to Low-Anxiety Scenarios   In the 9th and 10th treatment sessions, the therapist initiates and continues to practice the FEAR plan with low-level anxiety-provoking situations using exposure strategies in both imaginal and in vivo scenarios. It is important to "acknowledge that this portion of treatment will provoke greater anxiety" (Kendall et al., 2003, p. 85).

The ninth session begins with a shift from learning skills to practicing the learned skills in real situations (the fear hierarchy is reviewed). Imaginal exposure exercises are implemented using the FEAR plan with low-anxiety situations (coping modeling) followed by in-session exposure exercises (e.g., for students with SAD, naturally occurring scenarios can be created in schools with the help of teachers and guidance counselors). In order to assess the extent to which the child experiences distress during exposure exercises, the subjective units of distress scale (SUDS) may be used. The therapist and child plan for additional exposure exercises to be implemented at home with the parents.

Imaginal and in-session exposure exercises with low-level anxiety-provoking situations (implementation of FEAR plan through coping modeling) are continued through the 10th session. One anxiety-provoking scenario may have several anxiety-provoking elements, which should be tackled one at a time. It is important that the therapist collaborate with the child in planning more challenging situations to practice during the following treatment session.

Sessions 11 and 12: Exposure to Moderate-Anxiety Scenarios   During these sessions, the child practices the FEAR coping plan in situations that produce moderate anxiety. In addition to using imaginal and in-session exposure to practice the FEAR plan, the therapist may want to initiate the child's first out-of-office exposure.

Sessions 13 and 14: Exposure to High-Anxiety Scenarios   Sessions 13 and 14 focus on the application of the FEAR plan to situations that produce high anxiety. Imaginal exposure exercises with high-level anxiety-provoking situations are implemented via modeling and role-playing exercises. Throughout these two sessions, the child is reminded to use relaxation exercises to help control anxiety levels. As the child masters the imaginal exposure exercises, in-session exposure exercises are implemented with high-level anxiety-provoking situations.

The idea of a commercial is introduced in session 14 as an informational piece, created by the child, to tell children how to manage anxiety. Producing a commercial will allow the child to act and feel like an expert on his own treatment and will provide a venue for the practitioner to observe what the child has learned over the course of therapy. The commercial can also be shared with others as evidence of the child's accomplishments.

Sessions 15 and 16: Making the Commercial   During sessions 15 and 16, the child continues to engage in in-vivo exposures in high-stress situations and to practice the FEAR plan. The therapist also begins to address anticipated concerns with termination while reinforcing the therapist's confidence in the child's ability to continue to progress on his own. Time is allotted in between sessions to allow the child to practice the FEAR coping skills on his own. As such, telephone check-ins are scheduled in between sessions as a means of providing more distanced support from the therapist.

The child, together with the therapist, begins to more actively plan the commercial. By session 16, the therapist reviews and summarizes the Coping Cat program. The commercial or audiotape "testimonial" is made, and the child's family is invited to view the commercial with the child and therapist.

Termination Session   The termination session, scheduled 1 week following the 16th session, is an opportunity for the therapist to provide feedback to the child and family on the child's overall progress in treatment and to comment on the child's strengths and weaknesses.

During this session, the child is presented with a certificate of completion ("goodbye ritual"), and the therapist establishes posttreatment plans with the parent that focus on helping the child to maintain and generalize his newly acquired skills. A check-in call is scheduled in 4 weeks, and future booster sessions are offered thereafter if needed.

Tools and Practice Example

Practice Example

Diego is an 8-year-old boy in the third grade, living in a single-parent home with his mother, Ms. Peña. His teacher, Miss Phillips, referred him to the school-based mental health clinic (SBMHC). Miss Phillips reported that Diego has been excessively absent in the last couple of months. When he does attend class, he arrives late, tearful, and in an irritable mood. When questioned about his tearfulness, he tells Miss Phillips that he feels sick and wants to go home. Attempts to go home are often unsuccessful. On these days, he seems distracted for most of the day and refuses to engage in school tasks. Miss Phillips reported that his behavior is worsening and is beginning to disrupt his learning.

The school-based therapist contacted Diego's mother following the teacher's referral. Ms. Peña recently started working in a perfume factory where she puts in long work hours and has an erratic work schedule. Although she acknowledged Miss Phillips's report of Diego's symptoms, she expressed that this is just a phase he is going through. Ms. Peña assured the therapist that she tries her best to bring Diego to school in order to force him to "get over it" but admits that she often gives in because "he acts up way too much." In addition, Ms. Peña expressed disappointment with the school staff for being so impatient with Diego and not understanding that his refusal to go to school is just a phase. In the spirit of building rapport with Ms. Peña, the therapist acknowledged Ms. Peña's frustrations in dealing with Diego's behaviors and invited her to come to the SBMHC with Diego for a preliminary assessment.

Assessing for Separation Anxiety Disorder

The therapist met with Diego and Ms. Peña to get some information about Diego's symptoms and to assess the extent of impairment they may be causing. Ms. Peña reported that Diego has been refusing to go to school for more than 3 months. His school avoidance leaves Ms. Peña feeling distressed, given that it interferes with her work and social life. On the days she is unable to get Diego to school, she calls in sick to stay at home and take care of him. On the days she does get to work, his morning tantrums make her late for work and his somatic symptoms require her to leave work early to pick him up from school. She also finds that she has little time for herself because of his refusal to go anywhere outside the home without her. In addition, Diego has been sleeping with Ms. Peña for the past 2 months because of recurrent nightmares that something "bad" is going to happen to her. Ms. Peña reported no other psychosocial stressors.

When it was Diego's turn to meet with the therapist alone, Diego appeared quite distressed about his mother leaving the room. Throughout the session, Diego consistently sought reassurance of his mother's whereabouts by opening the door of the therapist's office to see if she was still in the waiting room. The therapist used the SAD section of the Anxiety Disorders Interview Scale (ADIS; Silverman & Nelles, 1988) as a guide while interviewing Diego regarding his SAD symptoms. During the interview, Diego shared that when he thinks of something bad happening to his mother (e.g., car accident) his "tummy hurts real bad." Although Diego identified a few friends with whom he enjoys spending time, most of his social activities are limited to home since he refuses to go to a friend's home unless his mother accompanies him.

The assessment concluded with completion of the Screen for Anxiety and Related Emotional Disorders (SCARED; Birmaher et al., 1997) measure by both Diego and his mother. The therapist explained that the SCARED would be useful for assessing the severity of Diego's symptoms and monitoring his progress throughout treatment. Scores on the SAD subscale of the SCARED reflected significant impairment. After a careful review of Diego's symptoms, the therapist concluded that Diego met *DSM-IV-TR* diagnostic criteria for SAD and decided to use the Coping Cat program as the intervention of choice.

Implementing a 12-Week Coping Cat Program

Setting Up the FEAR Plan   The primary focus of the first phase of treatment was to help Diego learn the coping strategies of the FEAR plan. In order to help Diego link his bodily reactions to an emotion, the therapist and Diego played "feelings charades." Diego enjoyed playing the game and was able to identify feelings and their associated physical expressions. Diego then worked with the therapist to construct a fear hierarchy in which a low-anxiety situation was identified as sitting in the therapist's office alone while his mother stayed in the waiting area; a medium-level anxiety-provoking situation was identified as going to sleep by himself in his room; and a high-anxiety situation was spending a night at his grandma's house without contacting his mother. Beginning with the situation that caused the least stress, the therapist modeled the first step of the FEAR plan (F: Feeling Frightened?). Diego role-played a low-anxiety scenario where he recognized that the tightening of his chest was a clue that he was feeling anxious about not being able to check and see if his mother was still in the waiting room.

Mastering the second step in the FEAR plan (E: Expecting bad things to happen?) was not so easy. The therapist used the cartoons and empty thought bubbles in the Coping Cat workbook to help Diego master this concept. After much practice, Diego gradually was able to identify what thoughts made him anxious during his day-to-day experiences. The therapist coached Diego to use thoughts that reduce stress (coping self-talk) instead of those that induce it (anxious self-talk). The therapist and Diego practiced using coping self-talk when imagining Diego's fears of sleeping alone in his room. Diego repeated this exercise several times with different anxiety-provoking scenarios.

In the following sessions, the therapist and Diego explored some ideas about what he can do when he is anxious. During this problem-solving exercise (FEAR step A: Attitudes and Actions that will help?), Diego listed actions he could take, such as using deep-breathing exercises when alone in his room. The therapist referred to Diego's hierarchy of anxiety and modeled problem solving at bedtime. Diego recognized his anxious feelings and thoughts while getting ready to go to bed, joined in the role-playing, and acted out how he would listen to his favorite audio book while in bed.

Implementing the final coping step (R: Results and Rewards?) was challenging given the constant negative feedback Diego received from school staff and his mother in response to his SAD symptoms. Diego felt "bad" and undeserving of anything "good." His low self-esteem hindered his ability to evaluate his performance. The therapist worked with Diego on how to rate his own performance and praise his efforts even if the end result was not what he wanted. The therapist used Diego's past successes during session practices as examples of how Diego could rate himself positively. Diego enjoyed planning for potential rewards for successful efforts. When the therapist checked in with Ms. Peña, she expressed reluctance to reward Diego for behaviors such as going to school. She believed that Diego's attendance was to be expected and did not merit a reward. The therapist educated Ms. Peña on the importance of reinforcing positive behavior to sustain those behaviors that are desirable (i.e., going to school). Ms. Peña was receptive to the therapist's suggestions and rewarded Diego's efforts more consistently as she became comfortable with the concept of rewards.

By the end of the training phase, the therapist and Diego worked on creating a poster that illustrated the FEAR plan. Diego used bright-colored markers to detail each of the four steps to the FEAR plan while adding cut-outs from magazines that had phrases to help him recall different aspects of the plan. Diego then created a wallet-sized card and wrote the acronym FEAR on it. The FEAR card was in Diego's possession at all times and served as an anchor for him to refer to when confronting an anxiety-provoking situation.

Coping Cat Practice Phase   The main treatment goals of the second phase of treatment were to practice the FEAR plan in actual anxiety-provoking situations. Exposure to these situations was gradual, beginning with exposure to low-level situations and gradually progressing to higher-level situations.

During the beginning of the practice phase, the therapist met with Ms. Peña to review this phase of treatment. Ms. Peña was forewarned that Diego might appear more anxious in the next couple of weeks given his repeated exposure to anxiety-provoking situations. Ms. Peña was reminded of the importance of being a support for Diego and to continue praising his efforts and providing rewards for successes.

The first series of exposure sessions began with low-anxiety situations using both imaginal and in vivo exposure. For the imaginal exposure, the goal was for Diego to stay in his bedroom for 1 hour while his mother was cooking dinner in the kitchen. The therapist set up the situation as realistically as possible by hiding behind a bookcase in the office to represent the wall that separates Diego's room from the kitchen. Diego identified the stressor, used the feeling barometer to rate his anxiety, and problem solved how he would cope. The therapist later identified an anxiety-producing situation to be practiced in the office. Diego's goal was to stay in the therapist's office for the entire session without checking (e.g., opening the office door, calling out to his mother) to see if his mother was still in the waiting room. Additional in vivo exercises were practiced using low-level anxiety-provoking situations.

During the second series of exposures, the therapist referred to Diego's hierarchy of anxiety to select a situation of moderate anxiety for imaginal exposure. The first situation required Diego to imagine going to his cousin Jimmy's house to watch a movie without his mother. His mother would take him to Jimmy's home and pick him up when the movie was over. Through modeling and role-playing, Diego implemented the FEAR plan in this situation.

For the in vivo exposure, the goal was to implement the FEAR plan in the classroom upon arrival at school. The session was scheduled in the early morning and required collaboration between the therapist and Miss Phillips. On this day, Diego verbalized that he was feeling a bit queasy and recognized it was a signal that he was anxious because his mother had just dropped him off. Miss Phillips facilitated the exposure by reminding Diego to pull out his FEAR card. Diego sat through first period without requesting to go to the nurse's office. He was very proud of himself for his success and asked for his stickers as promised by Miss Phillips. Additional in vivo exposures for moderate-level anxiety-provoking situations were practiced in subsequent sessions.

The third in vivo exposure involved a high-anxiety situation. For Diego, this involved a one-night stay at his grandma's house without calling his mother. The therapist helped Diego to practice this situation in session by inviting his grandma to the office. The therapist coached his grandma on how to support Diego through the exercise. Diego identified the somatic cues (e.g., feeling sick) he experiences at grandma's house. He also identified for both his grandma and therapist his anxious thoughts about sleeping over without his mother (e.g., Mom will never come back to get me!) and how he would use coping thoughts instead (e.g., Mom has shown that she loves me very much and would not leave me at grandma's). Diego planned to evaluate his efforts the next morning and reward his successes. Grandma, armed with an understanding of Diego's action plan, detailed how she would support Diego by giving him reminders of the FEAR strategy, offering to participate in relaxation techniques, and praising his efforts throughout his stay. For additional support, the therapist arranged to conduct a telephone check that night to reassure Diego that she was confident he could do it on his own.

Termination   Diego was fully aware of the progress he had made throughout the course of treatment and was looking forward to sharing what he learned with other kids. Given the limited resources at the school, the therapist and Diego opted for creating a brochure to present his message to other children rather than filming a commercial. Multiple copies of the brochure were made so that he could distribute it to family and friends.

The therapist met with Ms. Peña and devised a maintenance plan for the coping skills learned by Diego. Ms. Peña reported a reduction in Diego's symptoms and seemed quite pleased with his progression throughout treatment. This was corroborated by the low SAD score on the SCARED measure completed by Ms. Peña and Diego. As a final reward for Diego's successful efforts, the therapist and Diego played basketball (Diego's favorite sport) in the school gym. The session ended with a goodbye ritual during which Diego was presented with a certificate of completion by the therapist in recognition of his participation in and successful completion of the Coping Cat program.

Resources

Coping Cat Program: Cognitive-Behavioral Intervention for Anxious Youth (Ages 8–13)

Philip C. Kendall, *Cognitive-Behavioral Therapy for Anxious Children: Therapist Manual* (2nd ed.). Temple University. www.workbookpublishing.com

Philip C. Kendall, *Coping Cat Workbook.* Temple University. www.workbookpublishing.com

Ellen Flannery-Schroeder & Philip C. Kendall, *Cognitive-Behavioral Therapy for Anxious Children: Therapist Manual for Group Treatment.* Temple University. www.workbookpublishing.com

Bonnie Howard, Brian C. Chu, Amy L. Krain, Abbe L. Marrs-Garcia, & Philip C. Kendall, *Cognitive-Behavioral Family Therapy for Anxious Children: Therapist Manual* (2nd ed.). Temple University. www.workbookpublishing.com

Philip C. Kendall & W. Michael Nelson III, *Managing Anxiety in Youth: The "Coping Cat" Video.* Xavier University. www.workbookpublishing.com

The C.A.T. Project: Cognitive-Behavioral Intervention for Anxious Older Youth (Ages 14–17)

Philip C. Kendall, Muniya Choudhury, Jennifer Hudson, & Alicia Webb, *The C.A.T. Project Workbook for the Cognitive-Behavioral Treatment of Anxious Adolescents.* Temple University. www.workbookpublishing.com

Philip C. Kendall, Muniya Choudhury, Jennifer Hudson, & Alicia Webb, *The C.A.T. Project Manual for the Cognitive Behavioral Treatment of Anxious Adolescents.* Temple University. www.workbookpublishing.com

Children's Books on Separation Anxiety

Elizabeth Crary & Marina Megale, *Mommy, Don't Go.* Reading level: Ages 4–8.

Irene Wineman Marcus, Paul Marcus, & Susan Jeschke, *Into the Great Forest: A Story for Children Away From Parents for the First Time.* Reading level: Ages 4–8

Judith Viorst, *The Good-Bye Book.* Reading level: Ages 4–8

Anxiety Organizations

Child & Adolescent Anxiety Disorders Clinic (CAADC). Temple University. 13th Street & Cecil B. Moore Avenue (Weiss Hall, Ground Level), Philadelphia, PA 19122. www.childanxiety.org

The Child Anxiety Network, Child and Adolescent Fear and Anxiety Treatment Program. 648 Beacon Street, 6th floor, Kenmore Square, Boston, MA 02215. 617-353-9610. www.childanxiety.net

Anxiety Disorder Association of America. 8730 Georgia Avenue, Suite 600, Silver Spring, MD 20910. 240-485-1001. www.adaa.org

Key Points to Remember

SAD is one of the most frequently reported disorders in the school setting. The literature on treating SAD indicates that CBT is the intervention of choice for treating the disorder. The Coping Cat program is particularly useful in treating

SAD in schools given its demonstrated effectiveness, transportability, and adaptability across diverse settings.

Implementing the Coping Cat program in the school setting requires some flexibility on the part of the school-based practitioner. Some of the factors that school-based therapists should keep in mind when implementing Coping Cat are summarized as follows:

- High comorbidity of SAD with other anxiety disorders requires that differential diagnoses be assessed thoroughly. This is especially true for children presenting with school refusal, given its similarity to school or social phobia.
- Teachers are instrumental in identifying SAD kids when provided with the resources to do so.
- Assessment of SAD is most comprehensive when multiple informants provide information on the manifestation of symptoms. Clinical interviews, self-reports (including parent versions), and teacher reports are strongly encouraged.
- The Coping Cat manual and accompanying workbook and notebook are essential tools for the delivery of CBT for SAD but must be used flexibly. Readers should obtain and read the manual prior to administering the treatment.
- Appropriate training and supervision are necessary for implementing Coping Cat.
- Family involvement throughout treatment will greatly enhance treatment effects. Parents are not only in the best position for reporting SAD symptoms but should participate actively in facilitating and reinforcing the strategies learned throughout treatment.

Effective Interventions for Students With Obsessive-Compulsive Disorder

Meghan Tomb
Lisa Hunter

Getting Started

Obsessive-compulsive disorder (OCD) is characterized by recurrent obsessions (which cause marked anxiety or distress) and by compulsions (which serve to neutralize anxiety) that are severe enough to be time consuming (i.e., take more than 1 hour a day) or cause marked distress or impairment in functioning (American Psychiatric Association, 2000). Obsessions are "recurrent, persistent ideas, thoughts, images, or impulses, which are ego-dystonic, and experienced as senseless or repugnant." Compulsions are "repetitive and seemingly purposeful actions that are performed according to certain rules, or in a stereotyped fashion" (Thomsen, 1998, p. 2). Compulsions act to neutralize the threat stemming from an obsession (Clark, 2000). OCD is not an exclusionary disorder and is often associated with major depressive disorder, other anxiety disorders (e.g., specific phobia, social phobia, panic disorder), eating disorders, and obsessive-compulsive personality disorder (American Psychiatric Association, 2000; March & Mulle, 1998). Symptomatology is similar in adults and children/adolescents with OCD; however, children may not recognize the obsessions and compulsions as excessive or unreasonable (American Psychiatric Association, 2000; Foster & Eisler, 2001; Wagner, 2003a). Table 5.1 shows the complete diagnostic criteria for OCD (American Psychiatric Association, 2000). See Chapters 4 and 6 for discussions of interventions for comorbid disorders of depression and other anxiety disorders.

It is important to note that some behaviors associated with OCD are common in the normal development of children. For instance, many children go through phases where they maintain superstitious beliefs, carry out certain rituals, such as bedtime rituals, or become fixed on a favorite number (Thomsen, 1998). However, these "normal" rituals typically dissipate by the age of 8 years, while children with OCD generally show an onset of the disorder after age 7. Only when rituals begin to interfere with daily life or cause marked distress should a diagnosis of OCD be considered. Washing, checking, and ordering rituals (see Table 5.2 for definitions) are particularly common, seen in about half the children with OCD (March & Mulle, 1998; Thomsen, 1998). However, these symptoms in children may not be ego-dystonic (disturbing to the self),

Table 5.1 Diagnostic Criteria for 300.3 Obsessive-Compulsive Disorder

A. Either obsessions or compulsions:

Obsessions as Defined by (1), (2), (3), and (4):
(1) recurrent and persistent thoughts, impulses, or images that are experienced, at some time during the disturbance, as intrusive and inappropriate and that cause marked anxiety or distress
(2) the thoughts, impulses, or images are not simply excessive worries about real-life problems
(3) the person attempts to ignore or suppress such thoughts, impulses, or images, or to neutralize them with some other thought or action
(4) the person recognizes that the obsessional thoughts, impulses, or images are a product of his or her own mind (not imposed from without as in thought insertion)

Compulsions as Defined by (1) and (2):
(1) repetitive behaviors (e.g., hand washing, ordering, checking) or mental acts (e.g., praying, counting, repeating words silently) that the person feels driven to perform in response to an obsession, or according to rules that must be applied rigidly
(2) the behaviors or mental acts are aimed at preventing or reducing distress or preventing some dreaded event or situation; however, these behaviors or mental acts either are not connected in a realistic way with what they are designed to neutralize or prevent or are clearly excessive

B. At some point during the course of the disorder, the person has recognized that the obsessions or compulsions are excessive or unreasonable. Note: This does not apply to children.

C. The obsessions or compulsions cause marked distress, are time consuming (take more than 1 hour a day), or significantly interfere with the person's normal routine, occupational (or academic) functioning, or usual social activities or relationships.

D. If another Axis I disorder is present, the content of the obsessions or compulsions is not restricted to it (e.g., preoccupation with food in the presence of an eating disorder; hair pulling in the presence of trichotillomania; concern with appearance in the presence of body dysmorphic disorder; preoccupation with drugs in the presence of a substance use disorder; preoccupation with having a serious illness in the presence of hypochondriasis; preoccupation with sexual urges or fantasies in the presence of a paraphilia; or guilty ruminations in the presence of major depressive disorder).

E. The disturbance is not due to the direct physiological effects of a substance (e.g., a drug or abuse of a medication) or a general medical condition.

(continued)

Table 5.1 *(Continued)*

Specify if:

> With poor insight: if, for most of the time during the current episode, the person does not recognize that the obsessions and compulsions are excessive or unreasonable.

Source: Reprinted with permission from the *Diagnostic and Statistical Manual of Mental Disorders,* Copyright 2000, American Psychiatric Association.

Table 5.2 Symptoms and Behavioral Manifestations of Obsessive-Compulsive Disorder

Obsessions

Behavioral Manifestations

Students may get "stuck," or fixated, on certain points and lose the need or ability to go on. Fixation on an obsessional thought may appear to be and is often mistaken for an attention problem, daydreaming, laziness, or poor motivation.

Examples in School Setting

- Fixation on a thought may cause distraction from the task at hand, which delays students in completing school work or following directions and can lead to a decrease in work production and low grades
- Fear of contamination, number obsessions ("safe" versus "bad" numbers), fear of harm or death

Compulsions
Washing/cleaning rituals

Behavioral Manifestations

These students may feel obligated to wash extensively and according to a self-prescribed manner for minutes to hours at a time. Others may be less thorough about washing or cleaning but may engage in the act frequently each day.

Examples in School Setting

- May appear as subtle behaviors not obviously related to washing or cleaning (i.e., going to the bathroom)
- Students may frequently leave the classroom to go to the bathroom in order to privately carry out cleaning rituals
- A physical sign of excessive washing is the presence of dry, red, chapped, cracked, or bleeding hands

(continued)

Table 5.2 *(Continued)*

Checking rituals

Behavioral Manifestations

The student may unnecessarily check specific things over and over again.

Examples in School Setting

- Getting ready for school, the student may check books over and over again to see if all the necessary books are there, sometimes causing lateness
- At school, the student may want to call or return home to check something yet another time
- The student may check and recheck answers on assignments to the point that they are submitted late or not at all
- Repeatedly checking a locker to see if it is locked
- Checking rituals may interfere with the completion of homework, can cause a student to work late into the night on assignments that should have taken 2 or 3 hours to complete

Repeating rituals

Behavioral Manifestations

The student repeats a behavior or task over and over again (often connected with counting rituals)

Examples in School Setting

- Repetitious questioning
- Reading and rereading sentences or paragraphs in a book
- Sharpening pencils several times in a row
- Repeatedly crossing out, tracing, or rewriting letters or words, erasing and re-erasing words
- May interfere with student's ability to take notes, complete computer-scored tests, and open locker

Symmetry/exactness rituals

Behavioral Manifestations

Obsessions revolving around a need for symmetry

Examples in School Setting

- Student may compulsively arrange objects in the classroom (e.g., books on a shelf, items on a page, pencils on a desk)
- Student may feel the need to have both sides of the body identical (e.g., laces on shoes), take steps that are identical in length, or place equal emphasis on each syllable of a word

Other compulsive behaviors

Behavioral Manifestations

Obsessional thoughts that lead to compulsive avoidance; individuals may go to great lengths to avoid objects, substances, or situations that are capable of triggering fear or discomfort

(continued)

Table 5.2 *(Continued)*

Examples in School Setting

- Fear of contamination may cause avoidance of objects in classroom (paint, glue, paste, clay, tape, ink)
- Inappropriately covering the hands with clothing or gloves or using shirttails or cuffs to open doors or turn on faucets
- If an obsessive fear of harm, may avoid using scissors or other sharp tools in the classroom
- Student may avoid using a particular doorway because passage through it may trigger a repeating ritual

Behavioral Manifestations

Compulsive reassurance seeking

Example in School Setting

- May continually ask teachers for reassurance that there are no germs on the drinking fountain or that there are no errors on a page

Behavioral Manifestations

Obsessions concerning fear

Example in School Setting

- Fear of cheating may cause students to compulsively seek reassurance, avoid looking at other children, and sometimes even to give wrong answers intentionally

and children do not frequently seek help. More commonly, parents will identify the problem and bring the child in for treatment. Like adults, children are more prone to engage in rituals at home than in front of peers, teachers, or strangers. This may make it difficult for school-based personnel (staff, practitioners) to identify children who are suffering quietly from OCD during school hours. Relatedly, gradual declines in schoolwork secondary to impaired concentration capabilities have been reported (American Psychiatric Association, 2000). Some of the common symptoms of OCD and ways these symptoms may be exhibited in the school setting are shown in Table 5.2.

What We Know

According to the APA (2000), community studies show that the estimated lifetime prevalence for OCD is 2.5% (Franklin et al., 1998) and the 1-year prevalence is 0.5%–2.1% in adults and 0.7% in children. More-recent reviews have reported lifetime prevalence rates of up to 4% (Foster & Eisler, 2001), with as many as 33%–50% of adults with OCD reporting onset of the disorder during childhood or adolescence (Franklin et al., 1998). There are not any differences in prevalence rates across different cultures (American Psychiatric Association, 2000). It is estimated that 1 in 200 children and adolescents has OCD (Adams, Waas, March, & Smith, 1994). Given this approximation, there may be 3–4 youths with OCD in an average-sized elementary school and possibly 20–30 in a large urban high school (Adams et al., 1994; March & Mulle, 1998). When left untreated, OCD can severely disrupt academic, home, social, and vocational functioning (Geller, Biederman, et al., 2001; March & Mulle, 1998; Piacentini, Bergman, Keller, & McCracken 2003). Without proper identification and treatment, these children and adolescents are at risk for significant difficulty in school.

Implications for School Social Workers and Other School-Based Practitioners and Staff

Classroom teachers and other school staff observe and interact with students on a daily basis for consistent periods of time and therefore have a unique opportunity to notice and identify OCD symptoms in children and adolescents (Adams et al., 1994). In some instances, school personnel may be the first adults in a child's life to identify potential OCD symptoms. It is essential, therefore, that "classroom teachers, school social workers, school psychologists, counselors, nurses, and administrators learn to identify OCD symptoms in the school setting, help make appropriate referrals, and assist, as appropriate, in the treatment of childhood OCD" (March & Mulle, 1998, p. 197).

School-based practitioners, like school social workers and counselors, play an important part in identifying children and adolescents who are suffering from OCD symptoms and in educating school personnel about OCD. When a child with OCD is properly identified and referred for services, the symptoms can be addressed, treated, and managed. If classroom teachers do not have the knowledge and tools to do this, symptoms may continue to impair the child's functioning on a greater scale and eventually cause the child to be unable to attend school (March & Mulle, 1998). One way that school-based practitioners can help this process is by educating school personnel on the specific ways that OCD symptoms can manifest themselves in the school setting. Information on OCD can be disseminated through teacher in-service trainings and seminars. These should include information on proper identification of OCD symptoms, referral options, and a description of available treatments for OCD. School-based practitioners may want to consult various resources in order to obtain the most up-to-date information on OCD and its treatment (Adams et al., 1994).

Teachers can be a valuable asset to school-based practitioners treating children with OCD. Teachers are in a position to report their own observations of the child in treatment as well as those of the child's peers in the classroom. Establishing a relationship with the teacher is imperative for this process. Teachers can also provide written records of social and academic problems the student is having (March & Mulle, 1998), as well as complete assessment measures. School-based practitioners should keep in mind that teachers may be more compliant in completing assessment measures for a referred student when the burden is kept low by short-form assessment measures (Velting, Setzer, & Albano, 2004).

What We Can Do

Cognitive-Behavioral Therapy as the First-Line Psychotherapy for OCD

After a school-based mental health practitioner diagnoses a child as having OCD, one of several different interventions may be implemented. Cognitive-behavioral therapy (CBT), alone or in combination with medication, represents the foundation of treatment for children and adolescents with OCD (American Academy of Child and Adolescent Psychiatry, 1998; March & Mulle, 1998) and is the basis for effective treatments for all anxiety disorders (Velting et al., 2004). For a complete review of the research literature supporting the efficacy of CBT for children and adolescents with anxiety disorders, see Kazdin and Weisz (1998), Ollendick and King (1998), and Albano and Kendall (2002). CBT programs for OCD utilize a combination of behavioral and cognitive information-processing approaches to alter symptoms. CBT aims to help the child with OCD to restructure unhealthy thoughts associated with the disorder in order to generate changes in the maladaptive behaviors that impair the child's daily home, school, and social functioning. The child learns specific strategies for coping with the disorder and, most important, for managing situations that may trigger certain thoughts and behavioral responses related to OCD.

The efficacy of CBT involving exposure and response prevention (E/RP) and pharmacotherapy with serotonin reuptake inhibitors (SRIs) is well established for adults (Franklin, Abramowitz, Bux, Zoellner, & Feeny, 2002; Franklin et al., 2003; Kampman, Keijsers, Hoogduin, & Verbraak, 2002). Although fewer data exist for the use of CBT for the treatment of pediatric OCD, it is believed to be a useful and successful treatment for youth (Franklin et al., 1998; March & Mulle, 1998; Southam-Gerow & Kendall, 2000). In an open trial, March et al. (1994) used an adapted version of CBT to treat 15 children and adolescents (6–18 years old) with OCD, most of whom had been previously stabilized on medication. The authors reported significant benefit immediately following treatment and at 6-month follow-up. At posttreatment, results demonstrated a mean reduction of 50% in OCD symptomatology on the Yale-Brown Obsessive Compulsive Scale (Y-BOCS) and clinically asymptomatic ratings on the National Institute of Mental Health (NIMH) Global OC Scale (March, Mulle, & Herbel, 1994). Eighty percent of patients were defined as responders to treatment. No patient relapsed after symptoms recurred, and booster sessions enabled six of the nine asymptomatic patients to stop taking medication without relapse (March & Mulle, 1998). In another open trial, Franklin et al. (1998), found CBT to be effective in reducing OCD symptoms. Twelve of 14 patients (10 to 17 years old) in this trial showed at least 50% improvement over their pretreatment Y-BOCS severity scores, and 83% remained improved in severity at follow-up. The results of both of these trials are comparable to treatment studies using pharmacotherapy only (Southam-Gerow & Kendall, 2000).

Despite general acceptance of CBT as the treatment of choice for OCD in children (Franklin et al., 1998; March & Mulle, 1998), there is a lack of randomized controlled trials of CBT against control and other active comparison treatments in the empirical literature (March, Franklin, Nelson, & Foa, 2001). The Pediatric Obsessive-Compulsive Disorder Treatment Study (POTS; Franklin, Foa, & March, 2003) is the first randomized trial in pediatric OCD that compares the efficacy of medication (sertraline), CBT for OCD, medication and CBT in combination, and a medication placebo. This study hopes to answer existing questions about the benefits and effectiveness of CBT and/or medication for the treatment of OCD. The current acceptance of CBT as the preferred treatment for OCD may be explained by the fact that E/RP is an integral part of any CBT protocol for OCD (Rowa, Antony, & Swinson, 2000). E/RP specifically has been proven to be an effective treatment for OCD (for reviews, see Abramowitz, 1998; Foa, Franklin, & Kozak, 1998; Stanley & Turner, 1995). In addition, studies measuring the effectiveness and transportability of CBT from research-based randomized controlled trials (RCTs) to clinical and school practice are being seen in the literature (Warren & Thomas, 2001). In addition to the CBT protocol outlined in this chapter, the reader is also directed to Aureen Pinto Wagner's CBT protocol for children with OCD (see Wagner, 2003a, for a review of this treatment protocol). Wagner's protocol, named RIDE Up and Down the Worry Hill (Wagner, 2002; 2003b), is a developmentally sensitive protocol designed as a flexible and feasible approach for clinicians in clinical settings treating children with OCD. Although comparative data do not exist for this protocol versus the protocol described in this chapter, both share many common features (Wagner, 2003a).

Pharmacotherapy

The literature on pharmacotherapy for pediatric OCD is more extensive than that of cognitive-behavioral treatment for OCD in children (Franklin et al., 2003). The medications most frequently used to treat OCD in children are SRIs. These include the tricyclic antidepressant (TCA) clomipramine, which is an SRI, and the selective serotonin reuptake inhibitors (SSRIs) fluoxetine, fluvoxamine, paroxetine, and sertraline. The majority of studies on psychopharmacology in pediatric OCD have focused on clomipramine (Franklin et al., 1998), which was approved by the FDA in 1989 for the treatment of OCD in children and adolescents aged 10 years and older (March & Mulle, 1998). See Chapter 12 for a review of psychiatric medications used with children and adolescents.

Though there have been fewer trials with the other medications listed above, all of the SSRIs are likely to be effective treatments for OCD in children and adolescents (Franklin et al., 2003; March & Mulle, 1998). Fluoxetine, fluvoxamine, and sertraline have all shown benefit in smaller trials but await further study on a larger scale. In a 12-week, double-blind, placebo-controlled trial, sertraline was found to be effective for pediatric OCD treatment, with 42% of patients rated as improved (March et al., 1998). Geller, Hoog, et al. (2001) reported the efficacy and safety of fluoxetine in the treatment of pediatric OCD after a 13-week double-blind, placebo-controlled clinical trial resulted in 55% of patients (7–18 years old) randomized to the medication being rated as improved. A more complete review of the research base for these medications is beyond the scope of this chapter. For additional information on recommended psychopharmacological treatment for OCD, see March et al., *The Expert Consensus Guideline Series: Treatment of Obsessive-Compulsive Disorder* (1997).

Although school-based practitioners are not responsible for prescribing medication to a child with OCD, they should be aware of the medications the child is taking. Practitioners should note any change in behavior, either improvement or otherwise, since the start of medication treatment. Practitioners providing psychotherapy to a child should be in close contact with the child's prescribing primary physician and/or psychiatrist. Keeping these lines of communication open is essential for ensuring the best possible treatment outcome for the child.

Assessment and Initial Evaluation

Proper assessment and evaluation is critical in the treatment of OCD. This assessment process should include an initial screening, telephone contact with parents, pretreatment evaluation (including a behavioral analysis), and referral. There are a number of assessment tools that school social workers and other school-based practitioners can use. For a list and description of assessment tools, see Table 5.3. After these preliminary measures, a first appointment is scheduled. Following this first meeting, the practitioner should provide feedback to the child, parent(s), and teacher(s) involved. Once a treatment program has been established, the student's services team should meet with the mental health practitioners involved to decide on school-based interventions. It is also important at this stage to devise a plan for keeping the lines of communication open among the student, the parents, and the school. This component will be essential for developing and implementing the treatment intervention that provides the greatest benefit to the student with OCD (March & Mulle, 1998).

Table 5.3 Recommended Assessment Tools

Assessment	Source	Description
NIMH Global Obsessive-Compulsive Scale	National Institute of Mental Health (public domain)	The scale is clinician-rated and used to generate a global rating from 1 to 15 that represents a description of the present clinical state of the patient. This rating is based on guidelines provided on the scale ranging from "minimal within range of normal or very mild symptoms" to "very severe obsessive-compulsive behavior."
Clinical Global Impairment Scale	National Institute of Mental Health (public domain)	This scale is clinician-rated and used to generate a global rating from 1 to 7 that represents how mentally ill the patient is at the current time, based on the therapist's clinical experience. The descriptions range from "normal, not at all ill" to "among the most extremely ill."
Clinical Global Improvement Scale	National Institute of Mental Health (public domain)	This scale is clinician-rated and used to generate a global rating from 1 to 7 that represents how the patient's condition has changed since the beginning of treatment. The descriptions range from "very much improved" to "very much worse."
Children's Yale-Brown Obsessive-Compulsive Scale[a]	Developed by Wayne K. Goodman, Lawrence H. Price, Steven A. Rasmussen, Mark A. Riddle, & Judith L. Rapoport Department of Psychiatry Child Study Center, Yale University School of Medicine;	The CY-BOCS is the most useful and widely used instrument, both clinically and in research. This scale is designed to rate the severity of obsessive and compulsive symptoms in children and adolescents, ages 6 to 17 years old. A clinician or a trained interviewer can administer the scale in a semistructured fashion. Ratings are generated from the parent's and child's reports, who are interviewed together, and the final rating is determined from the clinical

(continued)

Table 5.3 *(Continued)*

Assessment	Source	Description
	Department of Psychiatry, Brown University School of Medicine; Child Psychiatry Branch, National Institute of Mental Health	judgment of the interviewer. In total, 19 items are rated, and items 1–10 are scored for the total score, with 5 questions pertaining to obsessions and compulsions, respectively. Revised from an adult version, the interview contains questions regarding phenomenology of obsessions and compulsions, distress caused by the symptoms, control over OCD, avoidant behavior, pathological doubting, and obsessive slowness. The instrument is applicable for clinical use, particularly in describing symptoms and measuring any change in treatment (Thomsen, 1998).
Leyton Obsessional Inventory–Child Version	Berg, Whitaker, Davies, Flament, & Rapoport, 1988. © 1988 by Williams and Wilkins.	Transformed from a 65-item questionnaire (or card-sorting test) for adults, to a 20-item test for children and adolescents, this instrument can be used when screening for obsessive-compulsive symptoms, but does not specifically differentiate between obsessive traits and ego-dystonic symptoms (Thomsen, 1998).
Anxiety Disorders Interview Schedule for Children (ADIS-C)	Silverman & Nelles, 1988	Semistructured clinical interview for 6–17-year-olds, with child and parent as informants.
Multidimensional Anxiety Scale for (MASC)	March, Parker, et al., 1997	Self-report measure for 8-19-year-olds; child informant, 39 items total (10-item short form available). Children four subscales: physical anxiety, harm avoidance, social anxiety, separation anxiety.

[a] Investigators interested in using this rating scale should contact Wayne Goodman at the Clinical Neuroscience Research Unit, Connecticut Mental Health Center, 34 Park Street, New Haven, CT 06508 or Mark Riddle at the Yale Child Study Center, P.O. Box 3333, New Haven, CT 06510.

Overview of Cognitive-Behavioral Therapy for OCD

CBT is the most effective psychosocial treatment for OCD (March & Mulle, 1998). However, there is a lack of studies examining whether CBT protocols can be delivered by practitioners of all theoretical and clinical backgrounds with the same level of efficacy found in research trials (Velting et al., 2004). Similarly, the transportability of these treatments to nonresearch settings, such as schools, has not been examined extensively, though studies designed for this purpose are in progress (Albano & Kendall, 2002). When delivering CBT as treatment for anxious youth, school social workers and other practitioners are encouraged to be flexible, clinically sensitive, and developmentally appropriate (Albano & Kendall, 2002; Kendall & Chu, 2000). Keeping this in mind, practitioners in all settings seeking to use CBT must receive appropriate training and supervision (Velting et al., 2004). Below, the reader will find an overview of cognitive-behavioral therapy, as well as a more detailed description of a CBT protocol for OCD, developed by March and Mulle (1998). This description is not meant to replace the comprehensive protocol in *OCD in Children and Adolescents: A Cognitive-Behavioral Treatment Manual* (March & Mulle, 1998), and school social workers and other practitioners should not use it as such. At the end of this chapter, the reader will find a list of resources and information on how to obtain materials for use in the treatment of OCD, including the *CBT Manual for Children and Adolescents with OCD.*

The Treatment Process

Typically, CBT takes place over 12–20 sessions, depending on the severity and complexity of the case (March & Mulle, 1998). At the beginning of treatment, it is expected that the child has been through a pretreatment evaluation and assessment procedures. Though each session has its own specific goals, there are a few general themes consistent throughout treatment. Each time the practitioner meets with the child, he or she should

- check in with parents;
- review the goals for that session;
- review topics covered the previous session and any lingering questions or concerns the child may have;
- introduce new material for the current session;
- practice/role play new tasks;
- explain and administer homework for the coming week;
- provide any fact sheets pertinent to the topics covered at the end of the session (March & Mulle, 1998).

Keeping these common themes in mind, the CBT treatment process for OCD can be broken into two phases: the acute treatment phase and the maintenance treatment phase. In the acute phase, treatment is geared for ending the current episode of OCD. In the maintenance phase, treatment focuses on preventing any possible future episodes of OCD. These two phases are marked by the following components of treatment:

- *Education*: Education is crucial in helping patients and families learn how best to manage OCD and prevent its complications.
- *Psychotherapy*: Cognitive-behavioral psychotherapy is the key element of treatment for most patients with OCD. (This treatment may either be delivered in school or referred out to community-based programs, depending on the available resources.)
- *Medication*: Medication with a serotonin reuptake inhibitor is helpful for many patients. (March & Mulle, 1998)

Within these two phases, treatment is broken up into four general steps over the course of 12–20 sessions. The following steps are fully described in the next section:

- Psychoeducation (sessions 1–2, week 1)
- Cognitive training (sessions 2–3, weeks 1–2)
- Mapping OCD (sessions 3–4, week 2)
- Exposure/response prevention (sessions 5–20, weeks 3–18) (March & Mulle, 1998)

The length of each session may vary slightly and can depend on the schedules of the parent and child as well as the location of treatment. Ideally, each session should allow 50–60 minutes to cover all of the goals and any additional concerns raised by the child and/or parent. In a school setting, it may be difficult to schedule sessions for this length of time. Some school-based practitioners have modified this type of treatment to fit within one class period to avoid taking the child out of more than one class at a time. Generally, the time of each treatment session is arranged as follows:

- Check in (5 minutes)
- Homework review (5 minutes)
- Instruction of new task (20 minutes)
- Discussion of new homework (10 minutes)
- Review of session and homework with parents (10 minutes) (March & Mulle, 1998)

Step 1: Psychoeducation (Session 1)

During the first step of treatment, the practitioner is primarily focusing on establishing rapport with the child and parent as well as educating the family about OCD. This includes talking about OCD as a medical illness and giving the family a comprehensive knowledge base on treatment for the disorder.

Session I Goals

1. Establish rapport (initial interview). Treatment begins with the practitioner working to make the child feel safe and comfortable about being in therapy. One or both of the parents should be included in this first part of treatment, and initial conversation should be focused around the child's life apart from OCD. Once the practitioner begins to discuss OCD and how he or she will be working with the child and parent to establish the goals of treatment, the practitioner may be able to assess the level of understanding the family has of OCD and its treatment.

2. Establish a neurobehavioral framework.
   - As a first step in discussing OCD as a disorder, the practitioner provides a neurobehavioral framework around OCD for the child. This is extremely important during the onset of treatment in that it connects the disorder, OCD, and its symptoms with specific behavioral treatments and symptom reduction.
   - Within this discussion, the practitioner should use the neurobehavioral framework to compare OCD to medical illnesses, such as asthma or diabetes.
   - The practitioner should explain how OCD affects the brain and how it works to alter thoughts and behaviors. Symptoms of OCD, such as obsessions, can be described to the child as "brain hiccups."
   - The practitioner can use other illnesses to explain how treatment for OCD will work. Similar to insulin treatment for diabetes, the treatment of OCD may involve medication (SSRIs), and in both disorders, psychosocial interventions are used (i.e., diet and exercise for diabetes, CBT for OCD). Also, in both situations, not everyone completely recovers, so additional interventions are used to address any residual symptoms.
   - The practitioner may take this opportunity to use information from the child's psychiatric evaluation to answer questions about and discuss OCD. When working with children who are on medication for OCD, the practitioner may want to stress how medication and CBT can work together to provide an effective treatment for the child.

3. Explain the treatment process. During the first two sessions, CBT as a treatment is explained and discussed in detail, including the following key points:
   - The practitioner should review risks and benefits of behavioral treatment for OCD.
   - Components, expectations, and goals of the treatment are reviewed. This can be a time for questions from the parents and the child about all three of these things. The practitioner should make sure the child

understands each of the goals and what the different stages and components of treatment entail. Specifically, the child should have a grasp on E/RP and how they are connected. The child may be reassured that he or she will not have to do these things on his or her own but will have allies throughout treatment (practitioner, parents) and will be aided with a "tool kit" of coping strategies to use during these exercises.

- The practitioner lays out an expected time frame for treatment, which can be revisited throughout treatment and altered, based on the child's progress. The practitioner may want to use visual handouts to show what the timeline will look like.

4. Externalize OCD.
   - Practitioners may want to encourage younger children to give OCD an unfavorable nickname, putting OCD on the "other side" of the child. This allows the child to view OCD as something that can be fought rather than something associated with a bad habit or a bad part of his or her personality.
   - Discuss the concept of "bossing back" OCD.

5. Homework. The concept of homework is introduced and discussed. The practitioner should make it clear that the child will always have a collaborative say in what the homework will be.
   - The child should pay attention to where OCD wins and where the child wins in preparation for session 2.
   - If the child has not already done so, he or she should think about a nickname to be used for OCD.
   - The child and parents should review any materials given to them from the practitioner and generate any lingering questions they may have for the next session.
   - Parents should work on redirecting their attention toward those things the child does well and away from OCD-related behaviors.
   - When in a school setting, the practitioner may want to spend some time with the parents working on communicating with teachers about their child's OCD. The practitioner may also suggest ways in which teachers can use strategies in the classroom to help the child combat OCD.
   - The child is asked to practice the technique of bossing back OCD for homework.

Step 2: Cognitive Training (CT): Introducing the Tool Kit (Sessions 2–3)

During the second step of treatment, the practitioner introduces cognitive training (CT), which is training in cognitive tactics for resisting OCD (March & Mulle, 1998). This can be distinguished from response prevention for mental rituals. Using CT will work to increase a sense of self-efficacy, controllability, and predictability of a positive outcome for E/RP tasks.

Session 2 Goals

1. Reinforce information around OCD and its treatment (may be introduced in session 1).
2. Make OCD the problem.
   - Introduce cognitive resistance (bossing back OCD) to reinforce the concept that OCD is external to the child.
   - The practitioner should begin by asking some general questions around how OCD has been bossing the child around since the last session and how the child has successfully bossed OCD back. Some of the settings the practitioner may want to address include home, playing with friends, school, etc. When talking about school, the practitioner may want to ask questions around specific places and times in school and when the child is with specific people.
   - It is imperative during this time to frame E/RP as the strategy used in the child's "fight" against OCD and the practitioner and parents as the child's allies in this fight.
3. Begin mapping OCD.
   - Introduce the concept of a transition zone between territory controlled by OCD and territory under the child's control.
   - March and Mulle (1998) suggest using the C-YBOCS (Goodman et al., 1989a, 1989b) Symptom Checklist and the patient's history to inventory the child's OCD symptoms. The fear thermometer, introduced in step 4 below, is used as a guide to generate subjective units of discomfort scores (SUDS) for each item on the stimulus hierarchy formulated in session.
   - The child generates the stimulus hierarchy by ranking the OCD symptoms from the easiest to the hardest to boss back. After the child has ranked his or her OCD symptoms on the stimulus hierarchy, areas where the child's life territory is free from OCD, where OCD and the child each "win" some of the time, and where the child cedes control to OCD will become apparent.
   - The transition zone will become obvious as the symptoms are ranked.
4. Introduce the fear thermometer, which encompasses the concepts of talking back to OCD and E/RP.
5. Using the tool kit. Once the child learns self-talk (bossing back OCD) and how to use positive coping strategies, introduce the cognitive tool kit for use during exposure and response prevention (E/RP) tasks, which will ease the process as well as support its effectiveness for the child.

6. Homework.
   - The child should pay attention to any OCD triggers he or she can detect and build a symptoms list.
   - The C-YBOCS checklist can aid as a guide.

Step 3: Mapping OCD: Completing the Tool Kit (Sessions 3–4)

By the third step of treatment, the child has developed a knowledge base of OCD and a preliminary tool kit of strategies to fight OCD. At this point, the child can begin to work within his or her own experience with OCD, identifying specific obsessions, compulsions, triggers, avoidance behaviors, and consequences (March & Mulle, 1998).

Session 3 Goals

1. Begin cognitive training (CT). The purpose of CT is to provide the child with a cognitive strategy for bossing back OCD. By learning these strategies, the child further solidifies his or her knowledge base of OCD and its treatment, cognitive resistance to OCD, and self-administered positive reinforcement.
   - Child reinforcement.
     - Constructive self-talk: The practitioner should identify and help correct negative self-talk.
     - Cognitive restructuring: The practitioner helps the child directly to address any negative assumptions (e.g., risk of getting sick from touching a doorknob) feeding into the child's obsessions. This will help the child's willingness to participate in exposure tasks in later sessions.
     - Separation from OCD: Continue to externalize OCD by separating OCD from the child as something that just comes and goes.
   - Short-form cognitive training: The practitioner may help the child to review and keep these concepts separate by giving repeated examples or writing the concepts down on separate cards the child may take home.
2. Continue mapping OCD and review the symptom list (trigger, obsession, compulsion, fear thermometer).
   - Complete the symptom list (stimulus hierarchy) begun in session 1.
   - Identify obsessions and compulsions using the CYBOCS Symptom Checklist as a guide.
   - Link obsessions and compulsions with the child's specific triggers.
   - Rank each trigger, obsession, and compulsion according to fear temperature on a hierarchy (with the highest fear temperature on the top and the lowest at the bottom). The practitioner should be sure to get all of the details around each of these components from the

child using specific questions aimed at alleviating any embarrassment the child may have around these behaviors.

3. Learn to use rewards as a strategy. Verbal praise, small prizes, and certificates can be used as positive reinforcement to the child for bossing back OCD successfully and for making progress from session to session. These should be discussed with the child from the beginning of treatment.

4. Homework.
   - Have the child try to identify when OCD wins and when he/she wins as a lead-in to exposure and response prevention.
   - The child should practice cognitive interventions learned in sessions.

Session 4 Goals

1. Finalize the transition zone.
   - The child generates a stimulus hierarchy with the practitioner on paper, which shows where the child is completely free from OCD, where the child and OCD each win the fight some of the time, and where the child feels helpless against OCD.
   - The transition zone lies in the central region and is the point where the child has some success against OCD. Essentially, the transition zone can be identified where the child and OCD overlap.
   - The practitioner should express to the child that she or he is on the child's side as an ally in the area of the hierarchy where the child is free from OCD.
   - Throughout this exercise, the practitioner will help the child work within the transition zone, recognizing and using aspects of the transition zone that will help to guide graded exposure throughout later treatment. The transition zone is recognized as being at the lower end of the stimulus hierarchy, where the high end includes those areas in which the child feels helpless against OCD.

2. Finalize the tool kit in preparation for E/RP.
   - Solidify a method for selecting E/RP targets in the transition zone.
   - Review and use the fear thermometer with specifics from the child's symptom hierarchy.
   - Review and discuss additional cognitive strategies.
   - Review the rewards discussed as a strategy to fight OCD and identify any other rewards for bossing back OCD.

3. Assign trial exposure tasks.
   - Before moving on to the final and longest phase of treatment, some initial exposure and response prevention tasks may be introduced to determine the child's levels of anxiety, understanding of concepts and tasks, and compliance and/or ability to participate in this area of treatment.

- Some introduction to these tasks reinforces the notion that the child can successfully resist and win the fight against OCD.
- During this trial period, the practitioner should pay particular attention to the transition zone and whether targets within this zone have been placed correctly. Identifying mistakes in this area at this point in treatment will reduce the chance for hang-ups or misdirection later in treatment.
- Practice trial E/RP task in session.
4. Homework. The child should practice a trial exposure every day and pay attention to the level of anxiety felt during each exercise.

Step 4: Exposure and Response Prevention: Implement E/RP (Sessions 5–20, Weeks 3–18)

During the remaining sessions of treatment, graded E/RP is implemented. Some children may not need all of the additional 16 sessions. The practitioner also assists in imaginal and in vivo E/RP practice, which is actively associated with weekly homework assignments. *Exposure* occurs when the child exposes him- or herself to the feared object, action, or thought. *Response prevention* follows and is the process of blocking rituals triggered by the exposure to the feared stimulus and/or reducing avoidance behaviors (March & Mulle, 1998). The practitioner should continue to frame OCD as the enemy, with the child, parents, and practitioner all on the same side, fighting against OCD. Within this framework, the child may use the allies and the tool kit (from CT and E/RP) developed with the help of the practitioner to resist OCD. This resistance is practiced at home, in school, and throughout therapy. At the beginning of each E/RP session, the transition zone should be revisited and altered when appropriate. Throughout this process, the child should become more skillful and successful at resisting OCD. Relapse prevention should also be covered, usually in the last one or two sessions of treatment. In addition, within the main course of treatment, at least two sessions (besides the first one) should include the parents. Finally, one or more booster sessions should be scheduled after treatment is terminated. The first booster session should occur approximately 1 month after the end of treatment (i.e., week 24).

Session 5 Goals

1. Identify OCD's influence with family members.
   - The practitioner should discuss the impact that OCD may have on the child's parents and other family members.
   - OCD symptoms involving the child's parents may be identified and placed on the hierarchy with their own fear temperature.
2. Update symptom hierarchy.
   - At the beginning of each session using exposure and response prevention, it is essential to go back to the symptom hierarchy and make any changes and/or additions necessary.

- The fear thermometer will also change when the transition zone moves up the hierarchy as the child becomes more and more successful at bossing back OCD at different stages.

3. Continue imaginal and/or in vivo E/RP. There are a number of different components to consider when using exposure techniques.
   - *Contrived exposure* is shown when the child chooses to face a feared stimulus while *uncontrived exposure* is shown when the child comes into contact with the stimulus unavoidably. With contrived exposure, the child is working to end avoidance while uncontrived exposure will force the child to pick RP targets.
   - The practitioner can also introduce the child to exposure for obsessions and/or mental rituals where the child allows him- or herself time for obsessions.
   - After the exposure here, the practitioner helps the child to break the rules that OCD usually sets. Some ways to break these rules include:
     - delay the ritual
     - shorten the ritual
     - do the ritual differently
     - do the ritual slowly
   - The practitioner should assist E/RP by modeling the exposure task with and without telling the child.

4. Homework. The child should practice the chosen exposure or response prevention tasks daily. The practitioner should make sure the child has chosen an exposure that will be relatively easy as this will be the first time the child practices on his or her own. The child should be reminded to use all of the strategies in the tool kit.

Session 6 Goals
1. Identify areas of difficulty with E/RP.
   - Since the last session involved actually doing exposure and response prevention for the first time, the practitioner should try to identify any areas of difficulty or frustration the child is having with E/RP.
   - The practitioner should pay close attention to the child's levels of anxiety and how he or she manages the anxiety during the exposure task.

2. Continue therapist-assisted E/RP.
   - After any questions or concerns have been addressed, the practitioner should continue with assisted E/RP.
   - The tasks that are practiced in session should be among those chosen for homework.

3. Homework. The child should choose one exposure task to practice.

Family Session 1 (Session 7)

At this point in treatment, the practitioner should encourage the parents and/or family to participate in a family session.

Session 7 Goals

1. Include parents in treatment.
   - The primary goal of the family session is to make sure that the parents feel they are included in the treatment. The practitioner may need to review the purpose of treatment at the outset.
   - Discuss the role of parents in treatment as a supportive force for the child and completely separate from OCD itself. The practitioner should discuss with the parents the various roles they may play in the child's treatment and how to carefully manage their own behavior around the child, OCD, and treatment.
   - The practitioner should discuss with the child and parents ways in which the parents can engage in extinction strategies. Extinction procedures should always be discussed and approved by the child.
   - Discuss the possibility of family therapy.
2. Positive reinforcement. Make a plan for special occasions to recognize the child's success (ceremonies) and to inform significant others of the child's success (notifications).
3. Continue E/RP. The practitioner should continue with an exposure task in session with the child. Based on the discussion with the parents, the exposure task may involve them.
4. Homework. The child should choose an exposure task to practice at home. If the parents are involved in corresponding rituals, the homework may include practice around the parents.

Moving Up the Stimulus Hierarchy (Sessions 8–11)

These four sessions over 4 weeks cover similar material, each session building on the last one.

Sessions 8–11 Goals

1. Arrange rewards, ceremonies, and notifications.
   - The practitioner should review these three topics and decisions from the last session.
   - The practitioner should monitor how the child is responding to these reinforcements and whether they are a positive reinforcement to treatment. The practitioner may work with the child and parents to identify points where a ceremony is warranted and how to plan a party around accomplishments.
2. Address comorbidity and therapy needs. The reader is directed to the original treatment manual (March & Mulle, 1998) as well as *The Expert*

Consensus Guideline Series: Treatment of Obsessive-Compulsive Disorder (March, Frances, Kahn, & Carpenter, 1997), for recommendations and references on treatment for comorbidity.
- Any comorbidity that is present should be addressed, as well as any other therapy needs.
- Comorbid symptoms should be separated from OCD and treated as such.

3. Continue practitioner-assisted E/RP.
- Practitioner-assisted E/RP is continued with special attention to developmental considerations.
- The practitioner should continue to encourage the child to move up the symptom hierarchy, practicing harder exposure tasks as treatment continues.

4. Homework. Homework for each session should involve practice of skills learned within the session.

Family Session 2 (Session 12)

Session 12 Goals
1. Remap OCD.
- The practitioner should revisit how OCD involves and influences the parents and family of the child with OCD.
- The practitioner should remap OCD with the child and family and make any changes to the symptom hierarchy that has developed over the last four sessions of E/RP.

2. Implement extinction tasks. With the child's permission, the practitioner should implement extinction tasks with the parents working as co-therapists.

3. Continue E/RP.
- The child and parents may practice extinction tasks in session with the practitioner for those tasks in which the parents are enmeshed with OCD.
- For parents who are not involved directly with the child's OCD, the practitioner may begin to transfer some of the management decisions around choosing exposure tasks to the parents. With the child's permission, the parents may act as co-therapists in this sense. This decision may be influenced by the relationship between the parents and child as well as the parents' understanding of OCD and willingness to be involved in treatment.

4. Homework. The child may choose a new E/RP task to practice. In addition, an extinction procedure for the parents to practice for homework is chosen.

Completing E/RP (Sessions 13–18)

Sessions 13–18 Goals

1. Review child's overall progress. The practitioner should review the child's progress in treatment thus far.
2. Address plateaus.
   • The practitioner should address any areas where the child has exhibited a plateau point between easy and harder E/RP and the reasons for this.
   • If the child is having a particularly hard time moving to the next stage in the hierarchy, the practitioner may want to schedule a ceremony to officially congratulate the child on completing one stage and moving on to the beginning of another.
3. Choose harder E/RP tasks. The practitioner can move forward by considering harder E/RP tasks for the child to practice, with an especially hard E/RP for the following weekly session.
4. Address comorbidity. The practitioner should be aware at this point in treatment of any comorbidity the child is exhibiting. This should be addressed in treatment and discussed with the parents.
5. Homework.
   • The child should practice an E/RP task based on the updated stimulus hierarchy.
   • The child may want to ask a friend or family member for help in working on a difficult exposure task at home.

Relapse Prevention (Session 19)

Relapse prevention can be covered in one session but may extend to two or more depending on the needs of the child. The practitioner may assess how the child feels about possible relapse or even "slips" after ending treatment. During these sessions, the practitioner may set up imaginal exposures for the child to practice how he or she would react if a slip were to occur.

Session 19 Goals

1. Explain concept of relapse prevention.
   • Primarily, the child should understand that slips are not a loss of efforts up to this point.
   • The practitioner may openly discuss and address any fears and/or misconceptions the child has of relapse.
2. Provide opportunity for imaginal exposure of relapse. The practitioner may ask the child to think of an example in which he or she may slip and then successfully use the tool kit to boss back OCD. The child should express his or her anxiety levels throughout the exposure, and the

practitioner may help by suggesting specific tools to use (e.g., self-talk) in working through the exposure.

3. Address questions or concerns regarding the treatment. Since this session marks the last true treatment session, the child may have questions or concerns regarding the treatment and what happens after treatment.

4. Homework. The child should practice a relapse prevention task either imaginal or in vivo.

Graduation (Session 20)

The main purpose of this "graduation" session is to have a celebration for the child on completion of treatment.

Session 20 Goals

1. Celebrate the child's accomplishments. During this final session, the main focus is on celebration of the child's accomplishments during treatment.

2. The practitioner should present the child with a certificate of achievement.

3. Notify friends and family members. The child is encouraged to share his or her success with friends and family members.

4. Parents check in. The practitioner should check in with the parents at the end of this last session to address any lingering concerns regarding treatment and OCD.

5. Homework. Homework for the child should be simply to share his or her success with friends and family and to frame the certificate of achievement.

Booster Session (Session 21)

A booster session is scheduled at 4 weeks to reinforce the strategies learned throughout treatment.

Session 21 Goals

1. Celebrate the child's accomplishments since graduation.

2. Review the tool kit.

3. Reinforce relapse prevention.

4. Plan further notifications regarding the end of treatment.

Tools and Practice Examples

Assessment Instruments

In order to make a diagnosis of OCD in children and adolescents, a thorough review of the patient's behavior must be coupled with psychiatric interviews that are specific to an OCD diagnosis (Thomsen, 1998). Table 5.3 lists several assessment tools that may be helpful in the process of diagnosing OCD.

Resources

OCD-Specific Organizations

Obsessive-Compulsive Foundation, Inc.

676 State Street

New Haven, CT 06511

Phone: 203-401-2070

Fax: 203-401-2076

E-mail: info@ocdfoundation.org

http://www.ocfoundation.org

- Videotapes on OCD in school-aged children
- Reading materials
  - Treatment
  - Symptoms
  - Comorbidity
- List of other resources and Web sites on OCD

OC Information Center

2711 Allen Boulevard

Middleton, WI 53562

608-836-8070

Anxiety-Specific Organizations

Anxiety Disorders Association of America

6000 Executive Boulevard, Suite 513

Rockville, MD 20852

301-231-9350

Child & Adolescent Anxiety Disorders Clinic (CAADC)

Temple University

13th Street & Cecil B. Moore Avenue (Weiss Hall, Ground Level)

Philadelphia, PA 19122

www.childanxiety.org

Child Anxiety Network

Child and Adolescent Fear and Anxiety Treatment Program

648 Beacon Street, 6th Floor, Kenmore Square

Boston, MA 02215

617-353-9610
www.childanxiety.net

Publications on OCD for Practitioners, Children, and Families

March, J., Frances, A., Kahn, D., & Carpenter, D. (1997). The Expert Consensus Guideline Series: Treatment of obsessive-compulsive disorder. *Journal of Clinical Psychiatry, 58*(Suppl. 4), 1–72.

March, J. S., & Mulle, K. (1998). *OCD in children and adolescents: A cognitive-behavioral treatment manual.* New York: Guilford. www.guilford.com

Rapoport, J. (1991). *The boy who couldn't stop washing.* New York: Penguin.

VanNoppen, B., Pato, M., & Rasmussen, S. (1997). *Learning to live with obsessive compulsive disorder,* 4th ed. Milford.

Wagner, A. P. (2000). *Up and down the worry hill: A children's book about obsessive-compulsive disorder.* Rochester, NY: Lighthouse Press.

Wagner, A. P. (2002). *Worried no more: Help and hope for anxious children.* Rochester, NY: Lighthouse Press.

Handouts, Tips for Parents, and Guidelines

Expert Knowledge Systems
P.O. Box 917
Independence, VA 24348
www.psychguides.com

OCD Support Groups

http://groups.yahoo.com/group/OCDSupportGroups/links

Practice Example: Background and Reason for Referral

Maria is a 10-year-old Hispanic female in the fifth grade, living with her mother and two older brothers. Her two brothers are significantly older and do not spend a lot of time with Maria. Maria's mother, Ms. Alba, works two jobs, and Maria is often at home by herself. Maria was initially referred to the school-based health clinic at the beginning of the school year by her teacher, who was concerned because he noticed that she was leaving to go to the bathroom a lot and had very red, chapped hands. Maria was assessed by the health clinic and referred to the partnering school-based mental health clinic for further assessment when it became apparent she had underlying symptoms in addition to those exhibited physically.

Jennifer, a social worker at the clinic, contacted Ms. Alba and obtained a verbal report over the phone of Maria's behavior at home. At home, Ms. Alba reported, Maria was very concerned with cleanliness and often spent hours rearranging her room, placing and replacing toys and books on her shelves. Ms. Alba also continually had trouble getting Maria out of the apartment on time for school because Maria would insist on checking to make sure her bed was made correctly and to make sure she had all of her school books in her bag. This could sometimes go on for 30 minutes to an hour and caused Ms. Alba to be late to work on a regular basis. Around meal times, Maria would insist on washing her plate, glass, and hands numerous times before and after her meal. Ms. Alba also noticed Maria had been staying up much later than usual since the start of the school year, completing her homework. Ms. Alba hadn't worried too much about this because she assumed that Maria had more challenging homework to do since she had moved into the fifth grade. Ms. Alba agreed to come into the school-based mental health clinic with Maria to meet with Jennifer for an initial screening and evaluation.

Jennifer also met with Maria's teacher to get a better sense of how Maria behaved in the classroom. Maria's teacher had noticed that Maria seemed extremely anxious when working in certain areas of the classroom and tended to go to the bathroom following activities in other areas of the classroom, including the reading circle and arts and crafts corner. When working at her desk independently or in a group, Maria always seemed to be falling behind, and her teacher would often catch her retracing one word or sentence over and over again. When working on writing assignments or math problems, Maria would sometimes get stuck on the first sentence or problem, erasing and rewriting the same thing over and over again. Maria seldom finished an assignment and would often be blamed or teased for incomplete work when working in a group.

Assessment

Given the information provided by the mother, teacher, Maria, and intake evaluation, Maria was diagnosed with OCD according to the *DSM-IV-TR* (American Psychiatric Association, 2000).

Other tha n OCD-related symptoms, Maria did not exhibit any impairment or symptoms for any other Axis I or II *DSM-IV-TR* diagnoses. She had had no previous psychiatric history, and her medical and developmental histories were normal. Nothing remarkable or traumatic had occurred in Maria's life at home or at school recently other than the reported symptoms. Jennifer scheduled a first session with Maria and her mother to begin CBT for OCD. After the initial screening following standard clinic procedures, Jennifer completed an intake evaluation with Maria. Jennifer administered the symptom checklist from the Children's Yale-Brown Obsessive Compulsive Scale (CYBOCS) to determine if specific OCD symptoms were present. Jennifer assigned a baseline score on the CYBOCS showing significant impairment and gave a global rating using the NIMH Global Obsessive-Compulsive Scale. Jennifer also rated Maria's global symptom severity and functional impairment using the Clinical Global Impairment Scale. Jennifer continued to give global ratings after each session using these two scales. Beginning with session two of Maria's treatment, Jennifer assigned a global rating after each session using the NIMH Global Improvement Scale, to monitor functioning and improvement across sessions. Jennifer also checked in with Ms. Alba after each session to address any lingering questions and discuss what she and Maria covered in session.

Implementing the CBT for OCD in Children and Adolescents Treatment Program

Step 1: Psychoeducation and Building Rapport

At the beginning of treatment, Jennifer took some time to talk to Maria about what she likes to do in and out of school, with her friends and family. Maria reported that she likes to spend time with her mother when she is not working. She does not have many friends her own age and does not really like to play games with other children because they get annoyed with her for "ruining" the game by repeating certain steps and movements. Jennifer made an effort to also establish rapport with Ms. Alba by empathizing with her frustrations around struggling in the morning with Maria to get out of the house, as well as dealing with Maria's other behaviors associated with OCD.

Next, Jennifer explained OCD as a type of "hiccup" in Maria's brain that sometimes tells Maria what to think and how to act. While describing the treatment process to Maria and Ms. Alba, Jennifer explained how they will be working together to help Maria "boss back" her OCD. She asked Maria to think of a nickname to give her OCD. Maria chose to call her OCD "Weird Worry" and identified some of her "weird worries" as staying clean; not getting germs from food, other kids, or things in the classroom; keeping her room and desk neat; getting her homework right; and making sure she hasn't forgotten anything when she leaves her apartment. She explained that she makes sure these things don't happen by always washing her hands when she does something new, making sure she cleans and tidies her room before she goes to bed and to school, and checking her assignments over and over again to make sure they are the right answers, at home and at school.

At the end of the first session, Jennifer explained how "homework" would be used during treatment. Jennifer assured Maria that she wouldn't have to write anything for homework outside of treatment, but that treatment homework would involve practicing and thinking about things they talked about and did in session. Maria agreed to this, and after the first session, Jennifer asked her to think about Weird Worry until the next session and look out for where, when, and how Weird Worry bothers her.

Steps 2 and 3: Mapping OCD and Cognitive Training

Over the next three sessions, Jennifer continued to work on showing Maria that OCD is the problem and that Maria can develop skills to boss back and control Weird Worry. Maria practiced resisting her OCD and reported that she had tried to resist copying over her work by telling Weird Worry to go away. During these reports, Jennifer asked Maria about her level of anxiety when resisting Weird Worry. Jennifer explained to Maria that they would begin "mapping" her OCD by labeling the degree of anxiety she experiences over different obsessions and compulsions. Jennifer introduced Maria to the concept of the "fear thermometer" and explained how it would be used to rate her anxiety. Jennifer explained that Maria will rank her specific OCD symptoms/triggers on a scale of 1 to 10. Jennifer helped Maria to write down her specific triggers, obsessions, compulsions, and fear ratings on a chart and labeled this symptom hierarchy as the "Weird Worry List." Jennifer explained she would be helping to coach Maria through this list from the lowest to the highest point, and they would only move on to the next level when Maria was comfortable.

After the symptom hierarchy was complete, Jennifer and Maria determined where in Maria's life she was free from OCD, where she shared control with Weird Worry, and where Weird Worry had complete control over her. Jennifer explained they would be working primarily in the middle area, the transition zone, and would slowly move the transition zone up the hierarchy until Weird Worry did not have any areas of control. Through CT instruction, Jennifer reassured Maria that she could do this by using her tool kit of strategies created in treatment, including bossing back OCD, remembering that her worries/obsessions are just OCD, or Weird Worry, and are separate from her compulsions, and that she didn't have to pay attention to Weird Worry. Jennifer wrote these steps on a card for Maria to carry around with her. Maria continued to think about her symptom hierarchy for homework and began practicing the cognitive strategies she had learned.

At the end of session four, Maria had finalized her symptom hierarchy, including the transition zone, and had a complete tool kit of strategies she was comfortable using in fighting Weird Worry. Jennifer also set up a variety of appropriate rewards for levels of achievement that Maria had agreed upon, including small prizes and certificates.

Step 4: Exposure and Response Prevention (E/RP)

At the beginning of this step of treatment, Jennifer explained to Maria that they would be moving on to put E/RP into action. Maria had been practicing not erasing and rewriting her answers so many times and reported her anxiety was much lower when she only copied her answers 5 times instead of 10. Since this symptom target was low on the symptom hierarchy, Jennifer suggested they try practicing the exposure in vivo so Jennifer could help coach Maria through it. Jennifer reminded Maria of her tool kit, and by the end of the exercise Maria had done a few math problems without copying over the numbers. Maria expressed confidence that she could work on this over the next week using her classroom homework as the exposure.

Over the next couple of sessions, Maria reported to Jennifer that she was able to practice resisting Weird Worry by not copying over her answers for classroom homework. She practiced the E/RP at home and was able to reduce her anxiety so she did not copy some of the questions in her homework and, finally, her entire homework. Jennifer rewarded these accomplishments with praise and asked Maria to identify some new targets from higher up on the symptom hierarchy.

As a higher-anxiety exposure, Maria thought that she might be able to try getting through an activity in the classroom without washing her hands repeatedly afterward. Jennifer suggested trying this as an imaginal exposure first, asking Maria to imagine how she would feel if she participated in this activity and then did not wash her hands before moving on to the next activity. Maria used examples of self-talk to explain how she would lower the anxiety she would feel resisting Weird Worry. Jennifer then set up an in vivo exposure where Maria read her a story and then bossed back OCD by not washing her hands afterward. Jennifer coached Maria through the process of self-talk and pushing away Weird Worry and the urges to wash her hands. Although Maria did not make it through the response prevention the first time without washing her hands, she limited the time spent on scrubbing her hands with soap. After a few sessions of practice, Maria's anxiety around this target had diminished. Jennifer rewarded Maria for her efforts throughout her attempts and Maria agreed to practice resisting this urge in class.

Family Sessions

During the E/RP step in treatment, Jennifer scheduled two family sessions with Maria and Ms. Alba. Jennifer began the sessions by reviewing Maria's homework and answering any questions Ms. Alba had. Jennifer asked how Weird Worry might affect members of Maria's family. Maria talked about how Weird Worry bosses around her mom and what the fear temperature would be for her if Ms. Alba didn't listen to Weird Worry. Ms. Alba had noticed that Maria was working on practicing the exposures at home but still expressed some frustration with the time she had to take to accommodate Maria's anxiety over dirtiness in the apartment. Ms. Alba had to wash Maria's bed sheets almost every day and wash the dishes multiple times a day or else Maria would not eat off them. Jennifer reiterated the importance of Ms. Alba as a cheerleader for Maria and helped her to think of ways she could help Maria complete an exposure task at home. At first, Ms. Alba was reluctant to reward Maria for eating her dinner without washing the dishes so many times because Ms. Alba believed this was something Maria should be doing anyway. After Jennifer explained the importance of positive reinforcement from her, Ms. Alba agreed to try giving Maria small rewards for accomplishing exposure tasks such as this. Jennifer set up an in vivo exposure with Ms. Alba and Maria where Maria completed a task on her hierarchy with which she was comfortable (writing without retracing), and Ms. Alba practiced encouraging and praising her efforts. At the end of the session, Maria agreed to try sitting down to dinner without having Ms. Alba wash her dishes and glass so many times beforehand.

Throughout the E/RP step in treatment, which took place over 13 sessions in 14 weeks, Maria continued to practice in vivo E/RP as well as practicing at home and in the classroom. Jennifer continued to monitor Maria's progress through global ratings and check-ins with Ms. Alba. She also held conferences with Maria's teacher to discuss any progress or possible regression in the classroom, but the teacher reported only positive results. Jennifer worked with the teacher to come up with some small rewards and examples of praise the teacher could use without singling Maria out from the rest of the class.

Relapse Prevention
After the E/RP sessions were complete and Maria felt that Weird Worry had been won over, one session was devoted to discussing relapse prevention. Jennifer distinguished the concept of "relapse" from a "slip" in which Maria may feel some of her OCD symptoms coming back. Jennifer assured Maria that she should not think of possible slips as failure on her part but that they are normal occurrences that may come and go, which she can manage using the strategies learned and practiced while in treatment. Jennifer coached Maria through an imaginal exposure where she pictured herself having a slip in which she felt the urge to scrub her hands after sharing in an art project with classmates. Maria successfully used self-talk to extinguish the anxiety she felt during the exposure and felt confident she would be able to manage the same situation if it happened for real. Jennifer walked Maria through her symptom hierarchy and discussed ways in which Maria could handle various slips for each symptom. Jennifer checked in with Ms. Alba and discussed the upcoming graduation with her and Maria as well as the process for booster sessions in the future if Maria or Ms. Alba felt they were needed.

Graduation
This final session of treatment focused solely on Maria's accomplishments since first coming to the mental health clinic. Maria reflected on the treatment process and recalled specific advances she had made up the symptom hierarchy as well as all of the times she won and gained control over OCD. Jennifer supported this realization by sharing the declining scores on the CY-BOCS and the increase in global ratings over the course of Maria's treatment. Jennifer presented Maria with a certificate of achievement and encouraged Maria to share her certificate as well as her success with her friends and family members. Jennifer checked in with Ms. Alba as well to address any remaining questions she had about the treatment and what would happen now that Maria was not in treatment. Ms. Alba seemed confident that Maria had the tools to manage her OCD on her own with Ms. Alba as the primary cheerleader. Jennifer scheduled one booster session for

the following month and reminded Maria that she could always come speak to her if she felt the need for additional booster sessions.

Key Points to Remember

OCD poses a significant risk to children and adolescents, with estimates of 1 in 200 children suffering from the disorder (Adams et al., 1994). School-based practitioners can play a valuable role in identifying, assessing, and treating children with OCD. Cognitive-behavior therapy, often in conjunction with pharmacotherapy, is the intervention most commonly used to treat OCD.

Though not thoroughly tested in school-based settings, CBT is an effective and useful treatment for school-based practitioners, given the brevity of treatment, flexibility, and transportability across settings and age groups. The school-based setting poses multiple challenges, however, and school-based practitioners should keep the following key points in mind:

- Training and supervision are crucial in learning and implementing cognitive-behavioral therapy.
- The *CBT Treatment Manual* for children and adolescents with OCD (March & Mulle, 1998) and the helpful handouts and tips within the manual are essential tools when providing this intervention.
- Teachers and parents can be valuable assets to the school-based practitioner in identifying, assessing, and treating the child. Practitioners are encouraged to provide teachers and parents in the school and community with information about OCD as an educational and preventive measure.
- Asking parents, teachers, and other informants to complete assessments about the child in treatment can help the practitioner to obtain a comprehensive picture of the child's behavior at the outset as well as the child's improvement throughout treatment. Practitioners should be aware of the time constraints on teachers' schedules and use appropriate assessment instruments (e.g., short version self-report assessments).
- Because OCD can be exhibited differently at home and school, ongoing communication among teachers, parents, and the practitioner is instrumental in the success of the treatment. School-based practitioners should collaborate with teachers and parents on scheduling sessions and sharing information so as to best fit the needs of all parties involved.

Effective Interventions for Adolescents With Depression

Jacqueline Corcoran
Jane Hanvey-Phillips

Getting Started

Depression occurs in about 2% of elementary-age children, but in adolescents, rates increase dramatically, making depression for this age group a significant mental health issue. For this reason, the focus on this chapter will be on depression in adolescence. Reviews of community studies have indicated lifetime prevalence rates for adolescent depression ranging from 15% to 20% (Birmaher et al., 1996; Lewinsohn & Essau, 2002). Point prevalence rates for major depression[1] in adolescents are estimated at between 4% and 8.3%; for dysthymia,[2] point prevalence rates range from 2% to 5% (Birmaher et al., 1996; Cottrell, Fonagy, Kurtz, Phillips, & Target, 2002). Rates of depression for females are double the rates of males (Birmaher et al., 1996; Lewinsohn & Essau, 2002). Depression in adolescents may also be comorbid with other disorders, such as anxiety disorders, attention deficit/hyperactivity disorder (ADHD), and substance abuse. Further, adolescent depression is a major risk factor for suicidal ideation, suicide attempts, and completed suicides (Cottrell et al., 2002; Waslick, Kandel, & Kakouros, 2002). See Chapter 10 on how to identify and prevent suicide in adolescents. Finally, adolescent depression presents risk for the continuation of depression into adulthood (Klein, Dougherty, & Olino, 2005). For these reasons, school social workers should demonstrate the knowledge and competence to assess for depression in teenagers and offer appropriate treatment and referrals.

What We Know

Intervention research has tended to focus on cognitive-behavioral models. *Behavioral* models focus on the development of coping skills, especially in the domain of social skills and choosing pleasant daily activities, so that the youth receive more reinforcement from their environments. *Cognitive* models include assessing and changing the distorted thinking that people with depression exhibit, in which they cast everyday experiences in a negative light. Interventions based on cognitive-behavioral models include the following components:

- the identification and restructuring of depressive thinking
- social skills training (how to make and maintain friendships)

- communication and social problem solving (how to share feelings and resolve conflicts without alienating others)
- developing aptitudes pertaining to self-esteem (establishing performance goals)
- progressive relaxation training to ease the stress and tension that can undercut enjoyment of activities
- structuring mood-boosting activities into daily life

Narrative reviews (Diamond, Reis, Diamond, Siqueland, & Isaacs, 2002) and meta-analyses (Cuijpers, 1998; Reinecke, Ryan, & Dubois, 1998) of cognitive-behavioral treatment for adolescents have indicated positive outcomes in terms of reduction of depression for up to 2 years' follow-up. The meta-analysis by Reinecke et al. (1998) was conducted on 24 control/comparison studies of cognitive-behavioral therapy (CBT), 14 of which had posttest information and 10 of which included follow-up data. All but one of the studies had as their subjects dysphoric[3] adolescents who were recruited from schools. A group therapy format was used in most studies. The overall effect size posttreatment was 1.02, whereas the overall effect size at follow-up was 0.61. These effect sizes are defined as "large" and "moderate," respectively, by Cohen (1988)—impressive findings for psychosocial treatment.

Another major review found a total of seven treatment-outcome studies involving children (grades three to eight) with depressive symptoms (Kaslow & Thompson, 1998). However, none of these studies met the criteria for well-established treatments. The work of one group of researchers, Stark and colleagues (Stark, Reynolds, & Kaslow, 1987; Stark, Rouse, & Livingston, 1991), merited the standard of a "probably efficacious treatment." The Kaslow and Thompson (1998) review also located seven treatment-outcome studies involving adolescents (ages 13–18) with either elevated depression scores or who had met DSM criteria for major depression or dysthymia. Since none of the studies compared an experimental condition with an already established treatment and none of the interventions had been examined by two or more research teams, criteria for a well-established treatment have not been met. However, the work of the research team of Lewinsohn and colleagues (Clark et al., 1995; Lewinsohn, Clarke, Hops, & Andrews, 1990; Lewinsohn, Clarke, Rhode, Hops, & Seeley, 1996) merited the standard of "probably efficacious treatment."

What We Can Do

Intervention in the school system for depression could include primary prevention (for all teens in a particular school); secondary prevention (targeting teens of parents who are depressed as these teens have a high risk of becoming depressed themselves); or tertiary prevention (targeting teens who test positive when screened for depression). It is highly recommended that the social worker and mental health counselors screen for depression in the school; unlike externalizing problems (aggression, acting-out behaviors), which are better identified by a teacher or parent, internalizing problems, such as depression, are more accurately reported by the adolescent (Cottrell et al., 2002; Mufson & Moreau, 1997). As a result, we recommend that school social workers and mental health counselors use measures of proven standardization to screen for depression. A review of this literature was drawn from Myers and Winters (2002). The interested reader may also consult Klein et al. (2005). Please see Table 6.1 for information on these measurement instruments.

Table 6.1 Measures for Youth Depression

Children's Depression Inventory (Kovacs, 1992)	• 27-item, self-report inventory for children from ages 8 to 13 • measuring severity (0 to 2) of overt symptoms of depression, such as sadness, sleep and eating disturbances, anhedonia, and suicidal ideation • modified from the Beck Depression Inventory for adults • translated into several languages	Multi-Health Systems 908 Niagra Falls Blvd. North Tonawanda, NY 14120-2060 800-456-3003 www.mhs.com
Reynolds Adolescent Depression Scale (Reynolds, 1987)	• measures *DSM-III* criteria for depression over the past 2 weeks • has primarily been developed and used with school samples • recommended for screening, rather than outcome	Psychological Assessment Resources, Inc. P.O. Box 998 Odessa, FL 33549 800-383-6595 800-331-8378 http:www.parinc.com
Center for Epidemiologic Studies Depression Scale for Children (Weissman, Orvaschel, & Padian, 1980)	• comprises items empirically derived from adult depression scales • assesses symptoms over the past week • widely employed with adolescents	http://www.depression clinic.com/db/servlet/ TopicReq?Session ID=227809545. 1091164813041&Topic ID=3009&Action=view

(continued)

Table 6.1 *(Continued)*

Beck Depression Inventory II (Beck, Brown, & Steer, 1996)	• self-report measure with 21 items, each having four answer options • targeted audience includes depressed adults, adolescents, elderly individuals, inpatients, outpatients, primary care patients, patients with medical conditions • works well with a wide range of ages and cultures, both males and females	Harcourt Assessment 19500 Bulverde Road San Antonio, TX 78259

Empirically tested cognitive-behavioral treatment models are available for public use. Specifically, the Lewinsohn and Clarke curriculum, Adolescent Coping With Depression Course, is available on the worldwide Web (http://www.kpchr.org/public/acwd/acwd.html). A shortened version of this curriculum will be described in this chapter and is available from the second author. (For some other empirically validated manuals, please see the list at the end of the chapter.)

The present intervention uses a group format, consisting of six 1-hour sessions offered once a week. A variety of techniques are employed, including education, group discussion, role play, and behavior rehearsal. Homework is emphasized as an important component of the intervention, with students being told that the amount of effort they invest in homework is associated with the amount of improvement they will feel. Given that teenagers may have difficulty with written assignments, participants are given credit even if they try to do tasks and report the results of their attempts to the group. Reinforcement may involve candy or small novelty items that teens find desirable. It often helps to ask the students what they find rewarding.

To make the intervention generally available to a wide variety of students, inclusion and exclusion criteria are kept to a minimum. The primary inclusion criteria for prospective participants includes clinically significant depression as shown by scores on standardized measures that suggest depression (e.g., a score of 10 or greater on the Beck Depression Inventory [BDI]). Exclusion criteria include unwillingness to consent to the intervention and students who do not speak or understand English (unless the group is composed entirely of students who speak another language and a facilitator is available to speak the language effectively). Students who report suicidality or who are determined to be suicidal are referred for evaluation and additional intervention outside the school setting.

Session 1: Introduction to the Group and Social Skills

The purpose of the group is shared with the students; it is to help them learn skills for controlling their moods. The following introduces the connections among feelings, thoughts, and actions.

Students learn that the way they feel influences how they think and behave, which then influences their feelings and thoughts, and so on. They are told that when people "feel bad," they're less likely to engage in enjoyable activities, and they doubt their ability to be successful at those things (e.g., making new friends). When people are successful at some effort, they feel positive and gain self-confidence.

The facilitator then explains that they will work on changing *actions* by increasing pleasant activities, improving social skills, and developing effective communication and problem-solving skills. They will work on changing *thoughts* by stopping negative thoughts and increasing positive thoughts. They will work on changing *feelings* by changing their thoughts, changing their actions, and learning relaxation skills.

Rules for the group are then formulated. Although group members are encouraged to come up with their own rules, the following should be included:

- Avoid depressive talk.
- Allow each person to have equal time.
- Maintain confidentiality.
- Offer support that is constructive, caring, and nonpressuring.

The first topic for the group is social skills, which are discussed as important for positive interactions to occur and to build or improve relationships. Students are taught to make eye contact, smile, say something positive about other people, reveal information about themselves, when to start a conversation and what to say, and how to leave a conversation.

For the first session's homework, students are asked to practice their newly acquired skills at least twice in the upcoming week.

Session 2: Pleasant Activities

The session begins by asking students to report on their homework efforts from session 1. As an introduction to the topic for the day, students are told that pleasant activities are important for feelings of well-being. Teens are then given a list of possible activities to engage in during the upcoming week, including listening to music, hanging out with friends, and driving a car. It is recommended that cofacilitators brainstorm with the group about ideas for activities. Homework assigned for this session involves setting a reasonable goal for increasing the number of pleasant activities and then engaging in this number of activities during the upcoming week.

Session 3: Relaxation Training

Students are informed about the role of stress and tension in depression. They are then informed that relaxation is likely to contribute to a reduction in both anxiety and depression. The facilitators guide the students through two different relaxation techniques: the Jacobson technique (progressive muscle relaxation) and the Benson technique (focusing on a word or phrase while doing progressive muscle relaxation). Homework for this session is to practice the Benson relaxation technique three times and to practice the Jacobson relaxation technique at least three times. The recommendation is made to do at least one of these techniques *every day* at a quiet time.

Session 4: Cognitive Restructuring

This session begins by educating students about the effects of decreasing negative thoughts and increasing positive thoughts. They are then taught how to replace negative thoughts with positive counterthoughts. Students are given instructions on how to use the A-B-C (activating event, belief, and consequences) technique to change their thoughts, and thus their moods.

To interrupt or stop negative thoughts, three techniques are taught:

1. Thought stopping. When alone and thinking negatively, students are instructed to yell "STOP" as loudly as possible and to then say, "I won't think about that any more." Students are told to gradually change from yelling to thinking "Stop," so the technique can be used in public.
2. The rubber band technique. Students are told they can wear a rubber band on their wrists and snap it every time they catch themselves thinking negatively. This technique should reduce negative thoughts.
3. Set aside worrying time. This involves scheduling a time each day to focus on troubling issues. The idea is to make an appointment with oneself for worrying; 15 minutes should be plenty.

Homework for this session is to use at least one thought-stopping technique at least two times during the week when negative thoughts cause problems.

Session 5: Communication Skills

This session involves a great deal of active participation from group members. Group members learn about appropriate responses that emphasize reflective, or active, listening with the facilitators modeling appropriate reflective listening techniques following a didactic presentation. Students are taught the difference between *understanding* and *judgmental* responses and are told that *understanding* responses promote healthier communication. Next, self-disclosure and the appropriateness of self-disclosure in given situations is addressed. Students are taught that appropriate self-disclosure includes talking about feelings related to events: "I feel _____ when you _____. I would prefer _____." They then practice this technique with their peers.

It is important to note that teens often have difficulty expressing negative feelings; therefore, in this session, they are educated about helpful ways to do this. Three possible situations are addressed: resisting peer pressure, telling a friend about something he or she did that bothered the person, and declining a friend's request for something. Students are assisted in identifying appropriate ways to express their feelings in these situations. For homework, group members are asked to use the self-disclosing format ("I feel...") two times in the coming week.

Session 6: Problem-Solving/Negotiation and Maintaining Gains

The problem-solving process is taught in order to work out situations with others that are bothersome. The process includes defining the problem, brainstorming, examining possible options, deciding on an option, implementing an option, and evaluating the implementation. The cofacilitators model the techniques in a role play, and group members practice.

During this final session, students are asked to "change gears" and prepare for the group's termination. They are told that, not uncommonly, group members feel a void when the group disbands. They are assisted in preparing for termination by reminding them to use the cognitive-behavioral coping skills they have been learning throughout the course. Students are given a "life plan" worksheet to identify potentially stressful life situations—both positive and negative—and the plans they can make to cope with these. They are also given information on the symptoms of depression and are strongly encouraged to contact a physician, school social worker, or therapist if they notice symptoms persisting for a period of 2 weeks. They are reminded that putting off the help they need won't make the depression go away. Finally, students are asked to complete a posttest measure of depression to determine their level of improvement (or decline) since the beginning of treatment. If appropriate and feasible, the measure could be used weekly to evaluate results via a single system design approach.

Use of Medications

For adolescent depression, selective serotonin reuptake inhibitors (SSRIs) (i.e., Prozac, Paxil, Celexa, Zoloft), as compared to tricyclic antidepressants, have shown greater therapeutic effectiveness and fewer adverse effects. Indeed, the tricyclic antidepressants are not recommended for children, given the lack of evidence to support their use (Hazell, O'Connell, & Heathcote, 2003). Concerns about suicidality in children and adolescents who have taken medication have led the United Kingdom to ban the use of antidepressants for youth. However, a recent study showed that a 12-week course of medication and psychotherapy (cognitive-behavioral therapy) was more effective than either medication or psychotherapy alone, producing an improvement rate of 71% (Treatment for Adolescents With Depression Study Team, 2004). At the same time, medication alone showed more improvements than psychotherapy alone, which was not statistically significant from the placebo condition.

Often, medication must be administered in the school setting. This may be the case because the student has a dosing schedule requiring administration during the time he or she is at school, or may occur if a child forgets to take medication at home. As McCarthy, Kelly, and Reed (2000) note, budget cuts in a time of increasing demand for school-based health services require more unlicensed assistive personnel (UAP) or students themselves to administer medication at school. Controversy concerns the administration of medication by nonmedical personnel and their ability to read health care provider orders, to properly store medications, to monitor students for side effects, and to dispense medications accurately. An additional area of concern is the need to have parental permission to dispense needed medications at school (McCarthy et al., 2000). For parents who do not realize the importance of medication compliance, obtaining permission to dispense medication at school may be difficult. In addition, it may be necessary for students to keep medication at home *and* at school, creating a financial burden for the family. Finally, there is the potential for students to abuse medication at school if proper monitoring is not in place. This might include selling or trading medication with other students or taking the wrong dose of their own medication. Clearly, medication issues create a dilemma for effective management in the school setting.

Challenges With School-Based Interventions

Although school-based interventions provide access to services that might otherwise be unavailable to depressed teens, they are not without challenges. Confidentiality remains one of the chief concerns in the implementation of interventions in the school setting, both in terms of identifying those at risk and in providing a confidential environment for provision of interventions (Atkins, Graczyk, Frazier, & Abdul-Adil, 2003; Satcher, 2004). Additional difficulties include integration of services with other providers outside the school and obtaining support from school personnel to facilitate interventions (Satcher, 2004). Parents also play a significant role in the success of school-based interventions. Without their consent, interventions may be prohibited for students; therefore it is necessary to educate parents, as well as students, about the intended outcomes of participation in school-based interventions. Despite these challenges, the benefits of providing interventions are likely to outweigh the difficulties of implementation.

Tools and Practice Examples

The following list provides an overview of interventions used with depressed students in the school setting.

Manuals

Clarke, G., Lewinsohn, P., & Hops, H. (1990). The adolescent coping with depression course. Available: http://www.kpchr.org/public/acwd/acwd.html.

Mufson, L., Dorta, K. P., Moreau, D., & Weissman, M. M. (2004). *Interpersonal psychotherapy for depressed adolescents* (2nd ed.). New York: Guilford.

Stark, K. (1990). *Childhood depression: School-based intervention.* New York: Guilford.

Stark, K., & Kendall, P. (1996a). *Taking action: A workbook for overcoming depression.* Available: www.workbookpublishing.com.

Stark, K., & Kendall, P. (1996b). *Treating depressed children: Therapist manual for "Taking action."* www.workbookpublishing.com.

Weisz, J. R., Weersing, V. R., Valeri, S. M., & McCarty, C. A. (1999a). *Therapist's manual for PASCET: Primary and secondary control enhancement training program.* Los Angeles: University of California.

Weisz, J. R., Weersing, V. R., Valeri, S. M., & McCarty, C. A. (1999b). *Act and think: Youth practice book for PASCET.* Los Angeles: University of California.

Case Example

Leah Hernandez was a 15-year-old Hispanic girl who lived with her mother, stepfather, and older brother. There were economic difficulties, and the level of tension in the household was high. Leah's grades had begun to decline in the past few months; she was irritable and spent most of her free time sitting alone in her room or sleeping. At her school, social workers began screening students for depression, using the BDI, to identify students who could benefit from participation in a cognitive-behavioral intervention. Leah participated in the screening and obtained a score of 23, which is considered a moderate level of depression.

The social worker met with Leah privately to explain that a training course was being offered to help students manage their moods. Leah was agreeable to participating, but since she was a minor, the social worker had to contact Leah's mother, Gloria Perez, and described the program to her. Mrs. Perez agreed to allow Leah to participate.

The course began 1 week after the conversation with Leah's mother. Arrangements had been made for the students to be excused from class for an hour, and they were welcomed with doughnuts and soft drinks. Two social workers introduced themselves as the group facilitators, then explained the format of the course and the rules for participation. Leah was shy about role-playing in front of the other students, but said that having practiced starting a new conversation, it would probably be easier for her to do so on her own that week as homework.

During the session on pleasant activities, Leah reported that she rarely engaged in any activities she enjoyed. She told the group that her mother and stepfather would tell her she should be working rather than having fun. The social workers addressed this issue and encouraged Leah to identify activities that would not disrupt the household, such as listening to relaxing music in her room, writing poetry (which Leah said she used to enjoy), or taking bubble baths.

During the session on relaxation, the students were given the opportunity to practice progressive muscle relaxation skills. At first, Leah reported that she felt awkward trying to relax with other people in the room, but found she was able to follow instructions easily after the social worker told all of the students to close their eyes so nobody was looking. Leah reported feeling calm and comfortable at the end of the session and willingly practiced the relaxation skills at home during the week.

Leah realized during the session on cognitive restructuring that she usually exaggerated negative experiences and minimized positive experiences. During the time Leah was participating in the group, she failed a math test and told one of the social workers, "I'm just stupid. That's why I failed." The social worker pointed out that Leah usually passed tests and, in fact, her grades had been improving recently. Leah was able to acknowledge this and stated that she would ask for help before the next math test and believed she could pass it then.

The session on communication skills focused on reflective listening and the use of "I feel…" messages. Leah had difficulty, at first, using "I feel" statements but eventually was able to understand the concept and was encouraged to practice at home. Leah reported that during the week, she and her mother had several positive conversations and that Leah's mood had improved as a result of them.

Leah was quiet during the session on conflict resolution. She appeared to attend to the discussion but did not participate. At the end of the group time, the social workers asked if she understood the concepts of brainstorming and problem solving as ways to reduce conflict. Leah replied that they seemed like good ideas, but she didn't think they would work with her family. The social workers encouraged Leah to present the material to her parents and to ask them to try the strategies. She agreed to do so. When she returned the following week, she reported that her mother tried to use brainstorming with her but her stepfather told her he wasn't going to negotiate anything with her; she would have to do things his way. The social workers helped Leah to identify cognitive coping strategies she could use when faced with her stepfather's unwillingness to change.

As part of the final group session, students identified gains made in treatment and planned for the future. During this session, Leah reported feeling a sense of contentment: Her grades had improved; conflict with her mother was greatly reduced; and she had found pleasant activities to do that did not upset the family.

Key Points to Remember

- Depressed adolescents are at risk for serious negative outcomes and can benefit from school-based interventions.
- Cognitive-behavioral group interventions have been shown to be effective and are recommended in the school setting.
- The recommended intervention includes attention to social skills, pleasant activities, relaxation, cognitive restructuring, communication, and problem-solving and negotiation skills.
- Homework assignments are important to the intervention.
- Assessment before and after the intervention is recommended.
- For adolescents with severe depression and/or suicidal ideation, adjunctive interventions are also recommended.

Notes

1. A *major depressive episode* is a period of at least 2 weeks during which a person experiences a depressed mood or loss of interest in nearly all life activities.
2. *Dysthymic disorder* represents a general personality style featuring symptoms that are similar to, but less intense than, those of major depression. This diagnosis requires 2 years of a continuously depressed mood (1 year for children and adolescents). It generally has an early age of onset (childhood through early adulthood) and produces impairments in school, work, and social life.
3. *Dysphoria* is depression that is subclinical in nature—when teens do not meet full criteria for either dysthymia or major depression.

Effective Interventions for Students With Bipolar Disorder

Kathleen A. Casey

Getting Started

Bipolar disorder, commonly referred to as manic-depressive illness, is among the least understood and most controversial psychiatric conditions in children. It is also one of the most severe, often creating significant impairment in school, family, and social functioning. Similar to other serious mental illnesses, early intervention and treatment of bipolar disorder is critical (Rivas-Vasquez, Johnson, Rey, & Blais, 2002). Despite the need for timely treatment and the steady increase in the diagnosis of bipolar disorder among school-aged children since the 1990s, there is a lack of empirical data to guide school social workers and school counselors in addressing this severe and chronic illness (Anglada, 2002). Indeed, to date, there are no evidence-based treatments specifically designed for youth under 18 years of age (Lofthouse & Fristad, 2004; National Institute of Mental Health, 2001).

In the absence of empirically supported treatments, the Clinical Child and Adolescent Division of the American Psychological Association recommends that practitioners utilize the most promising practices within the current literature (Kinscherff, 1999; Ollendick, 2003). To that end, this chapter translates the field's best practice information, including interventions currently undergoing clinical trials, to assist school personnel in recognizing, diagnosing, intervening with, and supporting students with bipolar disorder and their families. A list of additional resources is also included to aid teachers and counselors who wish to seek further assistance.

What We Know

Diagnosis
Bipolar disorder is a mental illness characterized by severe moods ranging between mania and depression. The American Psychiatric Association's *Diagnostic and Statistical Manual of Mental Disorders* (*DSM-IV*) classifies bipolar illness into four subtypes: bipolar I (BP-I), at least one manic or mixed episode; bipolar II (BP-II), at least one episode of major depression and hypomania; cyclothymia, alternating episodes of hypomania and symptoms of depression that fail to meet full

diagnostic criteria; and bipolar not otherwise specified (BP-NOS), symptoms that do not meet full criteria but include mood disturbance marked by significant impairment (American Psychiatric Association, 1994). School personnel may be more familiar with bipolar disorder in adults, which typically manifests distinct episodes of mania and depression as seen in bipolar I. Research suggests that BP-I is relatively rare in children and that, across the spectrum of other subtypes, their symptoms are expressed quite differently from adults (Lewinsohn, Klein, & Klein, 1995). For example, children tend to have much shorter mood phases or a more continuous series of changing moods rather than distinct episodes. In contrast to the classic manic behaviors of adults, such as elation, grandiosity, and spending sprees, children and adolescents are more likely to be highly irritable or quick to fly into a rage (Geller et al., 1998).

Since many of the symptoms associated with bipolar disorder, such as tantrums, high energy, and vivid imagination, are not uncommon among children in general, it can be very challenging for school personnel to distinguish appropriate developmental behaviors from the clinically abnormal (Fristad & Goldberg Arnold, 2004). While school social workers and mental health counselors should familiarize themselves with the primary indicators of bipolar disorder, the key determinants of a proper assessment are recognizing the signs and symptoms in terms of their intensity, duration, context, and presentation across multiple settings (Pavuluri, Naylor, & Janicak, 2002). The core features of bipolar disorder in children include

- Elated mood: excessive laughter, silliness, and giddiness. The child is often highly excitable, may joke constantly, and may seem excessively happy without apparent cause.
- Irritable mood: crabby, angry, and aggressive. The child may throw tantrums that involve screaming and throwing things. Some children display rage-like behavior or remain inconsolable for extended periods of time.
- Grandiose or inflated self-esteem: Beyond age-appropriate bragging, the child may make statements such as "I don't need to go to school. I am smarter than all my teachers," or "I am the best baseball player in the world, and I plan to play for the Red Sox next year."
- Decreased need for sleep: Children may repeatedly stay up late at night, refuse to go to bed because they feel wide awake, and after just a few hours of sleep wake up early in the morning full of energy. Whereas most children require between 9 and 11 hours of sleep, children experiencing mania or hypomania may only get 4 to 6 hours without feeling fatigued.
- Pressured speech: Children may describe a sense of having their thoughts race without being able to slow them down. They may talk persistently and demand constant attention and that someone listen to them.

- Frenzied activity: Similar to hyperactivity demonstrated by children with ADHD, kids in a manic state of bipolar disorder may be constantly moving from one activity to the next.
- Impulsive behaviors: Hypersexuality (not due to sexual abuse), hoarding, stealing, aggressive acts, or reckless behaviors.
- Depressive symptoms: Whiny, sad, crabby, and tearful without apparent cause. Thoughts of suicide and suicide attempts are also reported in about 25% of children with bipolar disorder (Geller et al., 2002).
- Psychosis: Hallucinations, delusions, or disconnected thoughts. See Chapter 8 for a discussion of psychotic symptoms in children and adolescents.

Specific *DSM-IV* criteria for bipolar I and II are displayed in Tables 7.1 and 7.2.

Since its recent recognition among professionals, bipolar disorder that emerges prior to age 18 has been referred to by several names, including pediatric bipolar, childhood onset, adolescent onset, prepubescent onset, and juvenile onset. Empirical studies suggest that there are two subtypes, which are commonly termed (1) prepubertal/early adolescent onset (PEA-BD) and (2) adolescent onset (AO-BD). PEA-BD includes children under age 12 and is characterized by irritability, rapid (i.e., more than four times a year) or continuous cycling, and high rates of co-occurring ADHD and conduct disorder (Findling, Gracious, & McNamar, 2001; Geller et al., 2002; Wozniak et al., 1995). AO-BD affects postpubescent youth, who tend to experience more distinct

Table 7.1 Core Features of Bipolar Disorder I: DSM-IV Criteria

- Manic mood symptoms: abnormally or persistently elevated, expansive, or irritable (for at least 1 week)

- Additional symptoms: 3 out of 7 (4 out of 7 if primary mood state is irritable)
  1. inflated self-esteem/grandiosity
  2. decreased need for sleep
  3. flight of ideas/racing thoughts
  4. poor judgment or hypersexuality
  5. distractibility
  6. foolish or reckless behavior
  7. talkative (increased volume, speed, amount)

- Mood disturbance is sufficient to cause marked impairment

- Symptoms are not due to physiological effects of a substance or to a general medical condition

Source: Reprinted with permission from the Diagnostic and Statistical Manual of Mental Disorders, Copyright 2000, American Psychiatric Association.

Table 7.2 Core Features of Bipolar Disorder II: DSM-IV Criteria

- Hypomanic mood symptoms: abnormally or persistently elevated, expansive, or irritable (hypomania alternating with depression) (for 4–7 days)

- Additional symptoms: 3 out of 7 (4 out of 7 if primary mood state is irritable)
  1. inflated self-esteem/grandiosity
  2. decreased need for sleep
  3. flight of ideas/racing thoughts
  4. poor judgment or hypersexuality
  5. distractibility
  6. foolish or reckless behavior
  7. talkative (increased volume, speed, amount)

- Mood disturbance is sufficient to cause marked impairment

- Symptoms are not due to physiological effects of a substance or to a general medical condition

Source: Reprinted with permission from the *Diagnostic and Statistical Manual of Mental Disorders,* Copyright 2000, American Psychiatric Association.

mood episodes than those with PEA-BD and have higher rates of comorbidity with substance abuse and anxiety disorders (Carlson, Bromet, & Sievers, 2000; Lewinsohn, Klein, & Seeley, 2000).

Current debate over the classification of bipolar disorder among children calls into question the diagnostic criteria of discrete mood episodes, the duration of the episodes, and the manifestation of manic symptoms (Leibenluft, Charney, Towbin, Bhangoo, & Pine, 2003). Both the adult and childhood literature suggest a spectrum of disorders and, as a result, experts recently introduced the term early-onset spectrum disorder (EOSD) as a more accurate description of bipolar disorder for individuals under age 18 (Lofthouse & Fristad, 2004).

Prevalence

The exact prevalence of bipolar disorder among children is largely unknown. There are no epidemiological studies specific to children, in part because the diagnostic criteria have been in a state of change, but primarily because its existence as a childhood disorder has only recently been acknowledged. Community school surveys of 14- to 18-year olds indicate prevalence rates of .12% for BP-I and 1% for BP-II and cyclothymia (Lewinsohn et al., 1995). Additional reports of symptoms associated with BP-NOS suggest a prevalence rate of 5.7%. Among adults, the prevalence of bipolar spectrum disorders is reported to be between 3% and 6%, with approximately 50% of those adults reporting symptoms that began in childhood or adolescence.

Causal Factors

Bipolar disorder is considered a biopsychosocial disorder because evidence indicates a biological basis upon which psychosocial factors exert significant influence (Pavuluri et al., 2002). More simply, biological factors likely cause the disorder and, perhaps, the course of mood cycling, but stressors within the child, family, school, and environment strongly affect outcomes. Genetic studies reveal that having a close relative with bipolar disorder increases the risk of developing the illness by 5%–10% (Craddock & Jones, 1999). Twin studies also offer compelling evidence of a genetic link in the onset of bipolar disorder (Badner, 2003).

Neurochemical, pharmacological, and neuroimaging studies also offer strong evidence of biological influences in bipolar disorder. For example, serotonin, dopamine, various hormones, such as cortisol, and calcium levels have all been implicated as causal factors (Findling, Kowatch, & Post, 2003). Recent studies using neuroimaging techniques reveal possible involvement of the brain's frontal–striatal–limbic regions (DelBello & Kowatch, 2003).

Psychological and social factors appear to affect the severity of the illness, relapse rates, and recovery time. Research in this area has focused on three main categories of stressors: high expressed emotion (EE) within families, degree of maternal warmth, and disruptions to sleep patterns. An overly critical or hostile family environment coupled with emotional overinvolvement among household members characterize a family with high expressed emotion. Several investigations have found that, among adults, high familial EE is associated with significantly higher relapse rates (Simmoneau, Miklowitz, & Saleem, 1998). Studies of children with bipolar disorder have focused more on the degree of maternal warmth and reveal that children who experienced low maternal warmth were four times more likely to relapse than those with high maternal warmth (Geller et al., 2000; Geller et al., 2003). Stress due to negative life events appears to increase recovery time by three- to fourfold in adults (Johnson & Miller, 1997). Recurrence rates, particularly for manic episodes, are also markedly increased by irregularities in sleep patterns (Malkoff-Schwartz et al., 1998).

What We Can Do

As with all mental health conditions in children, the hallmark of effective treatment is early identification and accurate assessment (Pavuluri et al., 2002). This is especially true for childhood bipolar disorder, which can have devastating consequences if undetected or improperly diagnosed (McClure, Kubiszyn, & Kaslow, 2002).

Pharmacotherapy

Given that comorbidity is more the rule than the exception for children with bipolar disorder, it is not surprising that multiple medications are often needed to achieve stability. In a recent study of youth between the ages of 7 and 18,

80% of children who were unresponsive to one mood stabilizer effectively responded to the use of two mood stabilizers (Kowatch, Sethuraman, Hume, Kromelis, & Weinberg, 2003). Another well-controlled study using valproate found significant improvement in the use of valproate in combination with quetiapine than valproate alone (DelBello, Schwiers, Rosenberg, & Strakowski, 2002). Among bipolar adolescents with symptoms of psychosis, better outcomes were reported for the combined use of lithium and antipsychotics than with lithium alone (Kafantaris, Coletti, Dicker, Padula, & Kane, 2003).

Many school-based practitioners may be aware of the recent media attention centered on the use of antidepressant medication with children. Some of this controversy stems from reports indicating that both selective serotonin reuptake inhibitors (SSRIs) and stimulants induce mania (Biederman et al., 2000; Oldroyd, 1997). There is some evidence that stimulant medication may induce mania in some children (DelBello et al., 2002). These studies have been criticized for methodological shortcomings and refuted by subsequent reports, but the debate continues. Given the current state of the evidence, experts recommend mood stabilizers as the primary pharmacological intervention, followed by a slow and cautious introduction of SSRIs or stimulants as needed (Findling et al., 2003).

Since the majority of children with bipolar disorder are on multiple medications, side effects are very common. Table 7.3 lists some of the most common side effects and accommodations that can be made within the classroom and school environment to support the student. See Chapter 12 for additional information on the potential side effects of medications. Most side effects are at their worst during the first few weeks of taking the medication, but some, such as weight gain, can remain and cause difficulty. The school social worker and school-based mental health practitioner can take several steps to maximize the child's compliance and comfort with medication maintenance. First, if medication must be taken during school hours, help ensure that the student can do this privately. Second, although privacy is important, safety is paramount. Be sure to inform the student's teachers and other school personnel who work directly with the child about the seriousness of side effects, such as stomach pain, vomiting, and dehydration. In case of these side effects, school staff should immediately contact a parent or other emergency contacts.

Psychosocial Interventions

Currently there are no evidence-based interventions for children with bipolar disorder, but a few clinical trials of the most promising interventions are under way. The interventions conform to the surgeon general's recommendations for treatment of childhood mood disorders by placing special emphasis on including families, determining functional status in addition to symptom severity, and including children with co-occurring disorders. They are also manualized and designed for practitioners to use flexibly (Pavuluri et al., 2002).

Table 7.3 Common Side Effects of Bipolar Medications and Suggested Classroom Accommodations

Side Effect	Accommodation
Increased thirst	Allow ongoing access to water and juice
Frequent urination	Allow unlimited access to the bathroom
Drowsiness	Arrange for frequent breaks or a delayed start time in the morning
Fluctuations in energy and motivation	Provide a flexible workload for the student to work on projects consistent with energy and focus
Difficulty concentrating and remembering instructions	Record assignments in a daily notebook, provide special reminders, identify a classroom aide to help student focus on tasks
Easily overheated or dehydrated from physical activity	Allow student to waive physical education class on hot days

Source: Adapted from the Child and Adolescent Bipolar Foundation's *Educator's Guide* (Anglada, 2002). A more detailed list of symptoms and accommodations may be obtained at www.bpkids.org

The Multi-Family Psychoeducation Group (MFPG) developed by Fristad and colleagues and its modified version, Individual Family Psychoeducation (IFP) share the following treatment goals for parents and their children:

- Increase understanding of the disorder, symptoms, and common comorbid conditions.
- Increase knowledge of medications, psychological treatments, and school-based interventions.
- Help parents and children avoid blame for the disorder and encourage a sense of responsibility for symptom management.
- Promote better management of symptoms.
- Enhance coping skills.
- Improve family communication and problem-solving abilities.
- Improve family and peer relationships.
- Expand social support.
- Promote cooperation and cohesiveness among caregiving adults.

MFPG uses a group format for the advantages it offers in terms of peer support, feedback, and in vivo practice. It consists of a 6-week, 90-minute session design, which begins with a brief check-in for parents and children to review the previous week's assignments. Children and parents meet in separate groups for the remainder of the session. A randomized pilot test of MFPG demonstrated increases in parents' knowledge, improved parent–child relationships, and increased social support. IFP allows the practitioner to work with families on an individual basis and uses sixteen 50-minute sessions. It includes an additional component called "healthy habits" to improve regular sleep patterns, nutrition, and exercise to combat the side effects of medication and prevent relapse. MFPG is being tested in a multiyear NIMH clinical trial, and IFP is being tested using a randomized control study.

Both MFPG and IFP combine education, skill building, and therapeutic techniques. The first 50% of the treatment is purely educational and guides families through developing and monitoring their own treatment goals, which they track on "fix-it lists." Parents also chart their child's moods to monitor the effects of medication. One of the most potent exercises, called "naming the enemy," helps both the child and parents distinguish the symptoms of the disorder from the child. The exercise involves dividing one sheet of paper into two columns; one column lists all of the child's symptoms, and the other column lists all of the child's positive qualities and strengths. Folding the page in half allows the family to see how symptoms can sometimes cover up the child's best characteristics and, conversely, how proper treatment can bring the child's finest attributes to the forefront. The remaining sessions combine coping-skills training with cognitive-behavioral techniques and problem-solving skills. Special emphasis is placed on anticipating times of added stress and developing the skills as a family to manage through them. The last session is dedicated to the child's strengths, areas in need of growth, and recommendations and resources. More detailed guidelines for both MFPG and IFP may be found in Fristad and Goldberg Arnold (2003).

The second manualized treatment being tested through an NIMH-sponsored clinical trial is Family Focused Treatment (FFT), which has been empirically supported for use with adults (Miklowitz & Goldstein, 1997). It is designed for adolescents aged 13 to 17 with BP-I. Similar to MFPG and IFP, it incorporates psychoeducation, problem-solving skills for the family, and communication skills. It places special emphasis on reducing EE, crisis management, and relapse management.

Perhaps most inclusive of the school environment, Pavuluri and colleagues have developed a treatment program called Child and Family Focused Cognitive-Behavioral Treatment (CFF-CBT) for bipolar disorder, also referred to as RAINBOW, for youth between the ages of 8 and 12. CFF-CBT is an adaptation of Miklowitz and Goldstein's model for adults and, like FFT, it is based on the premise that life stress, in combination with genetic and biological factors, causes an increase in mood symptoms. Reducing stress, improving coping skills, and enhancing family support are key targets of the intervention.

The treatment format calls for 12 sessions for parents and children. RAINBOW stands for

- The importance of *Routine*
- *Affect* regulation/anger control
- *I* can do it/self-esteem enhancement
- *No* negative thoughts
- *Be* a good friend/balanced lifestyle for all family members
- *Oh*, how can we solve it? (problem solving)
- *Ways* to seek and obtain support

RAINBOW emphasizes therapeutic support for parents in coping with their frustrations and questions. The treatment is designed in three phases:

- Phase I: therapeutic alliance, psychoeducation, role of medication
- Phase II (uses principles of cognitive behavior therapy): increase positive experiences, decrease negative consequences
- Phase III (uses interpersonal principles of problem solving): social skills, problem-solving skills, social support skills

The intervention is designed to be used flexibly. The treatment manual offers the following guidelines:

Sessions 1 and 2 (parents and child together): The emphasis of these sessions is learning about the illness as a brain disorder. The importance of maintaining regular sleep patterns, stress management, and medication adherence is specifically addressed.

Session 3 (parents only): Parents are taught skills to support their child in regulating emotions and ways to counteract dysfunctional thought patterns associated with bipolar disorder (e.g., grandiosity, paranoia, devaluing self and others).

Sessions 4–7 (child only): Emphasis is placed on the concept of regulating emotions and related skills. The therapist uses a mood chart to track progress across sessions.

Sessions 8–12 (alternate between parents only and joint therapy): Skill building for relapse prevention, problem solving, and social support skills are addressed.

The school is also a central component of treatment. The therapist provides a work folder of exercises that augment the weekly family sessions. Throughout all of the sessions, the therapist engages the child's teachers by requesting information on the child's classroom behavior and guiding them on classroom strategies to address the child's needs.

Tools and Practice Examples

Resources

- Child and Adolescent Bipolar Foundation. This national parent organization was formed in 1999 and provides education and online support. Its Web site, www.bipolarchildren.com, features a special section for educators that includes publications such as "The Student With Bipolar Disorder: An Educator's Guide."
- Juvenile Bipolar Research Foundation. This is a charitable organization founded in 2002 to support research in bipolar disorder among children. www.jbrf.org.
- Depression and Bipolar Support Alliance (DBSA), 730 N. Franklin Street, Suite 501, Chicago, IL 60610-7224. Phone: 312-642-0049. Fax: 312-642-7243. www.DBSAlliance.org
- Depression and Related Affective Disorders Association (DRADA), 2330 West Joppa Road, Suite 100, Lutherville, MD 21093. Phone: 410-583-2919. E-mail: drada@jhmi.edu.www.drada.org.
- Fristad, M., & Goldberg Arnold, J. (2004). *Raising a moody child: How to cope with depression and bipolar disorder.* New York: Guilford.
- Packer, L. E. *Classroom tips for children with bipolar disorder.* www.schoolbehavior.com.

Case Study: David

David, a 9-year-old student in the third grade, recently began acting out in the classroom by refusing to stay in his seat, constantly interrupting the teacher, and talking out of turn. He failed to turn in his assignments because he said he was too smart to have to do homework. His homeroom teacher referred him to the school counselor after he began bragging to other students that he drank beer, watched pornography, and had sex with girls in his room on the weekends. The counselor contacted David's mother, who denied his claims but shared concerns about her son's recent behavior. Although David had been diagnosed with ADHD at age 7, his behavior was only partially improved with medication. Recently, the medication has seemed to make him worse, and he complains that his brain feels like it has race cars in it. He has been staying up late at night watching TV and waking up before the rest of the family to draw in his art book or play with his Gameboy. When his parents insist that he go to bed at night, he flies into a rage and screams at everyone to leave him alone.

As David's case illustrates, the diagnosis of bipolar disorder is often complicated by other conditions that share similar symptoms and may coexist. In fact, it is extremely rare for a child with bipolar disorder to have only one diagnosis (Geller et al., 2000). The American Association of Child and Adolescent Psychiatry (AACAP) has issued practice guidelines for assessment that recommend the use of structured or semistructured interviews, such as the NIMH DISC-IV (National Institute for Mental Health Diagnostic Interview Schedule IV), K-SADS-PE (Kiddie Schedule for Affective Disorders in Schizophrenia for School-Age Children—Present Episode), and ChIPS (Children's Interview for Psychiatric Syndromes), to aid in assessment and differential diagnosis. The most widely used scales are available to practitioners on-line at www.bpkids.org. In addition, the school-based mental health practitioner should gather information from multiple informants, including teachers, parents, and the child, to obtain a thorough history and more comprehensive understanding of the child's functioning. Given the evidence of a strong genetic link, a detailed family history is also a critical aspect of the assessment process (American Academy of Child and Adolescent Psychiatry, 1997).

Once diagnosed, best practice and treatment guidelines recommend a combination of pharmacotherapy and psychosocial intervention. Medication, especially for manic symptoms, is a critical precursor to psychosocial treatment. In the adult literature, lithium, valproate, and carbamazepine have been shown to be efficacious (Keck & McElroy, 2002). Unfortunately, few well-controlled studies of medication use with children have been published. One notable exception is the research on lithium, which has demonstrated efficacy for adolescents with BP-I, BP-II, and comorbid substance abuse (Geller et al., 1998).

Key Points to Remember

Bipolar disorder in children has only been officially recognized since the 1980s and, as a result, evidence-based treatments have yet to be established. Several promising interventions are available to school-based practitioners, but more research is needed to provide specific school-based interventions. A thorough assessment using multiple informants, including parents, teachers, and the child, is an essential precursor to effective treatment. Clinicians should be especially attentive to the high comorbidity rate with bipolar disorder and to the developmental differences in symptom presentation. Medication to treat a child's mood symptoms must also precede psychosocial interventions. Finally, best practice dictates collaboration with parents and the child, education about the chronic condition, differentiation of symptoms from the child, and strategy development for relapse prevention and management. A list of references is included to guide practitioners to more detailed information.

Effective Interventions for Students With Schizophrenia and Other Psychotic Disorders

8

Susan Stone

Getting Started

Psychosis is a rare phenomenon among school-aged children but is perhaps the most critical of mental conditions for early identification and intervention. Little reliable literature exists regarding school-based identification and interventions for children with schizophrenia or other psychotic disorders. Much of the literature that does exist is flawed because of marked changes in recent years in the way childhood psychosis is both conceptualized and diagnosed (Lewis, 2002). Psychosis is a frightening and little understood cluster of symptoms that impairs reality testing and everyday senses and perceptions. Because of the lack of public awareness about psychosis, in general, and especially in children, school-based practitioners may be the first to be aware of the changes in a child's behavior that reflect the possibility of psychosis. Identification of psychosis is difficult in adults but even more difficult in young children, as youths often do not have the communication skills to convey such complex symptoms to adults. Identification is also clouded by the rich imaginary processes of children. Distinguishing between imagination and psychosis can be difficult, even for well-trained child psychiatrists. This is particularly true in very young children, who are unable to use and communicate about adult rules of logic or notions of reality (Caplan, 1994). This chapter will focus on ways to identify childhood psychosis, the various causes of childhood psychosis, medical treatment, and school-based supportive interventions that may assist children and families in managing this potentially life-threatening situation.

What We Know

What Is Psychosis?
In overly simplistic terms, psychosis is an impairment of "reality testing," characterized by the following symptoms:

- Thought disturbance, a term used to reflect disorganization in the way thoughts are put together and expressed. Another term to describe thought disturbance is "loosening of associations," meaning that the logical relationships between thoughts and feelings become jumbled. In children, thought disturbance might be mistaken for inattentiveness, as the child's thinking might appear to be "jumping" from one thought to another.

- Hallucination, a phenomenon which involves seeing, hearing, feeling, or smelling something that is not there. The most common form of hallucination is an auditory hallucination, or hearing a voice or voices when there is no one speaking. Auditory hallucinations are truly like voices from the outside—not thoughts from the inside. Often, children will answer "yes" when asked about hearing voices, when truly they are only referring to internal thoughts and worries. Visual hallucinations, which are less common, are brief, vague flashes of visual material. More detailed pictures, such as cartoon characters or people, are more likely to be imagination than psychosis. Tactile hallucinations, or feeling things crawling across the skin, are very uncommon in children. Olfactory hallucinations, or smelling characteristic odors that are not present, are often associated with seizure disorders.

- Delusions are generally defined as "fixed false beliefs." Children with delusions develop strongly held beliefs that cannot be swayed, despite confrontation with realities. The most common type of delusion is paranoid, or feeling that others are trying to hurt them. Especially in adolescence, paranoia can easily be mistaken for insecurity or difficulties in relating to peers. The reverse is also true. Delusions are very difficult to treat and tend to remain at least somewhat present even after treatment with psychotropic medications. Delusions often become even more "fixed" the more they are talked about; so attempting to argue a child out of a delusion is not advised.

Causes of Psychosis in Children

Schizophrenia is one of the least understood illnesses in the United States, largely because of media influence, confusing the clinical term *schizophrenia* with the lay term *split personality*. Schizophrenia is a very serious chronic mental illness, characterized by the psychotic symptoms (thought disturbance, hallucinations, and delusions) described above. While schizophrenia can appear in childhood, the more common course is for schizophrenia to emerge in early adulthood. The incidence of childhood-onset schizophrenia is approximately 1 in 40,000, contrasted with the incidence of schizophrenia in older adolescents and adults, which is approximately 1 in 100. (National Institute of Mental Health, 2003).

It is exceedingly rare to see schizophrenia emerge in children under the age of 6 (Werry, 1992). Very young children may have imaginary friends and fantasy thoughts, which are developmentally normal for this age. Concerns should arise, however, if a child of 7 years or older often hears voices, talks to himself or herself, stares at scary things that aren't there, and shows no interest in friendships.

Schizophrenia with childhood onset is conceptually the same as schizophrenia in adolescents and adults. In order to diagnose schizophrenia in childhood, the following must be present:

- at least two of the following: hallucinations, delusions, grossly disorganized speech or behavior, and severe withdrawal for at least 1 month;
- social or academic dysfunction; and
- continuous signs of the disturbance for 6 months. (Kaplan, Sadock, & Grebb, 1994)

Schizophrenia in adults is characterized by what mental health professionals refer to as a "chronic, deteriorating course." In children, however, consideration must be given to failure to achieve expected levels of social and academic functioning, instead of actual deterioration in functioning (Kaplan, Sadock, & Grebb, 1994). The symptoms of schizophrenia can often be managed with medications, but the illness itself is not curable, and often gets worse, even when adequate treatment is provided. Sadly, schizophrenia that appears at younger ages tends to be more resistant to treatment and have a worse prognosis (McClellan, McCurry, Snell, & DuBose, 1999).

Schizophrenia is a biological brain disease. Images obtained from high-resolution magnetic resonance images (MRI scans) repeatedly demonstrate brain dysfunction. There is also clearly a genetic component to schizophrenia, demonstrated by family histories of schizophrenia in persons with the disease, as well as twin studies (Kaplan et al., 1994). The prevalence of schizophrenia in the general population, for example, is approximately 1%, but children with two parents with schizophrenia have a 40% risk of developing the illness, and identical twins have a risk of almost 50%.

Other Causes of Psychosis in Children

Not all children and adolescents who exhibit psychotic symptoms actually have schizophrenia. Recent research has shown that schizophrenia tends to be over-diagnosed because of a lack of clarity about diagnostic criteria (Volkmar, 1996). The balance between overdiagnosis and early detection is important. While early diagnosis may dramatically affect the long-term prognosis, an erroneous diagnosis of schizophrenia can also have profound implications. All mental illnesses are stigmatizing in current society, but this is probably most pronounced for schizophrenia. The prognosis for children with other psychotic disorders is significantly better than for children with schizophrenia (McClellan et al., 1999). Anticipation of lifelong battles with psychosis, complicated by frightening information in the media, can send even the most stable families into turmoil. Sadly, many families dealing with psychosis in children and other family members are not stable, resulting in increased chaos and decreased ability to address the symptoms and follow through with treatment recommendations. A diagnosis of schizophrenia also has the unfortunate result of hampering future attempts to obtain health insurance. Thus, while early identification is important, the results of an erroneous diagnosis of childhood schizophrenia can have serious, lifelong implications.

Brief Psychotic Disorders

Some children exhibit psychotic symptoms that resemble symptoms of schizophrenia but that resolve over a relatively short period of time. This usually occurs in response to a significant stressful event, such as the death of a parent or sibling. Children with brief psychotic disorders may exhibit all of the characteristic features of schizophrenia, with the exception of significant deterioration in functioning or failure to meet expected social or academic functioning. Brief psychotic disorders are usually treated with medications and supportive therapy, much like schizophrenia, but it is important to attempt to discontinue the medications after a reasonable period of time to determine whether the underlying psychotic symptoms are still present.

Schizotypal Personality Disorder

A personality disorder is characterized by an inflexible pattern of behaviors that are maladaptive and interfere with normal functioning. While typically not diagnosed until adulthood, some personality disorders begin to reveal themselves in adolescence. One particularly severe personality disorder, schizotypal personality disorder, can easily be mistaken for schizophrenia. Children with schizotypal personality disorder may exhibit social isolation, eccentric thoughts, and bizarre behavior, but overt psychotic symptoms, such as hallucinations and outright delusions, are absent.

Mood Disorders With Psychotic Features

Children with mood disorders, such as major depression and bipolar disorder, can also exhibit psychotic symptoms. See Chapters 6 and 7 for information on symptoms of mood disorders. These symptoms may closely resemble the psychotic symptoms of schizophrenia, but there is a distinct mood component present as well.

Treatment of psychosis accompanying mood disorders requires treatment of both the mood disturbance and the psychosis. Typically, the psychotic symptoms resolve relatively quickly, at which time treatment can be exclusively focused on the mood disorder.

Pervasive Developmental Disorder

Pervasive developmental disorders, including autism, have often been confused with schizophrenia. See Chapter 9 for a discussion of autism and related disorders. In fact, much of the available literature about childhood-onset schizophrenia is now suspected of including numerous children with pervasive developmental disorders. While difficulty in social functioning, flat affect, and social withdrawal are present in both disorders, overt psychotic symptoms are usually absent in pervasive developmental disorders.

Attention Deficit Disorder and Obsessive-Compulsive Disorder

Other psychiatric disorders that may be confused with psychosis include attention deficit disorder and obsessive-compulsive disorder. In attention deficit disorder, attention problems and wandering thoughts may sometimes be misconstrued as hallucinations or evidence of a thought disorder. In obsessive-compulsive disorder, bizarre, ritualistic behaviors may also resemble the behaviors of children experiencing delusions. In neither of these disorders, however, would the overt presence of auditory hallucinations, frank delusions, or grossly disorganized thought processes be expected.

Drugs

Many illicit drugs currently available to children can cause significant psychotic symptoms. Most notable are cocaine, PCP, LSD, ecstasy, and inhalants. Psychotic states induced by drugs tend to be abrupt in onset and transient, whereas schizophrenia and psychoses associated with mood disorders tend to have a more gradual, insidious onset.

Medical Problems

There are a number of reversible medical problems that can cause psychotic symptoms, most notably brain tumors, thyroid imbalance, seizure disorders, and lupus, which is an autoimmune disorder. In addition, some medications can produce transient psychotic symptoms as a side effect.

Case Example of Differential Diagnosis

The following case example demonstrates the difficulty in distinguishing these conditions and issues.

Barry had always been a quiet kid. He never exhibited any behavior problems and did fairly well academically, but he never really seemed to fit in. When Barry entered high school, his grades started to fall somewhat. When he came home from school in the afternoons, he would go immediately to his room. He appeared to be distracted and often looked toward the ceiling. He stopped talking to his parents. He dropped out of sports. Often, when his mother would walk by his room, he would be talking to himself in a loud voice. The teachers noted that, while previously he would sit at the front of the class, he now sat at the back of the class and mumbled to himself often. Sometimes, when he was called on, his answers wouldn't make much sense, and the thoughts didn't connect very well. He would wash his hands several times per hour and seemed to be preoccupied with his health. He stopped eating in the cafeteria. The other kids began to steer clear of him.

Analysis

- "Always quiet." The fact that Barry has always been quiet only becomes significant after other psychiatric symptoms begin to emerge. A child who is quiet may be simply exhibiting shyness, or the quietness may indicate prodromal symptoms of an anxiety disorder, mood disorder, personality disorder, pervasive developmental disorder, or psychosis.
- "Did fairly well academically." While deterioration in functioning is necessary for a diagnosis of schizophrenia in adults, failure to achieve expected levels of academic and social functioning is a factor to consider in children. While some studies indicate some early language-related deficits (Kaplan et al., 1994), most youths with schizophrenia function in the average range of academic performance prior to the onset of their illness. The drop in Barry's academic functioning, however, does not alone indicate concern related to psychosis. Often children with mood disorders, attention deficit/hyperactivity disorder (ADHD), and Obsessive-compulsive disorder (OCD) exhibit worsening academic performance as well, especially as they reach the high school years.
- "Social withdrawal." Social withdrawal is also a nonspecific sign that is difficult to interpret. As most parents of adolescents know, withdrawal in the home environment is a developmentally normal behavior for youths in their teenage years. On the other hand, social isolation can reflect serious mood disturbance or psychosis. Social isolation from peers is a stronger indicator of a significant problem.
- "Distracted, looking toward the ceiling, talking to himself." None of these symptoms alone cause concern that Barry is psychotic but, taken together, they raise a significant concern that Barry is experiencing auditory hallucinations. Children with auditory hallucinations have more difficulty than adults in blocking out the voices, so they can be observed being startled or distracted for no apparent reason and can sometimes be heard responding to the voices.
- "Thoughts didn't connect very well." The prime indicators of a thought disturbance attributable to schizophrenia are speech and/or thought processes that are grossly disorganized. So, while a child with attention deficit disorder or a mood disorder may exhibit some disjointed and meandering thinking patterns, the level of disturbance does not meet the criteria of gross disorganization.
- "Washing hands, health preoccupation, stopped eating." As with the other symptoms in Barry's history, these symptoms could be associated with psychosis but could also be consistent with other psychiatric problems. Excessive hand washing, for example, is a common symptom of obsessive-compulsive disorder. Children who stop eating may be

exhibiting social anxiety or signs of an eating disorder. The key factor in interpreting these symptoms is to determine the reasons for the behavior.

What We Can Do

Assessment

As with all mental illnesses, assessment and diagnosis require a broad-based, biopsychosocial approach. Unlike other illnesses that are more common in children, however, most of the standardized assessment instruments helpful in the diagnosis of psychosis were designed primarily for use in adults (McClellan et al., 1999) (Box 8.1).

As demonstrated by Barry's case, early signs of psychosis can be fairly non-specific and can be easily confused with other social or psychological problems. Some things to look for are as follows:

- Changes in the way the child interacts with peers
- Changes at home noticed by the family (changes in behavior in school without changes in behavior at home may reflect peer/social issues)
- Internal preoccupation or distraction
- Exhibition of fright, without cause, or suspicious nature (might reflect paranoid delusions)
- Bizarre or disorganized behavior or speech

If there *is* evidence of psychosis, look for the following:

- Recent major stressors in the child's life (may reflect brief psychotic disorder)
- Recent physical evaluation (to rule out thyroid or other medical causes)

Box 8.1. Standardized Instruments

Structured Clinical Interview for *DSM-IV* (SCID) (First, 1997)
Schedule for Positive Symptoms (SAPS) (Andreasen, 1982)
Schedule for Negative Symptoms (SANS) (Andreasen, 1982)
Schedule for Affective Disorders and Schizophrenia for School
    Age Children (Kiddie-SADS) (Puig-Antich & Chambers, 1983)
Kiddie Formal Thought Disorder Rating Scale (Caplan, 1994)

- Recent neurologic evaluation and an EEG (to rule out seizure disorders)
- Recently started medications
- Sadness, irritability, or tearfulness
- Euphoria, with rapid speech and rambling thought process (may reflect bipolar disorder with psychotic features but, if acute onset, might also reflect drug use)
- Family history of any mental illness
- Suspicion of drug use

Psychotic disorders in children are not typically associated with mental retardation, but various developmental and learning problems may be present (Lewis, 2002). Psychoeducational testing should include assessment of intellectual level, assessment of adaptive behavior, and assessment of communication skills. Projective testing may also be helpful, as some children do not know how to describe their symptoms or do not exhibit flagrant thought disorder (Lewis, 2002).

Acute Intervention

Once psychosis has been identified in a child, regardless of the cause, certain steps must be taken immediately. Because people with schizophrenia are at a higher risk of suicide (Kaplan et al., 1994), the safety of the child is the first concern. Using a stepwise process in the development of a safety plan will help ensure that the complex factors associated with psychosis in children are addressed quickly and appropriately.

Step 1: Is Hospitalization Necessary?

The first critical component in the development of a safety plan is the assessment of whether the child can be maintained in the school or if hospitalization or another restrictive setting is necessary. Some children with suicidal thoughts talk about them readily, but others hide them, especially if the thoughts relate to command auditory hallucinations (voices that tell them to do something) or delusions. Even if suicidal thoughts are present, evaluation of the need for hospitalization can be complex. Psychiatric hospitalization, while sometimes necessary, can significantly increase the self-perceived stigma of mental illness for children. The decision about whether hospitalization is necessary must balance (1) the severity of the risk; (2) the stability and safety of the home environment; and (3) the ability to get the child into outpatient treatment immediately. Even if hospitalization is necessary, it will only be a short-term intervention; so efforts must begin immediately to establish a longer-term safety plan.

Step 2: Engaging the Family

Engaging the family is critical to treatment success for children with psychosis. Although this is true when working with any sort of mental or emotional disturbance, it is markedly increased when working with psychotic children, for a number of reasons. First, the often bizarre nature of the psychotic symptoms and behaviors can be very frightening for family members who have watched them develop over time. These behaviors, in addition to elements of social withdrawal, can result in the child becoming isolated or even ostracized within the family unit. Because of the genetic nature of many illnesses that result in psychosis, many family members will have previous experience of psychosis, leading to a variety of emotions. Although, as in other areas related to childhood psychosis, the data are limited; available literature suggests that families of children with psychosis have some disturbances in the patterns of communication. It is unclear whether these abnormalities are reactions to the child's disorder or if they reflect the same underlying vulnerability exhibited more directly in the affected child (Lewis, 2002).

The first intervention with the family should be education. Education should focus on dispelling myths about schizophrenia and psychosis and preparing families for the difficulties they will likely address in dealing with the illness. Because of recent negative media attention to the use of psychotropic medications in children, many families may be resistant to using medications to control the symptoms of psychosis. These concerns must be addressed directly, with emphasis on the fact that psychosis and schizophrenia are biological disorders that must be addressed just as other medical conditions. Emphasis must be placed on the necessity of remaining consistent in taking these medications, and side effects from the medications should be addressed immediately with the prescribing physician, rather than simply stopping the medication. School-based mental health professionals can often serve as useful liaisons between families and the formal mental health system, which can often be somewhat intimidating.

Because psychosis in childhood is so rare, it may be difficult to identify peer support for family members. Linking families to support systems for other serious mental illnesses, however, may have some benefit. Communication issues within families must be addressed in an effort to enhance strengths and maintain the availability of the child for educational and other interventions (Lewis, 2002).

Step 3: Treatment

School-based treatment of children with psychotic disorders requires the services of a multidisciplinary team of professionals, including school social workers and mental health counselors, special education services, consulting psychiatrists for pharmacotherapy, and case management (Policy Leadership Cadre for Mental Health in Schools, 2001).

Pharmacotherapy For the most part, the mainstay of treatment for schizophrenia and other psychotic disorders is antipsychotic medication. Unfortunately, as with the other issues in this area, the literature is extremely limited with regard to the benefit and safety of antipsychotic medication in children and adolescents (Schur et al., 2003). Furthermore, much of the literature that does exist addresses the use of antipsychotic medication for reasons other than psychosis, such as aggression or autism (Gage, 2003).

The first medications used in the treatment of psychosis in both children and adults were the "typical" antipsychotics, also known as traditional neuroleptics. While some children show little or no response to these medications, there is some evidence that these medications are moderately effective in dampening the symptoms of psychosis (Kaplan et al., 1994).

The major limitation to their use, however, in both children and adults, is the side-effect profile, including hand tremors, stooped posture, drooling, shuffling gait, restlessness, irritability, muscle spasms, and a relatively rare disorder called tardive dyskinesia, which involves involuntary muscle movements of the head, limbs, and trunk. Although the data are limited, there is some evidence that some of these side effects may be increased in children and adolescents (Findling, 2000).

Newer generation antipsychotics, referred to as the "atypicals," have emerged in recent years as an alternative option to the traditional forms. The first of these atypical agents was clozapine, and it has probably been the medication most studied in childhood-onset schizophrenia (Frazier et al., 1994; Kumra et al., 1996; Remschmidt, Schulz, & Martin, 1994; Turetz et al., 1997). Although it has proven to be effective in most of these trials, significant side effects can emerge from this medication, including drops in blood counts (necessitating frequent blood draws), weight gain (which appears to be more pronounced in children and adolescents) (Gage, 2003), and an increased risk of diabetes. Chapter 12 presents more information on the uses and side effects of psychotropic medications.

The keys to managing these side effects are analyzing the risks versus the benefits, making sure that the family understands these issues and agrees to using the medication, and minimizing dosages, to the extent possible. School social workers and other practitioners can be extremely helpful in assisting the family in monitoring the presence of side effects that may result in the child being resistant to taking the medications.

Kids Hate Medicines   While the symptoms of mental illness, especially psychosis, are incredibly troubling for children and adolescents, being seen as "different" by their peers may be even more troubling. Many youths would prefer to downplay their frightening symptoms when confronted with having to "go to the nurse's office" to take their medications. Parents of children with mental illness often relate significant difficulties with medication compliance. Here are a few strategies that seem to help:

- Normalize the illness. Emphasize that taking this kind of medication is much like taking an antibiotic for an ear infection or taking medicine for a cold.
- Monitor compliance regularly. Adolescents can be less than honest about whether or not they're taking the medications as prescribed.

A quick count of pills can make a big difference between response versus no response.

- Be vigilant about side effects. Often, the reluctance to remain on the medications is more about side effects. Younger children usually do not have the communication skills to talk about side effects, so things like dysphoria, sexual side effects, andextrapymidal side effects may have to be detected by observation rather than communication.

Psychotherapy   Studies of psychotherapy in children with psychosis are limited in number and validity (because of the diagnostic issues noted above), but there is some evidence that supportive psychotherapy may be beneficial (Cantor & Kestenbaum, 1986). Supportive therapy should focus on education about the symptoms and coping strategies for dealing with them. It is important to note, for example, that, even with treatment, delusions may not totally go away. Using supportive, behavioral techniques may assist the child in diverting attention away from delusional thought processes or hallucinations. The usefulness of intensive, insight-oriented therapy is much less clear (Lewis, 2002). The benefits of psychotherapy may ultimately be dependent on the level of adaptive functioning and communication skills.

Step 4: Academic Programming

Although the emergence of schizophrenia in young adults may present as an acute psychotic episode, research has shown that schizophrenia in children may emerge more gradually, preceded by developmental disturbances, such as lags in motor and speech/language ability. Some recent research has shown that the pathophysiology of schizophrenia may involve abnormal development of language-related brain regions (National Institute of Mental Health, 2003). As with other areas of this illness, academic programming must balance the specialized learning needs of the child with minimizing self-perceived stigma. The need for special education services will be dependent upon developmental delays and intellectual issues identified during psychological testing. It must be noted, however, that children with psychosis may be better functioning intellectually than other children in special education classes, necessitating specialized attention. Being placed in special education classes with children who have mental retardation or autism may actually increase the stigma and perception of self-shame. This decision must be made on a case-by-case basis.

Tools and Practice Examples

Although there is a dearth of research findings with regard to childhood psychosis, there are a number of Internet Web sites that provide up-to-date, valid information about childhood schizophrenia and psychosis:

www.webmd.com

www.schizophrenia.com

www.nimh.com
www.psychiatry24×7.com
www.nmha.com
www.psychdirect.com
www.mentalhealth.com
www.nami.org

Key Points to Remember

Early identification and intervention are critical for children with schizophrenia and other psychotic disorders. The diagnosis of these conditions can be difficult for a number of reasons, which include the rich imaginary processes of children and their relative inability to communicate the complex nature of psychotic symptomatology. Psychoses are generally biological conditions that may run in families. For this reason, a careful biopsychosocial assessment, including extensive family history, is necessary to arrive at a diagnosis. Because childhood psychosis is a very rare phenomenon, little literature exists about evidence-based practices. Development of a safety plan and engaging the family are critical first steps. Psychotropic medications may be helpful, but they often have difficult side effects, which may be more pronounced in children. Decisions about using these medications necessitate a careful analysis of risks versus benefits. Supportive psychotherapy has been generally shown to be effective, with special emphasis on education about the condition, treatments, and prognosis. Designing an educational program also requires a careful analysis of specialized needs versus minimization of stigma to the individual child. These decisions must be made on a case-by-case basis.

Effective Interventions for Students With Autism and Asperger's Syndrome

Michelle S. Ballan
Karen S. Hoban

Getting Started

Autism is a complex disorder defined by numerous developmental and behavioral features. The canopy of the autism spectrum is far reaching, with school-aged children and adolescents ranging from nonverbal with multiple developmental disabilities to mild Asperger's syndrome with advanced capabilities for mathematics and science. Autism spectrum disorders (ASDs), termed pervasive developmental disorders (PDDs) in the *Diagnostic and Statistical Manual of Mental Disorders* (*DSM-IV-TR*; American Psychiatric Association, 2000) and in the *International Classification of Diseases* (*ICD-10*; World Health Organization, 1992), is a term often used in educational and clinical settings to refer to various disorders spanning a severe form known as autistic disorder (AD), to a milder form called Asperger's syndrome or disorder (AS). If a child exhibits symptoms of AD or AS, but does not meet the specific criteria for either disorder, the child is diagnosed with an ASD identified as pervasive developmental disorder not otherwise specified (PDD-NOS) (American Psychiatric Association, 2000; Strock, 2004). Less common are two additional acute ASDs known as Rett's syndrome or disorder (RS) and childhood disintegrative disorder (CDD).

Students identified as having an ASD exhibit a tremendous range in symptoms and characteristics due to developmental maturity and varying degrees of associated cognitive limitations (Filipek et al., 1999). Many school social workers, psychologists, and special educators are familiar with the primary clinical symptomatology of the majority of ASDs, which typically falls within three major categories: (1) qualitative impairment in social interaction, such as gaze aversion or the absence of communication; (2) impairments in communication, such as mutism and lack of pretend play; and (3) restricted, repetitive, stereotyped behavior, interests, and activities, such as retentive motor mannerisms (American Psychiatric Association, 2000; Bregman, 2005). ASDs vary with respect to age of onset and associations with other disorders. Differences among ASDs appear to be linked to intelligence, level of adaptive functioning, and number of autistic symptoms rather than to the presence of distinct symptoms (Hollander & Nowinski, 2003, p. 17).

Since the 1990s, research has revealed an upward trend in the prevalence rate for ASDs (Fombonne, 2005; Fombonne, Du Mazaubrun, Cans, & Grandjean,

1997; Fombonne, Simmons, Ford, Meltzer, & Goodman, 2001; Yeargin-Allsopp et al., 2003) due largely in part to issues regarding diagnosis. An increase in the prevalence rate may be attributable to a diverse range of factors, such as the broadening of diagnostic concepts to include milder and more atypical variants (Bregman, 2005), greater awareness among parents and professionals, the prospect of securing specialized services or benefits for children due to educational funding formulas, and the extent to which families advocate for the diagnosis during assessment (Scott, Clark, & Brady, 2000). Fombonne (2005) reported an estimate of 60 out of 10,000 for the prevalence of all ASDs. The majority of studies report that ASDs are four times more common in boys than girls (Fombonne, 1999), and approximately 75% of all individuals classified with autism have measured intelligence in the range of mental retardation (Bryson & Smith, 1998). ASDs are often accompanied by a range of abnormalities within cognitive, adaptive, affective, and behavioral domains of development, deficits in executive functions, limitations in adaptive skills, learning disabilities, mood instability, stereotypic and self-injurious behaviors, anxiety disorders, and aggression (Bregman, 2005). One in four children with an ASD develops seizures, often beginning in either early childhood or adolescence (Volkmar, 2000), and the rate of tuberous sclerosis appears to be 100 times higher among children with ASDs (Fombonne, 2005).

An increase or variation in prevalence rates may also be due largely in part to the utilization of different diagnostic criteria for ASDs across research studies. There are varying diagnostic groups within ASDs and varying diagnostic criteria for assessment. However, the *DSM-IV-TR* (2000) and the *ICD-10* (1992) share general agreement regarding the almost identical criteria for the diagnosis of the five subtypes of PDDs or ASDs (AD, AS, PDD-NOS, RS, and CDD).[1] For the purpose of this chapter, two of the more common ASDs (AD and AS) seen among school-aged children and adolescents will be the focus. The *DSM-IV-TR* (2000) outlines specific criteria for AD (see Table 9.1) and AS (see Table 9.2).

The most notable difference between AD and AS involves age-appropriate communication skills. Communication is presumed to be within normal limits in children with AS, although as one might expect of a school-aged youth with severe limitations in recognizing and interpreting social messages, pragmatic deficits are frequent (Scott et al., 2000). Because pragmatic deficits constitute a core area of communication functioning, this minimizes the true differences between children diagnosed with AS and AD (Scott et al., 2000).

The *DSM IV-TR* (2000) specifies a set of criteria for AS and AD, which might lead one to believe that diagnosis of such disorders is made with ease. However, diagnosis can be difficult due in part to the lack of definitive diagnostic tests for AD or AS. There are currently no reliable physiological markers for diagnosis as there are in some other disabilities (i.e., the genetic markers associated with Fragile X syndrome). To make a diagnosis, clinicians frequently rely heavily on

Table 9.1 DSM-IV Diagnostic Criteria for Autistic Disorder

A. A total of six (or more) items from (1), (2), and (3), with at least two from (1), and one each from (2) and (3):

  (1) qualitative impairment in social interaction, as manifested by at least two of the following:
- (a) marked impairment in the use of multiple nonverbal behaviors such as eye-to-eye gaze, facial expression, body postures, and gestures to regulate social interaction
- (b) failure to develop peer relationships appropriate to developmental level
- (c) a lack of spontaneous seeking to share enjoyment, interests, or achievements with other people (e.g., by a lack of showing, bringing, or pointing out objects of interest)
- (d) lack of social or emotional reciprocity

  (2) qualitative impairments in communication as manifested by at least one of the following:
- (a) delay in, or total lack of, the development of spoken language (not accompanied by an attempt to compensate through alternative modes of communication such as gesture or mime)
- (b) in individuals with adequate speech, marked impairment in the ability to initiate or sustain a conversation with others
- (c) stereotyped and repetitive use of language or idiosyncratic language
- (d) lack of varied, spontaneous make-believe play or social imitative play appropriate to developmental level

  (3) restricted, repetitive, and stereotyped patterns of behavior, interests, and activities, as manifested by at least one of the following:
- (a) encompassing preoccupation with one or more stereotyped and restricted patterns of interest that is abnormal either in intensity or focus
- (b) apparently inflexible adherence to specific, nonfunctional routines or rituals
- (c) stereotyped and repetitive motor mannerisms (e.g., hand or finger flapping or twisting, or complex whole-body movements)
- (d) persistent preoccupation with parts of objects

B. Delays or abnormal functioning in at least one of the following areas, with onset prior to age 3 years: (1) social interaction, (2) language as used in social communication, or (3) symbolic or imaginative play

C. The disturbance is not better accounted for by Rett's disorder or childhood disintegrative disorder.

Source: Reprinted with permission from the *Diagnostic and Statistical Manual of Mental Disorders*. Copyright 2000. American Psychiatric Association.

Table 9.2 DSM-IV-TR Diagnostic Criteria for Asperger's Syndrome

A. Qualitative impairment in social interaction, as manifested by at least two of the following:

    (1) marked impairment in the use of multiple nonverbal behaviors such as eye-to-eye gaze, facial expression, body postures, and gestures to regulate social interaction

    (2) failure to develop peer relationships appropriate to developmental level

    (3) a lack of spontaneous seeking to share enjoyment, interests, or achievements with other people (e.g., by a lack of showing, bringing, or pointing out objects of interest to other people)

    (4) lack of social or emotional reciprocity

B. Restricted, repetitive, and stereotyped patterns of behavior, interests, and activities, as manifested by at least one of the following:

    (1) encompassing preoccupation with one or more stereotyped and restricted patterns of interest that is abnormal either in intensity or focus

    (2) apparently inflexible adherence to specific, nonfunctional routines or rituals

    (3) stereotyped and repetitive motor mannerisms (e.g., hand or finger flapping or twisting, or complex whole-body movements)

    (4) persistent preoccupation with parts of objects

C. The disturbance causes clinically significant impairment in social, occupational, or other important areas of functioning.

D. There is no clinically significant general delay in language (e.g., single words used by age 2 years, communicative phrases used by age 3 years).

E. There is no clinically significant delay in cognitive development or in the development of age-appropriate self-help skills, adaptive behavior (other than in social interaction), and curiosity about the environment in childhood.

F. Criteria are not met for another specific pervasive developmental disorder or schizophrenia.

Source: Reprinted with permission from the *Diagnostic and Statistical Manual of Mental Disorders*. Copyright 2000. American Psychiatric Association.

behavioral characteristics, which may be apparent in the first few months of a child's life or appear during the early years. The diagnosis of AD or AS necessitates a two-stage process composed of a developmental screening during "well child" checkups and a comprehensive evaluation by a multidisciplinary team (Filipek et al., 2000). Among the most promising first- and second-degree screening tools for AD are the Modified Checklist for Autism in Toddlers (M-CHAT; Robins, Fein, Barton, & Green, 2001) and the Screening Tool for Autism in Two-Year-Olds (STAT; Stone, Coonrod, & Ousley, 2000). For AS, the tools are the

Autism Spectrum Screening Questionnaire (ASSQ; Ehlers, Gillberg, & Wing, 1999) and the Krug's Asperger's Disorder Index (KADI; Krug & Arick, 2003)[2] (see Table 9.3). These screening instruments do not provide a diagnosis; instead they aim to assess the need for referral for possible diagnosis of AS or AD.

The second stage of diagnosing AD or AS should include a formal multidisciplinary evaluation of social behavior, language and nonverbal communication, adaptive behavior, motor skills, atypical behaviors, and cognitive status made ideally by an experienced multidisciplinary team composed of social workers,

Table 9.3 Screening Instruments for Autistic Disorder and Asperger's Syndrome

Instrument	Type of Screening	Age Level	Informant	Characteristics
Autistic Disorder				
M-CHAT (Robins et al., 2001)	Level 1	24 months	Parent	23-item checklist to examine child's developmental milestones
STAT (Stone et al., 2004)	Level 2	24–35 months	Clinician	12 activities for observing child's early social/ communicative behaviors
Asperger's Syndrome				
ASSQ (Ehlers et al., 1999)	Level 1	>6 years	Parent/ Teacher	27-item checklist for assessing symptoms characteristic of Asperger's syndrome
KADI (Krug & Arick, 2003)	Levels 1 & 2	>6 years	Individual with daily and regular contact with child for at least a few weeks	32-item norm-referenced rating scale for presence or absence of behaviors indicative of Asperger's syndrome

psychologists, speech language pathologists, psychiatrists, pediatricians, educators, and family members (Howlin, 1998; National Research Council, 2001). AD and AS often involve other neurological or genetic problems, thereby necessitating a first-line comprehensive assessment of medical conditions (Filipek et al., 2000). The diagnosis of AD or AS often entails a school-based social worker gathering information on developmental history, medical background, psychiatric or health disorders of family members, and psychosocial factors. In addition, a social worker typically conducts a social family history by assessing the child's parents, caregivers, and environmental setting (McCarton, 2003). Psychological assessment and communicative assessment via testing, direct observation, and interviews should also inform the diagnosis. The psychological assessment helps to develop an understanding of the cognitive functioning and should address adaptive functioning, motor and visual skills, play, and social cognition (National Research Council, 2001). Communicative assessment should address communication skills in the context of a child's development (Lord & Paul, 1997) and assess expressive language and language comprehension.

In addition, diagnostic instruments can be used to help structure and quantify clinical observations (see Table 9.4). The Childhood Autism Rating Scale (CARS; Schopler, Reichler, & Renner, 1986) is the strongest, best-documented, and most widely used clinical rating scale for behaviors associated with autism (Lord & Cosello, 2005, p. 748). Other instruments with strong psychometric data to support their use as a component of the diagnostic process include the Autism

Table 9.4 Diagnostic Instruments for Autistic Disorder

Instrument	Characteristics
CARS (Schopler et al., 1986)	15-item rating scale covering a particular characteristic, ability, or behavior on which children are rated after observation; can be administered by clinician or educator, and some studies have demonstrated use by parents
ADI-R (Lord et al., 1994)	93-item semistructured interview composed of three subscales (social reciprocity, communication, and restricted, repetitive behaviors); administered by a clinician to caregivers
ADOS (Lord et al., 1999)	Standardized protocol for the observation of social and communicative behavior of children who may have an ASD; administered by a clinician

Diagnostic Interview-Revised (ADI-R; Lord, Rutter, & Le Couteur, 1994) and the Autism Diagnostic Observation Schedule (ADOS; Lord, Rutter, DiLavore, & Risi, 1999). One promising instrument for measuring symptom severity is the Social Responsiveness Scale (SRS; Constantino, 2002). No diagnosis would be complete without documentation of a child's unique strengths and weaknesses, as this component is critical to designing an effective intervention program since unusual developmental profiles are typical (National Research Council, 2001).

Although several instruments have been proposed to formally substantiate a diagnosis of AS,[3] these instruments have little relationship to each other and have not been found to be reliable (Lord & Cosello, 2005). In addition to the aforementioned categories, when diagnosing AS, attention and mental control, auditory and visual perception, and memory should be assessed (DuCharme & McGrady, 2003). Additional observations may address components of topic management and conversational ability, ability to deal with nonliteral language, and language flexibility (National Research Council, 2001).

In regard to diagnosis, parents and professionals should serve as partners in reaching the best possible understanding of the child. The developmental, medical, and family histories that parents provide are crucial components of a diagnosis. Their description of their child's behavior across multiple settings is essential. The role of the professionals on the multidisciplinary team is to interpret the information that parents provide. Parents know their individual child better than anyone, but professionals can offer a broad view of what is typical and where the child might differ from the norm (Wagner & McGrady, 2003).

Once a diagnosis of AD or AS is provided, parents begin to explore early intervention services to treat their child. Although early intervention has been shown to have a dramatic impact on reducing symptoms and increasing a child's ability to develop and gain new skills,[4] it is estimated that only 50% of children are diagnosed with an ASD before kindergarten (Strock, 2004). Thus, upon diagnosis, school-based interventions for youth with AD or AS often become the immediate focus of parents. Unfortunately, parents are soon faced with a prolific body of literature and disparate professional advice composed to some extent of ineffective approaches and treatment fads. Among the recommended treatments are facilitated communication, holding therapy, auditory integration training, gentle teaching, and hormone therapies, such as secretin, which are not adequately supported by scientific evidence for practice, and research has actually demonstrated some of these treatments to be harmful (Jacobson, Foxx, & Mulick, 2005; Simpson et al., 2004; Smith, 1996).

Part of the problem is that research has not demonstrated a single best treatment program for children with ASDs. Gresham, Beebe-Frankenberger, and MacMillan (1999) used conventional standards of research design and methodology and the Division 12 Task Force on Empirically Supported Treatments for Childhood Disorders of the American Psychological Association to evaluate the empirical evidence for the efficacy and effectiveness of several of the most visible and frequently cited treatment programs for children with autism: the UCLA Young Autism Project, Project TEACCH, LEAP, applied behavior analysis programs, and the Denver Health Science Program (p. 559). Their evaluation documented no well-established or probably efficacious treatments for autism; however, almost all programs demonstrated significant developmental gains, particularly in measured IQ. Rogers (1998), however, aptly noted that it is essential to recognize that the lack of empirical demonstration of efficacy does not necessarily signify that a particular treatment is ineffective. Instead, it means that the treatment's efficacy has not been demonstrated in a carefully controlled and objective way (Gresham et al., 1999).

What We Know

School-aged children with ASDs face transitions to a new learning environment, socialization with new peers and adults, and departures from familiar routines and settings. Thus, many professionals agree that a highly structured, specialized program is optimal for this transition to an individualized learning environment. Among the many methods available for treatment and education of school-aged children with AD or AS, applied behavior analysis (ABA) has become the most widely accepted effective intervention model (Strock, 2004). A recent U.S. surgeon general's report (U.S. Department of Health and Human Services, 1999) noted that 3 decades of research has led to the demonstrated efficacy of applied behavioral methods in reducing inappropriate behavior and increasing communication, learning, and appropriate social behavior for children with ASDs. Two evidence-based practices, discrete trial training or teaching (DTT) and pivotal response training (PRT), which use the principles of ABA, have been demonstrated as effective skill-based and behavioral treatment strategies. For the purpose of this chapter, *evidence-based practice* is defined as "the integration of best research evidence with clinical expertise and [client] values" (Sackett, Straus, Richardson, Rosenberg, & Haynes, 2000, p. 1).

Hundreds of scientific studies have demonstrated the effectiveness of ABA in building important skills and in reducing problem behaviors in children with ASDs (e.g., Jacobson, Mulick, & Green, 1998; Lovaas, 1987; McEachin, Smith, & Lovaas, 1993; Smith, Groen, & Wynn, 2000), yet due to ethical and practical considerations (such as small sample size and the heterogeneity of participants), well-controlled studies with random assignment have been nearly impossible to conduct (National Research Council, 2001). Studies of ABA's effectiveness are primarily based on single-case design, with close to 100 published on children with autism since 1980. ABA as an umbrella term includes "numerous measurement procedures and many behavior-increase and behavior-decrease procedures that can be used singly or in combination to remediate various skill deficits and behavior problems" (McClannahan & Krantz, 2004, p. 93). The effectiveness of these more broadly defined ABA interventions for eliciting new skills and reducing problematic behavior has been documented by numerous studies (Anderson & Romanczyk, 1999; Harris, Handleman, Gordon, Kristoff, & Fuentes, 1991; Smith, 2001; Smith et al., 2000; Yoder & Layton, 1988, as cited in Paul & Sutherland, 2005, p. 949); however, this variation of treatment strategies causes problems with comparisons of ABA techniques. For this reason, the primary educational and treatment techniques of DTT and PRT are reviewed as important instructional systems of ABA (Arick, Krug, Fullerton, Loos, & Falco, 2005).

What We Can Do

Applied Behavior Analysis

ABA is a discipline devoted to understanding the function behind human behavior and finding ways of altering or improving behaviors (Cooper, Heron, & Heward, 1987). ABA involves systematically applying learning theory-based interventions to improve socially significant observable behaviors to a meaningful degree and seeks to demonstrate that the improvement in behavior stems directly from the interventions that are utilized (Anderson, Taras, & Cannon, 1996; Baer, Wolf, & Risley, 1968; Sulzer-Azaroff & Mayer, 1991). The emphasis is on teaching the student how to learn from the environment and how to act on the environment in order to produce positive outcomes for himself and those around him (Harris & Handleman, 1994; Koegel & Koegel, 1995; Lovaas, 1993, 1981; Lovaas & Smith, 1989; Maurice, Green, & Luce, 1996; Schreibman, Charlop, & Milstein, 1993).

Behavior analytic treatment systematically teaches measurable units of a behavior or skill. Skills that a student with autism needs to learn are broken down into small steps. This form of teaching can be utilized for simple skills, such as making eye contact, and complex skills, like social interactions. Each step is initially taught by using a specific cue and pairing that cue with a prompt. Prompts range from physical guidance to verbal cues to very discrete gestures. Prompts should be faded out systematically by decreasing the level of prompt needed for the student to perform the target skill until, ideally, the student can perform the skill independently. In addition, skills should be taught by a variety of individuals, including teachers, aides, social workers, speech pathologists, and parents. There is strong evidence that parents can learn to employ ABA techniques and that doing so helps them to feel better in general and more satisfied and confident in their parenting role (Koegel et al., 1996; Ozonoff & Cathcart, 1998; Schreibman, 1997; Sofronoff & Farbotko, 2002, as cited in Wagner & McGrady, 2003). However, students should not become dependent on a particular individual or prompt. The student should be reinforced immediately after responding appropriately. The reinforcement should be a consequence that has been shown to increase the likelihood of the student responding appropriately again (Cooper et al., 1987). Reinforcements will vary from student to student. Inappropriate behavioral responses (such as tantrums, aggressive acts, screaming/yelling, stereotypic behaviors) are purposely not reinforced. Often, a functional analysis of antecedents and consequences is performed to determine what environmental reactions are reinforcing such behaviors (Cooper et al., 1987).

ABA has been proven effective across different providers (parents, teachers, therapists), different settings (schools, homes, hospitals, recreational areas), and behaviors (social, academic, and functional life skills; language; self-stimulatory, aggressive, and oppositional behaviors). Professionals who use ABA systematically and regularly measure progress on behavioral targets, leading to numerous studies of the effectiveness of ABA approaches. However, as Green (1996) pointed out, it is still unclear what variables are critical to intervention intensity (number of hours, length of the intervention, proportion of one-to-one to group instruction) and what are the expected outcomes when intervention intensity varies. It is also unclear what particular behavioral techniques (discrete trials, incidental teaching, pivotal response training) are most likely to be successful for a given child with an ASD and in what proportions particular techniques should be used (Anderson & Romanczyk, 1999). The current research is limited in that it does not allow us to draw comparisons across studies. For a review of the effectiveness of more broadly defined ABA intervention studies, see Anderson and Romanczyk (1999); Matson, Benavidez, Compton, Paclawskyj, and Baglio (1996); National Research Council (2001); New York State Department of Health, Early Intervention Program (1999a); and Simpson et al. (2004).

Discrete Trial Training

It is important to understand that ABA is a framework for the practice of a science and not a specific program. Programs using ABA often utilize DTT, which represents a specific type of presentation of opportunities to respond. Discrete trial training is a specialized teaching technique or process used to develop many new forms of behavior (Smith, 2001) and skills, including cognitive, communication, play, social, readiness, receptive-language, and self-help skills (Newsome, 1998). In addition, DTT can be used to reduce self-stimulatory responses and aggressive behaviors (Lovaas, 1981; Smith, 2001).

Discrete trial training involves breaking skills into the smallest steps, teaching each step of the skill until mastery, providing lots of repetition, prompting the correct response and fading the prompts as soon as possible, and using positive reinforcement procedures. Each discrete trial has five separate parts: (1) cue: the social worker presents a brief clear instruction or question; (2) prompt: at the same time as the cue or immediately thereafter, the social worker assists the child in responding correctly to the cue; (3) response: the child gives a correct or incorrect answer to the social worker's cue; (4) consequence: if the child has given a correct response, the social worker immediately reinforces the response with praise, access to toys, or other activities that the child enjoys. If the child has given an incorrect response, the social worker says "no," looks away, removes teaching materials, or otherwise signals that the response was incorrect; and (5) intertrial interval: after giving the consequence, the social worker pauses briefly (1–5 seconds) before presenting the cue for the next trial (Smith, 2001, p. 86). The following is an example of DTT:

The social worker says, "Touch your nose." (verbal cue)

The student does not respond (response).

After a few seconds, the social worker places her hand on the student's hand. (prompt)

The child extends his index finger himself, and the social worker helps the child to touch his nose. (response)

The social worker says, "Yes, that is your nose. Good job touching your nose." (consequence)

This is an example of one trial. The correct response is considered a measurable unit of a skill. Data can be collected on the number of correct versus incorrect responses to chart a student's progress. This trial would be repeated approximately five times, as repetition of skills is a component of discrete trial teaching.

The social worker says, "What's your address?" (verbal cue)

The student says, "My address is 123 House Street, Maywood, New Jersey." (response)

The instructor gives the student behavior-descriptive praise (i.e., "Good, you said your address correctly") and 30 seconds to play with a toy of his choice. (consequence)

As one can see from the examples above, DTT can be used to teach starting from the most basic information up to slightly more advanced knowledge. Discrete trial teaching affords children with AS and AD opportunities to respond, which have been linked with improved performance on measures of academic achievement (Delquadri, Greenwood, Stretton, & Hall, 1983). This approach has also been credited with impressive gains in children with otherwise poor prognoses (Lovaas, 1987) and in accelerated skill acquisition (Miranda-Linne & Melin, 1992). An effective school-based intervention should prioritize discrimination issues by using DTT strategies that (1) carefully present stimuli in a systematic manner and with planned repetition; (2) provide a planned process for teaching the relationship of words to functional objects, people, and other important concepts; and (3) use systematic visual stimuli to teach important functional auditory discriminations (Arick et al., 2005, p. 1007). For studies documenting the effectiveness of DTT, see Cummings and Williams (2000); Dawson and Osterling (1997); Goldstein (2002); National Research Council (2001); Odom et al. (2003); Simpson et al. (2004); and Smith (2001).

Pivotal Response Training

PRT is a model that aims to apply educational techniques in pivotal areas that affect target behaviors (Koegel, Koegel, Harrower, & Carter, 1999). Pivotal areas when effectively targeted result in substantial collateral gains in numerous developmental domains. Pivotal areas of primary focus include (1) responding to multiple cues and stimuli (i.e., decreasing overselectivity by distinguishing relevant features); (2) improving child motivation (i.e., increasing appropriate responses, decreasing response latency, and improving affect); (3) increasing self-management capacity (i.e., teaching children to be aware of their aberrant behaviors to self-monitor and to self-reinforce); and (4) increasing self-initiations (i.e., teaching children to respond to natural cues in the environment) (Simpson et al., 2004, pp. 114–115).

The goals of intervention in pivotal areas are "(1) to teach the child to be responsive to the many learning opportunities and social interactions that occur in the natural environment, (2) to decrease the need for constant supervision by an intervention provider, and (3) to decrease the number of services that remove the child from the natural environment" (Koegel et al., 1999, p. 174). Thus, the primary purpose of PRT is to provide children with the social and educational proficiency to participate in inclusive settings.

Designed on the basis of a series of studies identifying important treatment components, PRT in its fledgling stages used a discrete trial, ABA approach. Currently, PRT uses the principles of ABA in a manner that excludes negative interactions, reduces dependence on artificial prompts, and is family centered (Simpson et al., 2004, p. 114). Utilizing the strategies of PRT, target behaviors are taught in natural settings with items that are age-appropriate and meaningful as well as reinforcing to the child. PRT involves specific strategies such as (1) clear instructions and questions presented by the social worker, (2) child choice of stimuli (based on choices offered by the social worker), (3) integration of maintenance tasks (previously mastered tasks) (Dunlap, 1984), (4) direct reinforcement (the chosen stimuli is the reinforcer) (Koegel & Williams, 1980), (5) reinforcement of reasonable purposeful attempts at correct responding (Koegel, O'Dell, & Dunlap, 1988), and (6) turn taking to allow modeling and appropriate pace of interaction (Stahmer, Ingersoll, & Carter, 2003, p. 404). An example of using the specific steps of PRT to teach symbolic play might be as follows:

A child may choose to play with a doll. (choice)

The child is then given an empty cup and saucer, and asked, "What can we do with these toys?" (acquisition task)

The child is expected to use the teacup in some symbolic manner, such as having a tea party.

If the child does not respond, the social worker would model the symbolic behavior. (turn taking)

The teacup would then be returned to the child. If the child still does not respond, a new toy would be selected, or the social worker could assist the child.

When the child does respond, many of the child's dolls would be given to him to play with in any manner chosen, thus reinforcing the new behavior.

A more detailed description of using PRT to teach complex skills can be found in Stahmer (1999) and in *How to Teach Pivotal Behaviors to Children With Autism: A Training Manual* (Koegel et al., n.d.).

PRT has been adapted to teach a variety of skills, including social skills (Koegel & Frea, 1993), symbolic (Stahmer, 1995) and sociodramatic play (Thorpe, Stahmer, & Schreibman, 1995), and joint attention (Whalen & Schreibman, 2003). Parents have been trained to successfully implement PRT. Schreibman, Kaneko, and Koegel (1991) found that parents appeared happier and more relaxed when they used PRT methods with their children than when they used more structured teaching techniques (Bregman, Zager, & Gerdtz, 2005). For studies documenting the effectiveness of PRT, see Koegel, Koegel, Shoshan, and McNerney (1999); National Research Council (2001); and Simpson et al. (2004).

Last, due to the widespread use of various medications for symptoms associated with autism, a review of interventions for school-aged children would not be complete without a brief discussion of psychopharmacology.

Psychopharmacology

Psychopharmacological treatment of children with ASDs appears to be common in clinical practice via the use of atypical antipsychotics, serotonin reuptake inhibitors, stimulants, and mood stabilizers (Aman, Collier-Crespin, & Lindsay, 2000; Martin, Scahill, Klin, & Volkmar, 1999). It is estimated that as many as half of all individuals with a diagnosis of an ASD are treated with one or more psychotropic medications (Martin et al., 1999). However, few studies specifically targeting a sample of children with ASDs and adhering to conventional standards of research design and methodology with efficacious results were found. The Research Units on Pediatric Psychopharmacology Autism Network (2002) and Shea et al. (2004) completed large-scale multisite, randomized, double-blind, placebo-controlled clinical trials of risperidone in children with autism. Risperidone is known as an atypical antipsychotic and is frequently used for treating severe maladaptive behavior and symptoms associated with AD (McDougle et al., 2000), such as aggression, self-injury, property destruction, or severe tantrums. The studies provided convincing evidence that risperidone is safe and effective for the short-term treatment of severe behavioral problems. The focus on severe behavior problems leaves an open question about possible additive effects of medication and applied behavioral interventions (Scahill & Martin, 2005). For example, the improvement in serious behavior problems associated with risperidone may enable a child to participate in an inclusive setting with DTT techniques employed.

Additional randomized, double-blind, placebo-controlled clinical trials have been conducted to test the effects of liquid fluoxetine, donepezil hydrochloride, and amantadine. All three had efficacious findings to some extent. The clinical trial conducted to examine the selective serotonin reuptake inhibitor liquid fluoxetine yielded results that indicate that a low dose is more effective than a placebo in the treatment of repetitive behaviors in childhood and adolescents with ASDs (Hollander et al., 2005). The study of donepezil hydrochloride found expressive and receptive speech gains, as well as decreases in severity of overall autistic behavior after 6 weeks for the treatment group (Chez et al., 2003). Last, a randomized control trial of amantadine for childhood autism reported clinician-rated improvements on behavioral ratings but showed no difference between the placebo and the active drug for parent ratings (King et al., 2001). However, a large placebo response was also found in this group. It is important to strongly caution professionals and family members that there are no medications specifically targeting the core symptoms of social and language impairments of autism in children.

Tools and Practice Example

Increasingly, school-based social workers and other mental health professionals are providing collaborative consultation (Idol, 1988; Idol, Paolucci-Whitcomb, & Nevin, 1986) to general education teachers of students with disabilities, focused on problem-solving efforts to identify students' behavioral difficulties and to devise strategies to reduce the problems (Curtis & Myers, 1988, as cited in Pryor, Kent, McGunn, & LeRoy, 1996). The following case example illustrates a school social worker employing ABA and DTT to address the classroom behavior of a child with AD in an inclusive setting.

Practice Example

John is an 11-year-old Caucasian male currently enrolled in a public middle school in a blue-ribbon school district on the East Coast. John comes from an upper-middle-class family. Though John has no siblings, he has many relatives, including cousins in his peer group, with whom he interacts frequently. Between 2 and 2 1/2 years of age, John's language development regressed significantly. His parents noticed that he was not utilizing his functional language at the same level he had in the past, and he began to consistently make syntactic and pragmatic errors, such as pronoun reversal, and experienced difficulty answering simple what, where, when, and why questions. In addition, John began to exhibit strange behaviors, such as placing his toys in perfectly straight lines and verbally repeating television shows and commercials out of context. He exhibited additional impairments in his social interactions, including difficulty making and maintaining eye contact and an inability to understand nonverbal social cues, such as the curling of one's finger to mean "come here." John also exhibited a lack of social reciprocity. At this time, John's parents consulted a myriad of specialists to search for an explanation for their son's changes in behavior and speech. John was eventually assessed by a multidisciplinary team of professionals, which resulted in an Axis I diagnosis of 299.00 Autistic Disorder.

In concert with the parents' preference, John's school district enrolled him in a school that specialized in educating young children with autism. Due to the research evidence demonstrating the effectiveness of ABA methods with young children with AD in preschool settings, the school he attended utilized this systematic approach to teach students a continuum of skills and behaviors. A school social worker was assigned to support John in the school and home, guiding him in the areas of social interaction, functional language, academic skills, and decreasing inappropriate behaviors. She worked closely with the parents to further reinforce their instruction of the structured approach in an effort to incorporate ABA techniques into their everyday routine, thereby reinforcing John's skill set across persons and settings.

During his kindergarten year, John was enrolled part time in a regular public school. He went to his specialized school for children with autism in the morning, where he received intensive skill training through discrete trial teaching. In the afternoon, John was integrated into a regular kindergarten class in a public school. The school social worker stayed in this class with John for 1 hour per day to aid in generalization of the skills taught in his specialized school and in the home setting. Generalization of skills has been defined as an important aspect to consider in designing any intervention for children with autism (Prizant & Wetherby, 1998; Smith, 2001).

Two advantages to John's social worker shadowing him in the public school class were the opportunity to train the school staff in ABA principles and instruction and to gather data on John's behaviors and skill level in the school setting. For example, the social worker took occurrence/nonoccurrence data on John's "TV talk" (verbal repetition of lines from his favorite television shows). On a data sheet, she divided the school day into 5-minute intervals and took data on whether John exhibited TV talk or did not. The social worker marked each 5-minute interval with a "+" if John demonstrated TV talk or a "−" if no

TV talk occurred. This type of data was collected over a 3-day period during a 1-week interval. After the data collection was completed and the frequency of the behavior was established, the social worker performed a functional analysis of the behavior. The purpose of a functional analysis is to determine what environmental element is encouraging the student to engage in a particular behavior. To perform a functional analysis, the social worker took "ABC data." At each instance of the behavior, the social worker wrote down the (A) antecedent to the behavior: what occurred in the environment directly prior to the behavior being exhibited; the (B) behavior itself: exactly how the behavior was manifested, what the student said and did while participating in the behavior; and the (C) consequence(s) to the behavior: how the individuals in the environment responded to the behavior. Did the student receive attention? Was the student removed from a demanding task? After a functional analysis was performed on John's TV talk, the social worker established that John participated in the behavior to "escape" demanding social situations.

At this time, John was exhibiting noncontextual speech in the form of TV talk habitually throughout the day. The educator requested that the school social worker assist with the reduction of this behavior as it prevented John from interacting in a reciprocal way with his peers and caused many distractions for both John and his peers in relation to their learning. His social worker wrote a behavior modification plan to target this behavior. The plan was a differential reinforcement of appropriate behaviors (DRA). The DRA was selected as a treatment strategy as it enabled other school staff to be trained in the intervention techniques and built upon John's strengths by encouraging his appropriate behaviors. The DRA was executed throughout his day. When John would engage in appropriate activities without exhibiting TV talk, the social worker (or whoever was with him at the time) would sporadically give him a happy-face token, paired with social praise ("You're doing a nice job working on the puzzle"). When John would engage in TV talk, the social worker would give him a sad-face token paired with the verbal cue, "Tell me what you're doing now." This verbal cue taught John to comment on a present task rather than perseverate on television shows. When John earned five happy-face tokens, he was able to choose a preferred activity (e.g., working on the computer) to engage in for a 3-minute period. If John received five sad-face tokens before earning five happy-face tokens, he was given a verbal prompt, "You need to talk about what is going on in the [classroom], not about TV." The staff of both his specialized and inclusive schools was trained to implement the plan, as were his parents. John exhibited this behavior very frequently (some instance of TV talk occurred in 80% of the 5-minute intervals during data collection) when the behavior plan was initially implemented. With the consistency of the implementation, the behavior was reduced to one or two instances a day after 6 months and was eventually eliminated by the end of the school year.

John was mainstreamed into the public school, full time, with a one-to-one aide at the start of his first-grade year. He was able to complete the full curriculum with the help of the school staff, who worked with the school social worker to learn how to break down John's assignments into manageable steps. For example, stories read in class were broken down into "chunks" and paired with visual cues to aid in comprehension. He continued to receive ABA instruction and DTT after school with the social worker. The social worker utilized role-play techniques to teach social skills, breaking down the skills into manageable steps:

SW: I'm going to pretend to be Kyle. I'm on the playground with a soccer ball. You're going to walk up to me, tap me on the shoulder, look in my eyes and say, "Can I play soccer with you?" Get ready. Go!

John: [walks up, taps the social worker on the shoulder, looks in her eyes, but says nothing]

SW: Say, "Can I play soccer with you?" (verbal cue)

John: Can I play soccer with you?

SW: That was great! Let's try it again. (social praise used as positive reinforcement)

In the example, the social worker is breaking down a social interaction into small, teachable steps. After John mastered this first step of playground interaction (initiating play) in several different play scenarios, the social worker expanded the recess role-play scenes to teach John how to maintain extended play periods. During lunch time and recess at the school, John's social worker would shadow him and deliver verbal cues such as "Ask Kyle, 'Can I play with you?'" or gestural prompts (i.e., point at a peer with whom he can play). The verbal cue was also paired with the gestural prompt: pointing at the peer while modeling "Can I play with you?" These strategies aimed to help John generalize the skills he learned during his therapy sessions. Again, the school staff was also taught these prompts to assist with John's socialization throughout the school day. For a child with AD to be included in a mainstream setting, he needs to be able to manage social experiences (National Research Council, 2001).

John's social worker continued to consult in the school setting. John was taught to respond to discrete hand gestures to help him to refocus on the teacher when environmental distractions would impede his concentration. If John would look out through the window when his teacher was speaking, the social worker would touch his shoulder, and when John looked up, she would tap her ear twice and point to the teacher. John was taught that this gesture meant "listen to the teacher." The school staff was taught to utilize these hand gestures as well. These discrete gestures kept John from standing out too much from his peers, as verbal redirecting would draw attention to him. Through the use of such gestures by various staff members, John's classmates also began to respond to the gestures when they became unfocused.

John is currently enrolled in a public middle school. He continues to complete the full curriculum and plays on his town soccer and basketball teams. John does continue to experience difficulty in the area of reading comprehension and in assessing social cues at times. However, the progress John has made is quite noteworthy. He is a friendly and empathic boy who excels in math and enjoys athletic activities. John's success could not have been accomplished without the support of a multidisciplinary team effort. John's school social worker, teachers, speech therapist, and occupational therapist all collaborated through the years to utilize similar strategies and target compatible goals. John's parents employed reinforcement strategies in the home by carrying over the skills targeted in therapy and at school.

Resources

Overview of AD and AS

http://www.autism-society.org
http://www.autisminfo.com
http://www.nichcy.org
http://www.aspergers.com
http://www.udel.edu/bkirby/asperger/aslink.html
http://www.autism-pdd.net/autism.htm
http://www.autismwebsite.com/ari/index.htm

Educational and Therapeutic Interventions

http://www.teacch.com
http://www.autism.org
http://www.cabas.com

Treatment Centers

http://www.pcdi.org
http://gsappweb.rutgers.edu/DDDC
http://info.med.yale.edu/chldstdy/autism
http://www.behavior.org
http://www.son-rise.org

Training Materials

Arick, J. R., Loos, L., Falco, R., & Krug, D. A. (2004). *Strategies for teaching based on autism research: STAR*. Austin, TX: Pro-Ed.

Freeman, S., & Dake, L. (1997). *Teach me language*. Langley, BC: SKF Books.

Koegel, R. L., Koegel, L. K., & Parks, D. R. (1990). *How to teach self-management skills to people with severe disabilities: A training manual*. Santa Barbara: University of California.

Leaf, R., & McEachin, J. (1999). *A work in progress*. New York: DRL Books.

McClannahan, L. E., & Krantz, P. J. (1999). Activity schedules for children with autism: Teaching independent behavior. Bethesda, MD: Woodbine.

http://www.dttrainer.com/pi_overview.htm

http://www.nationalspeech.com

http://rsaffran.tripod.com/

http://www.users.qwest.net/~tbharris/prt.htm

http://www.education.ucsb.edu/autism/behaviormanuals.html

Suggested Practice Exercise Related to Intervention

Consider that a parent has received a diagnosis of AD for his 5-year-old son. How would you begin to present the options for intervention? Describe your role as a social worker in providing the information.

Key Points to Remember

- Autism spectrum disorders are defined by clinical symptomatology that typically falls within three major categories: (1) qualitative impairment in social interaction; (2) impairments in communication; and (3) restricted, repetitive, stereotyped behavior, interests, and activities.
- One of the important characteristics of children with ASDs is uneven learning ability and skill levels, and as such, individualization of intervention is necessary.
- Applied behavior analysis is the most widely accepted effective intervention model for children and adolescents with AD and AS.
- Discrete trial training is a specialized teaching technique or process used to develop new forms of behavior and skills, including cognitive, communication, play, social, readiness, receptive-language, and self-help skills, as well as reducing self-stimulatory responses and aggressive behaviors.
- The primary purpose of pivotal response training is to provide children with the social and educational proficiency to participate in inclusive settings.
- Medication cannot be justified as the first line of treatment for AD, AS, or the associated symptoms.
- Behavioral treatments are most successful when applied across settings and persons in the child's life.

Despite the promising treatment effects produced by the interventions reviewed above, existing treatments need to be refined and evaluated with rigorous testing procedures to establish efficacy. A primary goal of the research should be to determine the types of interventions that are most effective for children with different subtypes of ASDs and with specific characteristics, since the characteristics of children with ASDs and their life circumstances are exceedingly heterogeneous in nature (National Research Council, 2001). Regardless of the intervention selected, it is essential that strategies be devised to take advantage of the unique constellation of strengths and characteristics of the learner with AS or AD and to modify contexts to support the learning and behavioral style of the individual student (Klin, McPartland, & Volkmar, 2005).

The focus in this chapter has been geared toward the school social worker and mental health practitioner working with individual students in school settings. Equally important in sustaining gains in behavior and skill acquisition with school-aged children and adolescents with AD and AS are issues surrounding classroom management, group skill-based interventions, especially for students with AS, and working collaboratively with parents, teachers, peers, and school administrators to promote skill generalization across settings and persons in addition to sustaining change.

Notes

1. It should be noted that in addition to the diagnostic criteria for AS delineated in the *DSM-IV-TR* (2000) and the *ICD-10* (1992), there are at least five very different conceptualizations of AS (Ghaziuddin, Tsai, & Ghaziuddin, 1992; Klin & Volkmar, 1997; Leekam, Libby, Wing, Gould, & Gillberg, 2000; Szatmari, Bryson, Boyle, Streiner, & Duku, 2003), which represent to some extent the major differences in the conceptualization of this disorder (e.g., Asperger's syndrome as a milder form of autism, different conceptions of the timing when motor skills should be taken into account, etc.).

2. Level-one screening measures for autism are used to identify children at risk for autism from the general population, while level-two screening involves the identification of children at risk for autism from a population of children demonstrating a broad range of developmental concerns (Stone et al., 2004).

3. There are two instruments specifically designed as diagnostic tools for Asperger's syndrome: the Asperger's Syndrome Diagnostic Interview and the Australian Scale for Asperger's Syndrome. Both require further testing to determine their reliability and validity prior to use as diagnostic instruments.

4. See Rogers (1998); National Research Council (2001); and New York State Department of Health, Early Intervention Program (1999b) for a complete review of evidence-based early intervention programs.

School-Based, Adolescent Suicidality

Lethality Assessments and Crisis Intervention Protocols

Albert R. Roberts

Getting Started

Every 17 minutes, someone in this country commits suicide. This equates to 83 suicides each day throughout the United States. Suicides and suicide attempts take place in every age group, ethnic and racial group, gender, socioeconomic status, and geographic area (U.S. Department of Health and Human Services, 2001). Suicide is a prevalent social problem and public health problem for adults and youths. Adolescents and young adults seem to be especially vulnerable. More specifically, suicide is the third leading cause of death among young people between the ages of 15 and 24; accidents and homicides are the first and second. Suicide attempts have occurred among children as young as 7 years of age (Roberts & Yeager, 2005). Early detection and identification of acutely suicidal adolescents have the potential to dramatically decrease the prevalence of this significant social problem throughout the United States. Most children and youth who have ideas and thoughts about suicide exhibit specific warning signs, symptoms, gestures, and behaviors, which can be recognized by school social workers, mental health consultants, and crisis counselors who are trained in suicide assessment and crisis intervention.

School social workers and mental health consultants to the schools can develop competency in evidence-based suicide risk assessments and interventions. For the most part, suicidal behaviors and impulses are temporary and transient. Evidence-based studies have indicated that most individuals who have killed themselves have given some type of prior warning (Jobes, Berman, & Martin, 2005). The school social workers and mental health counselors are therefore in pivotal life-saving positions. Effective lethality assessments and evidence-based crisis intervention can certainly save lives, especially since most suicidal youth are ambivalent.

Here are three important operational definitions:

1. Suicide: the deliberate, intentional, and purposeful act of killing oneself
2. Ambivalence: having two mixed and opposing feelings at the same time, such as the desire to live and the desire to die

3. Lethality: the potential for a specific method and suicide plan to actually end the individual's life

What We Know

Suicide Warning Signs and Risk Factors

It is important to be aware of precipitating factors or events, risk variables, and biological or sociocultural factors that seem to put youths at imminent risk of deliberate self-harm and suicide attempts. Common triggering or precipitating events, also known as *the last straw*, include rejection or humiliation, such as a broken romance, being repeatedly bullied or teased, intense verbal abuse by parents, or the death of a parent. The key to whether or not a significant stressful life event leads to suicide or to a productive life is based on the internal meaning and perceptions that each person attaches to the event. For example, Dr. Viktor Frankel lost his wife and entire family in the concentration camps during World War II but instead of giving up, Frankel decided that no matter what torture the Nazis administered, they could not take away his will to live. His classic book, *Man's Search for Meaning*, has inspired hundreds of thousands of readers to never give up and to do their very best to lead productive lives devoted to helping others. Since the late 1970s, a number of risk variables, or suicide warning signs, have been documented (Beck, Brown, & Steer, 1997; Beck, Brown, Steer, Dahlsgaard, & Grisham, 1999; Beck & Lester, 1976; Berman, 1975; Berman & Jobes, 1991; Jobes, Berman, & Martin, 2005; Kovacs, Beck, & Weissman, 1976; Maris, Berman, Maltsberger, & Yufit, 1992; Roberts, 1975, 1991). These include the following:

Intense emotional pain
Extreme sense of hopelessness and helplessness about oneself
Socially isolated and cut off from other young people
Giving away important personal possessions
Prolonged feelings of emptiness, worthlessness, and/or depression
Prior suicide attempts
Mental confusion
Prior family history of suicide
Past psychiatric history
Presence of weapon
Alcohol or substance abuse
Anger, aggression, or irritability
Childhood physical or sexual abuse
Sleep disturbances
Loss of positive motivation

Loss of interest in pleasurable things

Poor personal cleanliness

Excessive focus on death and dying

Specific clues to suicide include statements such as "Life sucks and I might as well end it all," "I'd be better off dead," "I wish I was dead," "I am planning on killing myself," "I bought a new dress to be buried in," or "I borrowed my uncle's gun in order to shoot myself at midnight."

The National Mental Health Association has developed the following list of warning signs of someone considering suicide:

- Verbal suicide threats, such as "you'd be better off without me around"
- Expressions of hopelessness and helplessness
- Personality changes
- Depression
- Daring or risk-taking behavior
- Previous suicide attempts
- Giving away prized possessions
- Lack of interest in future plans

All school social workers and mental health counselors should be aware of the following scales for use in assessing suicide ideation and depression:

- Beck Hopelessness Scales
- Beck Depression Inventory
- Rosenberg Self-Esteem Scale
- Linehan Reasons for Living Scale
- Brown–Goodwin Aggression Scale
- Buss–Durkee Hostility-Guilt Inventory
- Spielberger State-Trait Anxiety Scale
- Plutchik Impulsivity Scale
- Self-Rated Problem Solving Inventory
- Suicide Ideation-Worst Pt.
- European Parasuicide Study Interview Schedules I and Isl
- ICD-10 Diagnostic Schedule
- Personality Assessment Schedule

Within the current care environment, social workers are required to determine imminent, moderate, and low suicide risk. In doing so, the individual practitioner is required to assign the patient to the most appropriate level of care. The implementation of Roberts's seven-stage model provides appropriate interventions for resolution of moderate and low suicidal ideation immediately upon the individual seeking assistance. In addition, application of the seven-stage model can provide insight in a nonthreatening manner to assist the patient in develop-ment of cognitive stabilization when completing the initial assessment and when the appropriate intervention protocol is followed.

What We Can Do

School Social Workers and Crisis Intervention Center Collaboration

Several states, including Florida, Georgia, Illinois, Massachusetts, Minnesota, New York, Ohio, Pennsylvania, Texas, Utah, Washington, and Wisconsin, maintain several 24-hour telephone crisis intervention and suicide prevention programs. These programs usually work closely with school social workers and other mental health professionals in the community. This service provides a lifeline as well as an entry point to behavioral health care for persons with major depression or suicidal thoughts and ideation. When crisis workers answer the cry for help, their primary duty is to initiate crisis intervention, beginning with rapid lethality and triage assessment and establishing rapport. In essence, crisis intervention and sui-cide prevention include certain primary steps in an attempt to prevent suicide:

Conduct a rapid lethality and biopsychosocial assessment.

Attempt to establish rapport and at the same time communicate a willing-ness to help the caller in crisis.

Help the caller in crisis to develop a plan of action that links him or her to community health care and mental health agencies. The most frequent outcome for depressed or suicidal adolescents is that they are either stabilized by the crisis social worker or transported to psychiatric screening and intake at a behavioral health care facility, hospital, or addiction treatment program.

The crisis intervention worker or mental health consultant assumes full respon-sibility for the case when a suicidal student arrives at school. The person cannot be rushed and handled simply by a referral to another agency. Crisis workers should follow the case until complete transfer of responsibility has been accomplished by some other agency assuming the responsibility. The crisis worker should com-plete the state-mandated mental health and psychiatric screening reports, which make an initial determination as to whether the person is a danger to himself or others. The ultimate goal of all crisis and suicide prevention services is to strive to relieve intense emotional pain and acute crisis episodes, while helping the person to find positive ways to cope with life (Roberts, 2000; Roberts & Yeager, 2005).

It is imperative for all crisis clinicians to establish rapport with the person in crisis by listening in a patient, hopeful, self-assured, interested, and knowl-edgeable manner. Skilled crisis workers try to communicate an attitude that the person has done the right thing by contacting them, and they convey willingness and an ability to help. An empathetic ear is provided to the person in crisis in order to relieve her intense stress by active listening. The crisis worker should relate to this person in a confidential, spontaneous, and noninstitutionalized manner (Yeager & Gregoire, 2000).

Suicide Assessment Measures and Tools

The author developed a seven-stage crisis intervention protocol in 1990 (Roberts, 1991). The most critical first step in applying Roberts's seven-stage crisis intervention model is conducting a lethality and biopsychosocial risk assessment. This involves a relatively quick assessment of the number and duration of risk factors, including imminent danger and availability of lethal weapons, verbalization of suicide or homicide risk, need for immediate medical attention, positive and negative coping strategies, lack of family or social supports, poor judgment, and current drug or alcohol use (Eaton, 2005; Eaton & Roberts, 2002; Roberts, 1991, 2000).

If possible, a medical assessment should include a brief summary of the presenting problem, any ongoing medical conditions, and current medications (names, dosages, and time of last dose). The highest suicide risk is among persons who express suicidal ideation, present with agitation and impulsivity, have a suicide plan, have access to a lethal weapon, exhibit poor judgment, are delusional and/or exhibiting command hallucinations, and are intoxicated or high on illegal drugs.

After listening to the story of the person in crisis and asking several key questions, the crisis worker makes a determination as to whether or not the individual has a high suicide risk. If the youth has a lethal method (e.g., a firearm) readily available and a specific plan for suicide, or has previously attempted suicide, then he is considered as having a high suicide risk. In sharp contrast, the youths evaluated as low suicide risk still need help, but they are primarily depressed and expressing ambivalent thoughts about what it's like to be in heaven versus hell. They have not yet planned the specific details of suicide. Other youths may be seeking information on how to help a friend or family member or about problems related to a broken romance, loneliness, or a sexually transmitted disease, or they may be in need of emergency medical attention due to illicit drug abuse.

With regard to inpatient versus outpatient psychiatric treatment, the most important determinant should be imminent danger—lethal means to suicide. It is also extremely important for crisis clinicians to make a multiaxial differential diagnosis using the *DSM-IV-TR*, which determines acute or chronic psychosocial stressors, dysfunctional relationships, decreased self-esteem or hopelessness, severe or unremitting anxiety, intimate partner violence, personality disorders (particularly borderline personality disorder), major depressive disorders, bipolar disorders, and comorbidity (American Psychiatric Association, 2003). See Chapters

12 and 11 for discussions on how to use the *DSM-IV-TR's* five multiaxial diagnostic criteria. Several recent studies have found that persons with suicide ideation have comorbid substance abuse and other mental disorders 60%–92% of the time (Roberts, Yeager, & Streiner, 2004). Making accurate assessments and predicting short-term risk of suicide (1 to 3 days) has been found to be much more reliable than predicting long-term risk (Simon, 1992). Other serious clues to increased suicidal risk are when a person has no social support network, poor judgment, or poor impulse control and adamantly refuses to sign a contract for safety (Rudd & Joiner, 1998).

Crisis Intervention

Crisis intervention with children and adolescents is difficult and is difficult to do well. As the acuity of mental health consumers increases and the service delivery system buckles under the increasing pressure of those seeking services, it becomes clear that specific and efficacious interventions and guidelines are needed to keep the process flowing. There is growing evidence of the risk factors for suicide, including a precipitating event, such as multiple stressors, a traumatic event, major depression, increased substance abuse, deterioration in social or occupational functions, hopelessness, and verbal expressions of suicidal ideation (Weishaar, 2004). For some individuals, dealing with ambivalence— simultaneous thoughts of self-harm and thoughts of immediate gratification and satisfaction—is a day-to-day event. For some, the thought of suicide mistakenly appears to be an immediate fix to an emotionally painful or acutely embarrassing situation that seems insurmountable.

For the depressed, impulsive, and chemically dependent youth, suicide may seem like the easy way out of a downward spiral of emotional pain. Therefore it may be helpful to include a working definition of crisis:

> *Crisis*: An acute disruption of psychological homeostasis in which one's usual coping mechanisms fail and there exists evidence of distress and functional impairment; the subjective reaction to a stressful life experience that compromises the individual's stability and ability to cope or function. The main cause of a crisis is an intensely stressful, traumatic, or hazardous event, but two other conditions are also necessary: (1) the individual's perception of the event as the cause of considerable upset and/or disruption; and (2) the individual's inability to resolve the disruption by previously used coping mechanisms. Crisis also refers to "an upset in the steady state." It often has five components: a hazardous or traumatic event, a vulnerable state, a precipitating factor, an active crisis state, and the resolution of the crisis. (Roberts, 2002)

The definition of a crisis stated above is particularly applicable to youths in acute suicidal crisis because these individuals usually seek help only after they have experienced a hazardous or traumatic event and are in a vulnerable state, have failed to cope and lessen the crisis through customary coping methods, lack family or community social supports, and want outside help. Acute psychological or situational crisis episodes may be viewed in various ways, but the definition we are using emphasizes that a crisis can be a turning point in a person's life (Roberts & Yeager, 2005).

Crisis intervention generally refers to a social worker, behavioral clinician, or crisis counselor entering into the life situation of an individual or family to alleviate the impact of a crisis episode in order to facilitate and mobilize the resources of those directly affected. Rapid assessment and timely intervention on the part of crisis counselors, social workers, psychologists, or child psychiatrists is of paramount importance.

Crisis interveners should be active and directive while displaying a nonjudgmental, accepting, hopeful, and positive attitude. Crisis interveners need to help crisis clients to identify protective factors, inner strengths, psychological hardiness, or resiliency factors that can be utilized for ego bolstering. Effective crisis interveners are able to gauge the seven stages of crisis intervention, while being flexible and realizing that several stages of intervention may overlap. Crisis intervention should culminate with a restoration of cognitive functioning, crisis resolution, and cognitive mastery (Roberts, 2000).

Tools and Practice Examples

Below is a case scenario. How would one assess the situation presented there and how should the school social worker or mental health counselor respond? These are discussed subsequently.

Synopsis: Maryann

Maryann has barricaded herself in the teachers' lounge for the past 2 hours. She has called her cousin on her cell phone to offer him her favorite CDs. Her mother, Mrs. Smith, is a social studies teacher in the school. Maryann has just broken up with her boyfriend and had a history of taking an overdose of sleeping pills 8 months ago in a similar situation.

On that previous occasion, Maryann had been rushed to the ER as she was distraught about the breakup with her previous boyfriend. Making matters worse, Maryann's father had died within the past year from cirrhosis of the liver. Maryann's mother usually drives her daughter home from school at 2:30 p.m. It is 4:30 p.m. and the janitor and Mrs. Smith recently found out that Maryann has barricaded herself in the teacher's lounge. Maryann has been crying. She refuses to come out, has barricaded the door with furniture, refuses to talk, and has asked her mother to put a large bottle of soda outside the lounge. Finally, Maryann said that she plans to sleep in the lounge and not come out until the morning. It is unclear whether Maryann has illegal drugs with her.

Application of Roberts's Seven-Stage Crisis Intervention Model

After reading the above case synopsis and reviewing the suicide risk assessment flow chart (Figure 10.1), would your preliminary rapid assessment rate Maryann as low, moderate, or high suicide risk?

It is important to keep in mind that while many persons at high risk of suicide have expressed/exhibited a specific suicide plan and availability of a lethal method (e.g., firearms or a rope or belt for hanging), there are exceptions. There is a relatively small group of individuals who do not talk to anyone before making a lethal suicide attempt but do give clear clues of imminent suicide risk, for example, the high school honors student who fails a course for the first time and can't sleep may be in imminent danger. Although he has never had a problem sleeping and has been an honors student for the past 3 years, he may magnify the inconvenience of retaking a course as the worst and most shameful thing ever. Another example would be a youth or young adult who never expressed paranoid delusions and now has expressed irrational fears that a violent gang with 100 members is after him and will try to kill him tonight. These delusions are an outgrowth of a drug-induced psychosis. *Psychiatric screeners, crisis workers, counselors, social workers, family members, and close friends should be made aware of the fact that a critical clue to suicidal ideation and/or suicide attempts includes a drastic change in behavior patterns, daily routine, or actions* (e.g., youths barricading themselves in their rooms for 24 hours and refusing to come out to eat or go to the bathroom, giving away prized possessions, having paranoid delusions or command hallucinations (e.g., hearing voices that tell them to harm themselves) for the first time, or talking about how wonderful it would be to go to heaven to be with a recently deceased and loving father) (Roberts & Yeager, 2005). See Chapter 8 for directions on how to recognize psychotic reactions in children and youths.

The school social worker needs to determine whether Maryann is between moderate and high risk of lethality and whether she needs to immediately call the 24-hour crisis center. The preliminary lethality assessment is based on the following six high-risk factors:

1. This is the first time that Maryann has ever barricaded herself in the teachers' lounge.
2. She seems to be depressed as shown by her not eating for 24 hours and crying for many hours.
3. She had made a suicide attempt previously, only 8 months ago.
4. She just gave away prized possessions—all of her favorite CDs.
5. Her father, to whom she was close, died less than 12 months ago.
6. She refuses to communicate with anyone.

You are the school social worker or crisis counselor, and you are dispatched to the school. The following application focuses on what you should say and

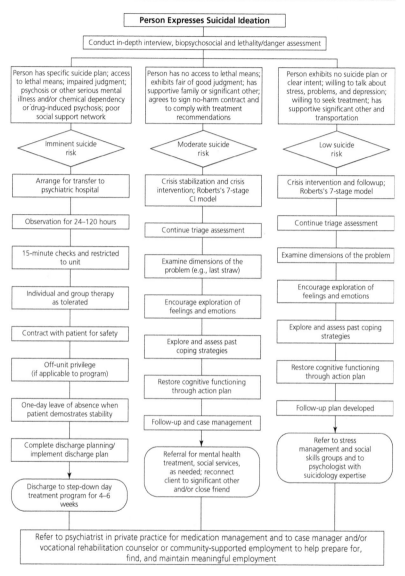

Figure 10.1. Suicide Risk Assessment and Intervention Flowchart.

Source: Roberts, A. R., & Yeager, K. (2005). Lethality assessments and crisis intervention with persons presenting with suicide ideation. In A. R. Roberts (Ed.), *Crisis intervention handbook: Assessment, treatment, and research* (3rd ed.). New York: Oxford University Press. Reprinted with permission.

do when you arrive. We describe this crisis situation with specific details and statements on ways in which to apply each of the seven stages in Roberts's crisis intervention model. First, it is important to be aware that stages 1 and 2 often take place simultaneously. However, in the case of life-threatening and high-risk suicide ideation, child abuse, sexual assault, or domestic violence, the emphasis is on rapid crisis, lethality, and triage assessment.

Stage 1: Assess Lethality by Talking Relatively Quickly to the Mother and Then Patiently to the Teenager

- Ask the mother if the daughter has been taking Acutane for acne. Then, ask the mother if Maryann was ever prescribed any antidepressant medication.
- If yes, does she know if the daughter has been taking her medication, what is the name of the medicine, and who prescribed it?
- Was it prescribed by a family doctor or a psychiatrist?
- Does Maryann have access to her medications or any other drugs?
- Also, upon arrival at the school or outside the teachers' lounge, ask the mother if anything has changed in the past 20–30 minutes (since they reached you) in her daughter's situation.

The crisis worker needs to obtain background information quickly from the mother: rapid collateral assessment. Next, give the mother something to do so she is not in the way (i.e., ask her to call the ex-boyfriend or Maryann's best girlfriend to obtain background data, especially whether Maryann has recently taken any illegal drugs).

- Assess Maryann's danger to herself and others (suicidal or homicidal thoughts), substance abuse history, and preexisting mental disorders.
- Ask questions about symptoms, traumatic events, stressful life events, future plans, suicidal ideation, previous suicide attempts, and mental illness.
- Ask about upcoming special events or birthday celebrations that Maryann may be looking forward to, or recollections of happy events or celebrations in the past that may well be repeated in the future (special events can instill hope for the future).
- Determine if Maryann needs immediate medical attention and if there are drugs, sleeping pills, or weapons in her possession.

Rapid Triage Assessment

1. The individual is a danger to herself or others and is exhibiting intense and acute psychiatric symptoms. These students generally require short-term emergency hospitalization and psychopharmacotherapy to protect them from self-harm or from harming other persons. (Priority I requires

emergency medical treatment, ambulance or rescue transport, and admission to a psychiatric screening center.)

2. The individual is in a precrisis stage due to ineffective coping skills, a weak support system, or ambivalence about seeking the help of a therapist. These students may have mild or no psychiatric symptoms or suicide risk. They may need one to three sessions of crisis counseling and referral to a support group.

3. The third type of student may have called a suicide prevention program or indicated to a friend or a teacher that she is sad, anxious, lonely, and/ or depressed (Roberts, 2002).

It is important to make a determination as to whether Maryann needs the mobile crisis intervention team to respond quickly to her home or school. In similar situations, the youth may have just attempted suicide or is planning to attempt suicide shortly or may be experiencing command hallucinations of a violent nature (Priority I). The student may be experiencing delusions and may be unable and fearful of leaving the teachers' lounge (Priority II), or she may be suffering from mood disturbances or depression and fleeting suicidal ideation, with no specific suicidal plan (Priority III: she is probably in need of an appointment with a caring social worker).

Stage 2: Establish Rapport

It is very important to introduce yourself as the school social worker or mental health counselor if Maryann has not met you before and speak in a calm and neutral manner.

- Social workers or mental health counselors should do their best to make a psychological connection to the 16-year-old in a precrisis or acute crisis situation.

- Part of establishing rapport and putting the person at ease involves being nonjudgmental, listening actively, and demonstrating empathy.

- Establish a bridge, bond, or connection by asking Maryann what CDs or posters she likes:
  "Do you have any posters on your wall at home right now?"
  "Do you have a favorite TV show?"
  "Do you have a favorite recording artist?"

- Another alternative approach is brief self-disclosure. For example:
  When I was 16 years old, my boyfriend broke up with me. I think I understand the emotional pain and sadness you are going through. I thought I loved my boyfriend very much. In fact, he was my first love. He broke up with me for another girl, and I was very sad, just like you. But, about 2 months after the breakup, I met someone else and we had a very enjoyable long-term relationship.

- Ask Maryann what her favorite dessert or candy is.
- It is important to understand that many adolescents are impulsive and impatient, may have escape fantasies, and are very sensitive and temperamental. As a result, do not lecture, preach, or moralize. Make concise statements, be caring, display keen interest, and do not make disparaging or insulting statements of any kind.

Stages 3 and 4 sometimes take place simultaneously.

Stage 3: Identify the Major Problem, Including Crisis Precipitants or Triggering Incidents

- Ask questions to determine the final straw or precipitating event that led Maryann into her current situation.
- Focus on the problem or problems and prioritize and focus on the worst problem first.
- Listen carefully for symptoms and clues of suicidal thoughts and intent.
- Make a direct inquiry about suicidal plans and nonverbal gestures or other communication (e.g., diaries, poems, journals, school essays, paintings, or drawings).
- Since most adolescent suicides are impulsive and unplanned, it is important to determine whether Maryann has easy access to a lethal weapon or drugs (including sleeping pills, methamphetamines, or barbiturates).

Stage 4: Deal With Feelings and Emotions and Provide Support

- Deal with Maryann's immediate feelings or fears.
- Allow the client to tell her story and why she seems to be feeling so bad.
- Provide preliminary empathy to the impact of Maryann's breakup with her boyfriend.
- Use active listening skills (i.e., paraphrasing, reflection of feelings, summarizing, reassurance, compliments, advice giving, reframing, and probes).
- Normalize the client's experiences.
- Validate and identify her emotions.
- Examine her past coping methods.
- Encourage ventilation of mental and physical feelings.

Stage 5: Exploring Possible Alternatives

First, reestablish balance and homeostasis, also known as equilibrium:

a. Ask Maryann what has helped in the past; for example, what did she do to cope with the loss and grief of losing a loved family member after her father passed away?

b. Initiate solution-based therapy (e.g., use a full or partial miracle question): Let's just suppose that you made it home today and went to sleep and overnight a miracle happened, but you did not know it happened, and you changed your mind about dying. What would be the first thing you would notice that was different when you woke up?

c. Ask her about bright spots from her past (e.g., hobbies, birthday celebrations, sports successes, academic successes, vacations).

d. Mutually explore and suggest new coping options and alternatives.

e. It is important for the crisis worker to jog the client's memories so she can verbalize the last time everything seemed to be going well and she was in a good mood. Help the client to find untapped resources. If appropriate, it may be helpful to mention that you have specialized in helping youths and have helped hundreds of other teens in crisis.

f. Provide Maryann with a specific phone number of a therapist and a plan to follow. The therapist needs to be someone who is willing and able to work with challenging and difficult adolescents in crisis.

Stage 6: Formulating an Action Plan

In this stage, an active role must be taken by the crisis worker; however, the success of any intervention plan depends on the client's level of involvement, participation, and commitment. The crisis worker must help Maryann look at both the short-term and long-range impacts in planning intervention. The main goals are to help the client achieve an appropriate level of functioning and maintain adaptive coping skills and resources. It is important to have a manageable treatment plan, so the client can follow through and be successful. Do not overwhelm the client with too many tasks or strategies, which may set the client up for failure.

Clients must also feel a sense of ownership in the action plan, so that they can increase the level of control and autonomy in their lives and to ensure that they do not become dependent on other support persons or resources. Obtaining a commitment from the client to follow through with the action plan and any referrals are important activities for the crisis worker, which can be maximized by using a mutual process in intervention planning. Ongoing assessment and evaluation are essential to determine whether the intervention plan is appropriate and effective in minimizing or resolving the client's identified problems. During this stage, Maryann should be processing and reintegrating the crisis impacts to achieve homeostasis and equilibrium in her life.

Termination should begin when the client has achieved the goals of the action plan or has been referred for additional services through other treatment providers. It is important to realize that many suicide-attempt survivors may need booster sessions from time to time or longer-term therapeutic help in working toward crisis mastery.

Stage 7: Follow-Up Phone Call, In-Person Appointment
for Booster Session, or Home Visit

Let Maryann know that she can call you, and give her your beeper number. Let her know that the beeper is for an emergency. In addition, depending on the crisis worker's assessment when leaving the school, it would be useful to schedule a follow-up with the therapist to whom Maryann is being referred, so that there is a team approach. Follow-up also may include a session with the school social worker or crisis worker scheduled for 2 days or one week later (Roberts & Yeager, 2005).

Recommended Web Sites for Further Information

American Association of Suicidology (AAS): www.suicidology.org
American Foundation for Suicide Prevention (AFSP): www.afsp.org
Canadian Association for Suicide Prevention: www.suicideprevention.ca
Crisis Intervention Network: www.crisisinterventionnetwork.com
International Association for Suicide Prevention (IASP): www.med/iasp
National Alliance for the Mentally Ill (NAMI): www.nami.org
National Institute of Mental Health (NIMH): www.nimh.nih.gov
National Strategy for Suicide Prevention: www.mentalhealth.org/
    suicideprevention
Suicide Information and Education Center: www.siec.ca

Key Points to Remember

School-based suicide prevention programs for youths can be effective when school social workers attempt to enhance students' protective factors and resilience, support them through therapeutic groups, and educate teachers on suicide risk factors at staff workshops. It is also imperative that school social workers have strong links to learning disability specialists, crisis workers, mental health professionals, and family counselors.

Because of the increasing need for mental health professionals to work within time-limited environments, there is a critical need to find evidence-based approaches to suicide prevention with increasingly complex youthful populations. Schools face these challenges every day. The overriding goal of this chapter has been to provide a realistic framework for school-based suicide prevention and to examine different methods of suicide lethality assessment and crisis intervention. School social workers and other mental health consultants to schools should consistently consider comprehensive suicide risk assessment strategies, the utility of instruments to assess and reassess students' status, the amount of time available, prior suicide family history, and the cost and potential outcome of chosen interventions. Application of best practices and systematic approaches such as the seven-stage crisis intervention model will assist social workers by providing a stable framework for addressing crises within a continuously changing care environment. It is the challenge of all mental health practitioners to develop their skills in rapid assessment, risk and rescue strategies, problem-solving methods, and building on the strengths of the suicidal youth as outlined by the seven-stage model.

Effective Strategies for Working With Students Who Have Co-Occurring Disorders

Stephen J. Tripodi
Johnny S. Kim
Diana M. DiNitto

Getting Started

In this chapter, adolescents who have a mental disorder and a substance use disorder are referred to as having co-occurring disorders. More than 50% of adolescents with a substance use disorder have a co-occurring mental disorder, and approximately 43% of adolescents receiving mental health services have been diagnosed with a substance use disorder (Substance Abuse and Mental Health Services Administration, 2002a).

The mental disorders that most commonly co-occur with substance use disorders are conduct disorder (CD), attention deficit/hyperactivity disorder (ADHD), depression, bipolar disorder, and posttraumatic stress disorder (Substance Abuse and Mental Health Services Administration, 2002b) (see Table 11.1). As many as 80% of adolescents in treatment for substance abuse have CD, between 20% and 40% have ADHD, up to 50% have mood disorders, and up to 40% have at least one anxiety disorder (Substance Abuse and Mental Health Services Administration, 2002b). Alcohol and drug use, combined with changes that occur during puberty, affect brain development and neuroendocrine systems that can exacerbate disorders such as CD, ADHD, and mood or anxiety disorders (Riggs, 2003).

What We Know

Though researchers have begun to study adolescents with co-occurring disorders (Kaminer, Tarter, & Buckstein, 1999; Matson & Bamberg, 1998; Wise, Cuffe, & Fischer, 2001), controlled studies are needed on the effectiveness of various treatment approaches for adolescents with co-occurring disorders. While there are evidence-based practices for working with adolescents who have substance use disorders and adolescents with mental disorders (e.g., multisystemic therapy has been used with both types of disorders), currently there is no intervention with a strong evidence-base for working with adolescents

Table 11.1 Definitions for Most Common Mental Disorders That Co-Occur With Substance Use Disorders in Adolescents

Conduct Disorder:

Repetitive and Persistent pattern of behavior in which the basic rights of others or major age-appropriate societal norms or rules are broken.

Attention-Deficit/Hyperactivity Disorder (ADHD):

Persistent pattern of inattention and/or hyperactivity-impulsivity that is more frequent and severe than is typically observed in individuals at a comparable level of development (criterion A).

Some hyperactive-impulsive or inattentive symptoms that cause impairment must have been present before age 7 (criterion B).

Some impairment from the symptoms must be present in at least two settings (criterion C).

There must be clear evidence of interference with developmentally appropriate social, academic, or occupational functioning (criterion D).

Major Depressive Disorder:

A period of at least 2 weeks during which there is either depressed mood or the loss of interest or pleasure in nearly all activities. With children and adolescents, the mood may be irritable rather than sad. The individual must also experience at least four additional symptoms drawn from a list that includes changes in appetite or weight, sleep, and psychomotor activity; decreased energy; feelings of worthlessness or guilt; difficulty thinking, concentrating, or making decisions; or recurrent thoughts of death or suicidal ideation, plans, or attempts.

Bipolar Disorder:

A clinical course that is characterized by the occurrence of one or more manic episodes or mixed episodes. Episodes of substance-induced mood disorder (due to the direct effects of a medication, other somatic treatments for depression, a drug of abuse, or toxin exposure) or of mood disorder due to a general medical condition do not count toward a diagnosis of bipolar disorder.

Posttraumatic Stress Disorder:

Development of characteristic symptoms following exposure to an extreme traumatic stressor involving direct personal experience of an event that involves actual or threatened death or serious injury or other threat to one's physical integrity; or witnessing an event that involves death, injury, or a threat to the physical integrity of another person; or learning about unexpected or violent death, serious harm, or threat of death or injury or injury experienced by a family member.

Characteristic symptoms include persistent reexperiencing of the traumatic event, persistent avoidance of stimuli associated with the trauma and numbing of general responsiveness, and persistent symptoms of increased arousal.

(continued)

Table 11.1 *(Continued)*

Bulimia Nervosa:

Binge eating and inappropriate compensatory methods to prevent weight gain. The self-evaluation of individuals with bulimia nervosa is excessively influenced by body shape and weight. To qualify for the diagnosis, the binge eating and the inappropriate compensatory behaviors must occur, on average, at least twice a week for 3 months.

Source: American Psychiatric Association. (2000). *Diagnostic and statistical manual of mental disorders* (4th ed. text revision). Washington, DC: Author. Reprinted with permission from the *Diagnostic and Statistical Manual of Mental Disorders*, Copyright 2000. American Psychiatric Association.

who have co-occurring disorders. The lack of specific information is unfortunate, because, as discussed in previous chapters, rates are high for co-occurring mental health disorders (e.g., depression and anxiety) and co-occurring mental and substance use disorders.

This chapter suggests techniques for school social workers and other mental health counselors to use in working with students who have co-occurring disorders. These techniques include educating students on co-occurring disorders, screening and assessment procedures, working with the adolescent's family, creating a therapeutic alliance with the client, roles of the multisystemic school counselor, relapse prevention, and referral sources.

What We Can Do

Increasing Staff, Students, and Families' Knowledge of Co-Occurring Disorders

Efforts to assist students with co-occurring disorders are more effective when school social workers and similar professionals collaborate with teachers, administrators, and families. These groups often know little about this topic, so offer to organize in-service trainings for teachers and other staff. This may also increase administrators' support for services. Training should focus on topics such as identifying symptoms and behaviors typical of substance abuse, mental illness, and co-occurring disorders. Inviting staff from local mental health and substance abuse agencies to conduct or assist in this training and to inform school personnel about relevant community resources can also be helpful.

School social workers and other mental health counselors can also solicit teachers' invitations to give class presentations on mental health, substance abuse, and co-occurring disorders. This can arm students with knowledge and suggest ways through which they can help themselves or their friends. Students and teachers often know who is using drugs or exhibiting behavior common for adolescents with co-occurring disorders. For example, peers may know that a student is drinking or using nonprescribed drugs and discarding medication prescribed for a mental disorder.

Encourage school administrators or other personnel to send a letter to parents with information about substance use disorders, mental disorders, and co-occurring disorders; ways in which parents can help their child; and services the school's counseling department provides. Parents may not know how common it is for both types of disorders to occur together. Instruct teachers and students on how to refer students who may have co-occurring disorders. Send similar letters to teachers along with a form they can use to refer students.

Recognizing Students With Co-Occurring Disorders

Distinguishing normal adolescent developmental issues and acting-out behavior from behavioral problems resulting from chemical use alone or from co-occurring disorders can be difficult. Substance use disorders and mental disorders may occur independently of each other; a mental disorder may place the adolescent at greater risk for a substance abuse disorder; or alcohol or drug abuse may result in temporary mental disorder syndromes (Substance Abuse and Mental Health Services Administration, 2002a). An accurate mental disorder diagnosis may require that the adolescent be alcohol- and drug-free for a period of time.

Regardless of the specific disorders, adolescents with co-occurring disorders tend to act out, exhibiting anger and hostility toward their parents and other authority figures and gravitating toward peers who also use chemicals to assuage their pain (Evans & Sullivan, 2001). Figure 11.1 depicts predictors of co-occurring disorders, along with school-related problems, legal problems, and other common problems.

Conveying Information to Parents

Family members are often confused and hurt by the adolescent's behavior and may blame the child or themselves. Social workers and mental health counselors should explain that no one is at fault, and expressing shame to their child about his or her disorders or behaviors may ultimately lower the child's self-esteem and decrease the chances of a successful outcome. The school social worker and other mental health counselors must inform parents that professional help is likely necessary. This might mean referral to a substance abuse counselor, mental health therapist, self-help group, and/or a psychiatrist for medication. Parents should be directed to participate in their child's assessment and treatment.

Adolescent substance users are often manipulative and tend to use inconsistent parental behavior to their advantage. Parents should be encouraged to remain consistent in providing encouragement; to reward positive behavior and

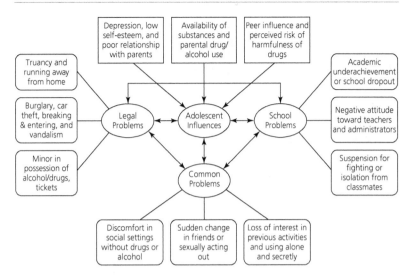

Figure 11.1.

abstinence, including short periods of abstinence; and to follow through on consequences for negative behaviors, even though it may be difficult to do so.

Screening and Assessment

Two helpful standardized instruments for screening adolescents for co-occurring disorders are the Drug Use Screening Inventory (DUSI) (Rahdert, 1991) and the Problem-Oriented Screening Instrument for Teenagers (POSIT) (Tarter, 1990). Table 11.2 shows the completion time, required reading level, and the domains measured for both of these instruments.

Initial screening may indicate the need for a comprehensive assessment. Assessment provides an opportunity to look at the adolescent's life in a holistic manner, and it allows the social worker and other school-based practitioners to develop the necessary rapport to establish a beneficial therapeutic alliance with the adolescent and his or her family. A thorough assessment considers the adolescent's strengths; home and living situation; relationship to child welfare, mental health, juvenile justice, and school systems; educational history; family history of substance abuse and mental health problems; and medical status (U.S. Department of Health and Human Services, 1993).

Parents' or guardians' presence at the initial interview enables the social worker and school-based practitioner to obtain an early developmental history and assess family dynamics (Riggs, 2003). The social worker and mental health counselor should assess how the family enhances or reduces the potential

Table 11.2 Screening Instruments for Adolescents With Co-Occurring Disorders

Drug Use Screening Inventory (DUSI) and Problem-Oriented Screening Instrument for Teenagers (POSIT)

Completion time	30 minutes
Required minimum reading level	Fifth grade
Domains measured	Substance abuse
	Psychiatric disorders
	Behavior problems
	School adjustment
	Health status
	Peer relations
	Social competency
	Family adjustment
	Leisure recreation
	Vocational status
	Aggressive behavior/delinquency

Sources: Rahdert, E. R. (1991). *The adolescent assessment/referral system manual* (DHHS Publication No. ADM 91–1735). Rockville, MD: National Institute on Drug Abuse; Tarter, R. (1990). Evaluation and treatment of adolescent substance abuse: A decision tree method. *American Journal of Drug and Alcohol Abuse, 16,* 1–46.

for success by determining if there is active substance abuse or mental illness in other family members (Zweben, 1994). The social worker and counselors should also explore how the family views mental illness and addiction (psychological problem, illness, weak character, or the results of negative peer influences) (Zweben, 1994). Guidelines for enhancing screening and assessment include the following:

- Interview the parents or guardian first.
- Interview the adolescent separately to elicit information he or she may not feel comfortable disclosing in front of parents.
- Be straightforward with the adolescent.
- Be empathic, nonjudgmental, and supportive with all.
- Ask the adolescent about patterns and frequencies of use for each substance, triggers for using, perceived motivation for using, consequences for using, and treatment goals.
- To supplement information, collect data from the adolescent's family, available case studies, the school system, and health care providers. (Evans & Sullivan, 2001; Riggs, 2003; U.S. Department of Health and Human Services, 1993)

In addition to standardized instruments, Evans and Sullivan (2001) recommend the following techniques to improve the adolescent's self-report history:

- Use open-ended and specific questions.
- Recognize vague answers and be gently persistent in getting specifics.
- Periodically summarize the client's feedback.
- Avoid argumentation and confrontation.
- Express empathy through reflective listening.
- Affirm the client through compliments.
- Avoid taking the client's defenses personally.
- Avoid discussions of rationalizations.
- Start with neutral questions and ask sensitive questions later.
- Ask about past behavior before current behavior.

Major acute psychiatric symptoms, such as manic episodes, hallucinations, psychotic depression, or suicide indicators, require emergency evaluation for possible hospitalization and need for medication (Chatlos, 1994). See Chapter 10 for suicidality assessment.

Working With Adolescents Who Have Co-Occurring Disorders

Social workers and other professionals should not wait until substance abuse treatment is completed to treat the mental disorder (Riggs, 2003). The chances of a successful outcome increase when substance use and mental disorders are treated simultaneously. The adolescent also needs education to understand both disorders and their interactions (Chatlos, 1994). Education should include risk factors, precipitating events, and the progression of the problems. To assess the client's understanding of his or her co-occurring disorders, the social worker and school-based practitioner might ask, "What do you see as the relationship between your substance use disorder and your mental disorder?" (Manwani & Weiss, 2003). The social worker and counselors should focus on current instances of negative consequences or outcomes to enable the adolescent to recognize the effect that drug use has had on his or her life (Evans & Sullivan, 2001).

A therapeutic alliance between the school-based practitioner and the adolescent is critical. Confrontation, a technique that counselors commonly use with clients who have a substance use disorder, is not as effective as establishing trust and credibility through a positive therapeutic alliance using support, empathy, reflective listening, and validation techniques (Manwani & Weiss, 2003).

Adolescents with co-occurring disorders require a comprehensive and individualized treatment plan that may include individual therapy, group therapy, family involvement, educational services, and medication compliance, if applicable (Substance Abuse and Mental Health Services Administration, 2002a). The social worker and mental health counselors should encourage parents to commit to involvement in the treatment plan and family therapy in order to create a supportive family recovery environment (Chatlos, 1994).

During the first few counseling sessions, the school-based practitioner must work with the adolescent to establish goals in order to eliminate substance use and begin to address the co-occurring disorders and other issues (Riggs, 2003). Following goal identification, the social worker and mental health counselors should create a contract with the adolescent, identifying peers with whom he or she should and should not associate (e.g., law-abiding versus non–law-abiding peers), places that should be avoided, specific hours to be at home, specific hours for homework, and times for attending mutual-help groups (Chatlos, 1994). Family members should be encouraged to join community support groups like Al-Anon (for families of individuals with alcohol problems) or the National Alliance for the Mentally Ill (for families of individuals who have mental illness) and study groups for parents regarding their children's substance use disorder and mental disorder (Substance Abuse and Mental Health Services Administration, 2002a). Siblings of adolescents with co-occurring disorders or adolescents with co-occurring disorders who have substance-abusing family members might be encouraged to attend a group like Alateen. For more information, visit the Web sites of Al-Anon, Alateen, and the National Alliance for the Mentally Ill.

Each parent or guardian involved should be asked to list situations where their adolescent's drug use affected them personally in order to enable the adolescent to recognize the consequences of his or her substance use (Chatlos, 1994). Review the list in a joint session with the parents and client. If the parents cannot be involved in the client's treatment (e.g., due to incarceration), ask the client to list how his or her substance use and recent behavior affected family and friends. Adolescents often have difficulty considering future consequences. Asking the adolescent to consider a lifetime of abstinence may be overwhelming and engender hopelessness. The social worker and other school-based practitioners should focus on the here and now, encouraging the adolescent to think about one day at a time.

If the adolescent has successfully abstained from substances in the past, the school-based practitioner should compliment that accomplishment, state how difficult that must have been, and ask how the client was able to refrain from drugs. As the adolescent maintains increased periods of abstinence, the school-based practitioner should help him or her identify areas in which his or her life is improving (Evans & Sullivan, 2001). The school-based practitioner should also compliment clients when their behavior supports maintaining stability, such as taking psychotropic medications as prescribed, participating in therapy, controlling anger, and engaging in healthy activities. Help the adolescent to identify areas where improvement in the mental disorder has resulted in changes in other areas of life, such as less acting out in the classroom. Work with the adolescents to identify reasons that they were able to behave properly in the classroom. Compliment these achievements and other positive gains to help them create those conditions more often. Inability to remain abstinent or exacerbation of mental illness may necessitate referral to residential treatment.

Multisystemic therapy (MST) is used with adolescent substance abusers and appears to fit the needs of adolescents with co-occurring disorders. MST appears to be effective in reducing acting-out behaviors, particularly illegal behaviors (Henggeler, 1999; Keys, 1999; Schoenwald, Brown, & Henggeler, 2000). MST's goals are to empower the adolescent's primary caregivers with the skills needed to address the youth's behavior problems and to empower youths to cope with the various systems in their lives (Henggeler, 1999; Schoenwald et al., 2000). MST requires knowledge of the multiple and interrelated systems (family, school, peers, and community) operating in the adolescent's life (Keys, 1999).

Implementing empirically based services is an integral aspect of MST (Henggeler, 1999; Schoen-wald et al., 2000). Approaches commonly incorporated are structural family therapy, cognitive-behavioral therapy, and behavioral parental training. The counselor should choose services based on the client's individual needs. As noted in Table 11.3, the multisystemic school counselor often acts as a school-community liaison, integrated services team member, group process facilitator, systems change agent, and family advocate (Keys, 1999).

Enhancing Adolescents' Motivation

The University of Rhode Island Change Assessment Questionnaire (URICA) is a tool to measure level of motivation to change and may be useful with adolescents (Greenstein, Franklin, & McGuffin, 1999). The adolescent's level of motivation will determine the approaches the school social worker and other mental health counselors employ. Evans and Sullivan (2001) have adapted a four-level model of motivation specifically for adolescents with co-occurring disorders (originally created by Osher & Kofoed, 1989): (1) engagement, where providers work to convince clients that treatment has some value (perhaps through films, peer groups, or other techniques appealing to adolescents); (2) persuasion, which consists of attempts to convince the client of the need for help, perhaps through values clarification exercises; (3) active treatment with an emphasis on developing skills and attitudes needed to maintain sobriety and mental health; and (4) relapse prevention, in which the adolescent incorporates techniques to sustain the skills needed to maintain abstinence and mental health, such as use of an ongoing self-help group.

Relapse Prevention

Relapse prevention is a vital component of treatment for those with co-occurring disorders. Help the adolescent identify effective methods to deal with alcohol or drug cravings and ways to recognize and avoid situations that present

Table 11.3 Roles of Multisystemic School Counselor

School–Community Liaison	Integrated Services Team Member	Group Process Facilitator	Systems Change Agent	Family Advocate
• Have knowledge of community resources from other agencies conform to school guidelines • Assure that treatment plans from other agencies conform to school guidelines	• Conduct meetings with applicable professionals, such as mental health professionals, child welfare professionals, juvenile justice professionals, and substance abuse counselors	• Help create a warm climate • Establish group norms • Manage dominant group members • Empower reticent members • Negotiate conflicts between professionals	• Become a social advocate working to effect changes in policy	• Teach family how to access community services • Assure family members they are welcome at school and at meetings no matter how serious their child's behavior was

Source: Keys, S. (1999). School counselors' role in facilitating multisystemic change. *Professional School Counseling, 3*(2), 101–108.

a high risk of relapse for both substance use and mental disorders (Manwani & Weiss, 2003). Role playing may help to decrease the chances of substance use relapse. The role playing may include presentation of mock situations in which friends or family members overtly or covertly encourage the client to use drugs, of how to cope with emotions without using drugs under such situations, and how to socialize and have fun while remaining clean and sober. The situations that create the highest risk for adolescent relapse for substance use and mental illness include negative emotional states like stress and interpersonal conflict (Roget, Fisher, & Johnson, 1998). Other high-risk situations include urges and temptations (parties where drugs are present), positive emotional states (the desire to celebrate achievements), negative physical states (such as sickness or physical injury), and positive interpersonal contact (interactions with potential dating partners) (Roget et al., 1998).

Before concluding treatment, a relapse prevention plan should be developed to help all of the parties involved in the adolescent's treatment. Roget et al. (1998) recommend incorporating the following in relapse prevention plans:

- Probation terms (if applicable to the client's legal situation)
- Family rules
- School attendance and grade requirements
- Participation in aftercare (e.g., outpatient therapy group or mutual-help group)
- Agreement to participate in drug testing
- Relapse consequences
- Compliance incentives (initially, a reward for each week of sobriety)

The social worker and other counselors should educate families that the overwhelming majority of individuals with substance use disorders relapse at least once. Expecting relapse does not mean accepting relapse. Parents should continue to implement immediate consequences, should relapse occur.

Referrals

The American Society of Addiction Medicine (ASAM) Patient Placement Criteria for the Treatment of Substance-Related Disorders is a good tool to consult with when considering a referral to outpatient services, intensive outpatient services with partial hospitalization, residential and intensive inpatient services, and medically managed intensive inpatient services (Mee-Lee, Shulman, Fishman, Gastfriend, & Griffith, 2001). For example, outpatient treatment is often appropriate when an adolescent suffering from co-occurring disorders admits that he or she has a problem, is not in immediate danger, and has an intact support group (Mee-Lee et al., 2001). When circumstances indicate that residential treatment is needed, the social worker and other practitioners should look for a controlled milieu such as a therapeutic community that can address both mental and substance use disorders. Therapeutic communities have had positive outcomes with substance-abusing adolescents (DeLeon, 2000). Treatment centers that utilize immediate consequences, both positive and negative, and a reduction of privileges for upper-level residents (with longer treatment tenure and positive behavior) when lower-level residents misbehave may increase the likelihood of a successful outcome (Evans & Sullivan, 2001).

Tools

Table 11.4 summarizes the approaches presented in this chapter to help adolescents with co-occurring disorders to lead more successful and productive lives. Social workers, counselors, teachers, and other school staff need patience as well as expertise to work with youth who have co-occurring disorders. Social workers or other professionals should not blame themselves when clients misbehave or relapse. Social workers and other school mental health counselors should have a support network to discuss the challenges they face working with adolescents who have co-occurring disorders, partake in enjoyable and healthy activities, and realize the importance of perseverance for both themselves and their clients.

Key Points to Remember

- Substance abuse and mental disorders frequently coexist.
- The mental disorders that most commonly co-occur with substance use disorders are conduct disorders, attention deficit hyperactivity disorder, depression and other mood disorders, bipolar disorder, and posttraumatic stress disorder.
- Two helpful standardized instruments for screening adolescents for co-occurring disorders are the Drug Use Screening Inventory and the Problem Oriented Screening Instrument for Teenagers.
- To be effective with students who have co-occurring disorders, school professionals must make use of best practices in the treatment of the substance use and mental disorders.
- The mental disorder and the substance use disorder should be addressed simultaneously.
- School professionals will need a strong treatment support base rooted in the community and family to be effective with students who have co-occurring disorders. Referrals to the community are usually necessary.

Table 11.4 Summary of Techniques and Interventions for Working With Adolescents Who Have Co-Occurring Disorders

Educating Teachers and Staff	Educating Parents and Family Members	Increasing Adolescent's Motivation	Working With Adolescents
• Organize in-service training for teachers and other staff • Invite staff from local mental health and substance abuse agencies to conduct or assist in this training • Solicit teachers' invitations to give class presentations on mental health, substance abuse, and co-occurring disorders • Instruct teachers and students on how to refer students who may have co-occurring disorders • Encourage school administrators or other personnel to send a letter to parents with information about substance use disorders,	• Explain to family that no one is at fault and discourage parents from expressing shame to their child • Inform parents that professional help such as a psychiatrist or substance abuse counselor may be necessary • Parents should be directed to participate in their child's assessment and treatment • Parents should be encouraged to remain consistent in providing encouragement and rewarding positive behavior like abstinence • Parents should be encouraged to follow through on consequences	• Encourage adolescent that treatment has value • Encourage adolescent of the need for help • Use active treatment with an emphasis on developing skills and attitudes necessary to maintain sobriety and mental health • Incorporate techniques to help adolescent sustain skills needed to maintain abstinence and mental health	• Screen the adolescent using the DUSI or the POSIT • Do not wait to treat the mental disorder until the completion of substance abuse treatment • Educate adolescent on both disorders and their interactions • Focus education on risk factors, precipitating events, and progression of the problems • Develop therapeutic alliance by using support, empathy, reflective listening, and validation techniques • Establish goals with the adolescent in order to eliminate substance use and begin to address the comorbid disorders and other issues

(continued)

Table 11.4 *(Continued)*

Educating Teachers and Staff	Educating Parents and Family Members	Increasing Adolescent's Motivation	Working With Adolescents
mental disorders, and co-occurring disorders	for negative behaviors even when difficult		• Develop comprehensive and individualized treatment plan that includes individual therapy, group therapy, family involvement, educational services, and medication compliance if needed • Encourage parents' involvement in the treatment plan and family therapy in order to create a supportive family recovery environment

- Multisystemic therapy may be a promising treatment option. Utilizing the adolescents' strengths and complimenting small behavioral changes are important. Ongoing management of multiple issues and relapse prevention are also important parts of effective interventions for co-occurring disorders.

12

Psychopharmacological Treatment for Child and Adolescent Mental Disorders

Kia J. Bentley
Kathryn S. Collins

Getting Started

Psychopharmacological treatment as an attempt to respond to students' social, emotional, and behavioral issues began during the 1930s and since the 1980s has been rapidly increasing as the treatment of choice by many health and mental health care providers (Olfson, Marcus, Weissman, & Jensen, 2002; Popper, 2002). Of particular interest is that despite the widespread use of psychotropic medications, with a few exceptions, the specific effectiveness of most of these drugs in children and adolescents has not been thoroughly researched, *and* they are most commonly used in ways not yet approved by the Food and Drug Administration (FDA) (Center for Mental Health in Schools at UCLA, 2003). Thus, it seems that proactively treating mental disorders in children and adolescents using knowledge acquired from research and real-world experiences with adults is an accepted and understandable approach that seeks to help reduce real pain, distress, and dysfunction in young human lives. The thinking of many practitioners and parents is that the positive impact of medications—or, better said, the hope and promise of it—is sufficiently beneficial to outweigh the potential harm of psychopharmacological agents; therefore the use of a wide variety of psychiatric medications is a viable but not much-needed option.

What We Know

Understanding Common Mental Disorders

Obviously, children and adolescents can and do experience the entire range of social, emotional, and behavioral problems, which are associated with significant distress to the students and their families, schools, and communities. Mental health problems are thought to affect 1 in 5 students at any given time, while 1 in 10 students experience serious emotional disturbances that severely disrupt their daily functioning (U.S. Department of Health and Human Services, 1999). When left undiagnosed and untreated, mental health problems can contribute to school failure, family conflicts, drug and alcohol abuse, violence, and suicide. School social workers can help by explaining that epidemiological studies indicate that mental and emotional disorders in children and adolescents, like those in adults, are primarily related to some complex interplay of biological and environmental factors (Rutter, 2000, 2002). It is important to note that mental disorders can remit or endure over the life span. School social workers and school-based mental health counselors can work with others (e.g., nurses, psychologists, psychiatrists, pharmacists) to develop psychoeducational programs and materials to teach students and parents about common disorders and their treatment. Such education can have an empowering effect, strengthen coping skills, provide emotional support, increase clients' hope, and promote good communication, among other things (Bentley & Walsh, 2006). Some common categories of disorders found in childhood include anxiety and mood disorders, attention deficit and disruptive disorders, autism and other pervasive developmental disorders, eating disorders, schizophrenia, and tic disorders (American Psychiatric Association, 2000).

Understanding Medications and Their Specific Use in Children

The five classes of medication are antipsychotic medications, antidepressants, anti-anxiety medications, mood stabilizers, and stimulants. Medications from all five drug classes are used with children and adolescents experiencing mental, emotional, and behavioral disorders. An important trend is that a physician's choice of type of medication may be only in part related to a student's diagnosis. That is, it is overly simplistic to say that depression will be treated with an antidepressant, anxiety with an anti-anxiety (anxiolytic) medication, attention deficit/hyperactivity disorder (ADHD) with a stimulant, and so on. Instead, the choice may relate to concern over a particularly prominent symptom or the interplay of symptoms, the explicit avoidance of a side effect (in youth, e.g., weight gain, acne, tremors, confusion, effects on reproductive system or sexual functioning), and especially the past effectiveness of a specific drug in clinical trials or in real-world practice with adults. Thus, in practice, physicians, for example, might choose a selective serotonin reuptake inhibitor (SSRI) for a wide variety of concerns ranging from depression, obsessive-compulsive disorder, and conduct disorder to eating disorder, anxiety disorder, and ADHD (Magno-Zito et al., 2002). Another example is that while anticonvulsant medications have been used instead of, or in combination with, lithium for the treatment of bipolar disorder, some physicians are now prescribing small doses of an antipsychotic medication for bipolar disorder in youth, often in combination with more traditional mood stabilizers (Wilens & Wozniak, 2003). Lithium, a naturally occurring salt categorized as a mood stabilizer, also has been used to treat a range of disorders from the expected bipolar disorder to posttraumatic stress, aggression, and depression. One of the highest profile drugs currently in use is Strattera (atomoxetine), approved in November 2002 for the treatment of ADHD in both children and adults. Because it is a nonstimulant, it is thought to be safer and have less abuse potential. However, it is known to have other serious side effects, such as hallucinations and liver damage. A summary of key medications currently used with children and adolescents is provided in the "Tools and Practice Examples" section of this chapter (see also National Institute of Mental Health, 2004; Thomson Healthcare, 2003).

Controversy About the Use of Psychopharmacological Treatment With Children

Much controversy surrounds the practice of child and adolescent psychopharmacology, and the school social worker and mental health counselor sit right in the middle of it, that is, "at the nexus of the systems of home, school and community," as one social worker eloquently noted (Allen-Meares, 1991, p. 5). In embracing expanded roles in medication management, school social workers uphold their professional tradition of striving to keep students safe from harm or distress, in its many forms, and help to keep their schools on the forefront of our changing society's thinking about psychotropic medications for children and adolescents. We argue that school social workers and other mental health consultants have a crucial role of not only providing comprehensive biopsychosocial assessment information to health and mental health care providers and parents so that good decisions can be made around the prescription of psychotropic medications but also in helping to monitor the positive and negative effects of medications on students in the school system.

As new psychotropic medicines are introduced, as new methods of administration develop, and even as new philosophies about dosing and polypharmacy emerge, it will be important for school social workers and mental health counselors to expand their knowledge and skill base about the medications, so that they may promote the full quality of life and well-being of the students they serve, while helping to deter any negative outcomes. Toward this end, we start with the assumption that children and adolescents are both like adults and unlike adults, and these different dimensions affect pharmacological treatment and medication management. For example, the rates of absorption, distribution, and metabolism are quite different in children. Importantly, children and adolescents have different cognitive schema that may effect their descriptions of physiologic or psychological changes (Brown & Sammons, 2002). Yet, as human beings, children and adolescents have the same basic anatomy, functional systems, and all of the same basic emotional needs and psychological dimensions as everyone else. With that principle in mind, this chapter will offer ideas on four basic "how do you help" questions faced by school social workers working with children, adolescents, and their families:

- How do you help students and parents make sense of the controversy and ambiguity in child and adolescent psychopharmacotherapy?

- How do you help students and parents understand common mental disorders and the medications used to treat them?
- How do you help students and parents negotiate the referral processes and pharmacological assessment?
- How do you help students and parents in managing and monitoring medications?

Making Sense of the Controversy and Ambiguity in Child and Adolescent Psychopharmacotherapy

Worries About Physical and Psychological Developmental Impact

Clearly, one of the biggest concerns about the use of medication in children and adolescents relates to uncertainties about long-term effects, both physical and psychological. These are important considerations for which some assurances can be provided, but also a place where a healthy skepticism may be appropriate. It is true that most formal clinical drug research, both with children and adults, does not help us to understand the long-term effects of medications because studies tend to focus on initial effects over just a few weeks to a few months. A further bad news is that such lack of research opens the door to speculation and myth. For example, the early concerns that stimulants were associated with significant levels of stunted growth have been largely abandoned by most reputable providers. However, some Internet sites continue to relay what appears to be misinformation about this and closely related issues.

Another specific concern about children and adolescents who take psychiatric medications relates to the fact that brain and neurotransmitter development is occurring at the same time these drugs are being used (Floersch, 2003; Greenhill & Setterberg, 1993). What are the long-term developmental effects? Another concern: Do we fully understand how medication use should be adjusted to account for the physical development of children's renal functioning, gastrointestinal system, or hepatic enzyme system in their early years? Another compelling concern has been raised by Floersch (2003, p. 52) about the impact of taking psychiatric medication on the self-identity and psychological development of children and adolescents. This will be especially important as school social workers and mental health counselors listen to how students make sense of their medication experience. So, as we have noted, while some argue that children are, after all, human beings and thus clinical research in humans is relevant and useful, others argue that children are still other than and different from little adults; thus, given the intrusiveness of the intervention, extreme caution is called for.

Worries About Pathologizing Human Experience

Of equal concern is that the use of psychiatric medications in children represents an inappropriate "blaming the victim." A number of vocal critics of medication use have noted that massive increases in the use of medication with kids in recent years has led to an underemphasis on other potential culprits in the seeming rise of mental, emotional, and behavioral difficulties in children, that is, the larger social context and poor school and community supports. Admittedly, it could be said that dramatic prescription increases and expanded use of medications with children and adolescents are not necessarily problematic signs, but rather represent good news about the accessibility of treatment to those in need. However, there remains a pervasive feeling among many school social workers and others in the field that too many children are being medicated without sufficient cause (see below) and that we are neglecting other environmental influences on behavior, which might have an even more powerful impact. These things might include a lack of tolerance of difference among kids, poor parenting practices, misperceptions about what is developmentally "typical" in children and adolescents, the violent media and the tendency to rely on overstimulation, the drug culture, the cultural value of immediate gratification, or more school system-focused influences like lack of school resources, high student–teacher ratios, lack of teacher training, and low teacher salaries, to name a few.

Backlash About Medication in Schools

Fears about the overmedication of children are reflected in recent legislation that has been passed in Congress. In May 2003, the House of Representatives passed the Child Medication Safety Act of 2003 (H.R. 1170) authored by Representative Max Burns, a Republican from Georgia. Although it did not get out of committee in the Senate that year, it (now H.R. 1790) has been reintroduced in 2005 by Representative John Kline with 21 cosponsors and is in committee as of the time of this writing. The bill would require states that receive federal Department of Education funds for any program or activity to create and implement specific policies *prohibiting* school personnel from "coercing children to receive, or their parents to administer, a controlled substance in schedule II under the Controlled Substances Act, as a condition of attending school or receiving services." However, it does not prohibit classroom teachers or other school personnel from making *observations* about academic achievement and classroom behavior and relaying the information to parents or recommending evaluation regarding special education or related school and classroom services under the Individuals With Disabilities Education Act (IDEA). It should be noted that an amendment with softer wording prohibiting educational personnel from "requiring" medication for children as a condition for attending school or receiving services was attached to the reauthorization of IDEA (P.L. 108-446), which recently passed Congress. Further, the comptroller general of the Government Accounting Office (GAO) plans to research such issues as the variation of states' definitions of medication use and the extent to which school personnel actively influence parents to pursue medication, the prescription rates of psychotropic drugs used in public schools to treat children diagnosed with mental health disorders (with specific mention of ADD/ADHD), and the identification and prevalence of medications used both under the Controlled Substance Act and otherwise.

Many states are in various stages of enacting legislation specifically on this issue. Some states, such as Georgia, Washington, North Carolina, and Hawaii, have created legislation to investigate the prevalence and effects of psychotropic medications on children and develop recommendations on how to better monitor prescription rates. Other states, such as Connecticut, Maryland, Illinois, Colorado, Minnesota, and Virginia, require school policies strictly prohibiting school personnel from recommending or requiring psychotropic drug use. Further, legislation urges school personnel to use nonmedication alternatives only with students who have difficulty learning and/or who display hyperactivity or other behavioral disruptions. Connecticut, Minnesota, Utah, and Illinois have legislation prohibiting disciplinary actions, such as reports to child protection services or charges of neglect against parents who refuse to seek a prescription for or administer psychotropic medications. It is crucial for school social workers and other personnel to be aware of legislative activities in their respective states and school districts as well as the values (and fears and concerns) they represent.

Off-Label Use by Physicians

Another issue of some concern is the widespread "off-label" use of medications with children and adolescents. *Off-label use* refers to the use of a specific medication with children in spite of the fact that it has not yet been approved by the FDA for use with children in particular. Parents and teachers should know that this practice is not only very common but obviously also quite legal, as long as the drug has been studied and received approval for use in adults. Physicians know well that the FDA is after all about the development and marketing of drugs, not the regulation of the practice of medicine. Although off-label use represents up to three quarters of medication use with children, drug companies are not allowed to target their marketing or advertising of a specific nonapproved drug for use in children until sufficient safety and effectiveness has been established and FDA approval obtained. The lack of FDA approval, then, does not mean a drug is *not* safe or effective. Clinical trials with children and adolescents are relatively new (Wilens, 1999) and come with even more controversy, as we discuss below.

The Media and Clinical Drug Research With Children

Newspapers and magazines have been generously covering issues related to the testing and marketing of medications for children. Parents, social workers, and school-based mental health workers cannot help but be curious about them or, more likely, have serious questions and concerns. For example, in 2002, the issue of pediatric drug testing in general made it to the editorial pages of *USA Today* ("Why Give Kids Drugs," 2002, p. 12A). At issue was whether the FDA exceeded its authority in 1999 by requiring (one report used the word "forcing") drug companies to test their adult products on children prior to receiving approval for distribution to children. The rule, instituted mainly because of concerns around psychiatric medication use among children, was thought by most lawmakers, health care providers, and advocates to be a step *forward* in ensuring the safety of children. However, the Competitive Enterprise Institute, a think tank concerned about advancing free markets on numerous fronts, brought a successful lawsuit, which has led to alterations and an emphasis on the voluntary testing of many drugs.

The most prominent recent topic has been the FDA's concern about suicidal ideation and self-harm among some young (and not so young) users of the most popular type of antidepressant, the SSRIs. After a series of public hearings and in a surprise move in early 2004, the FDA asked the manufacturers of 10 different SSRI antidepressants to strengthen or add a suitable warning about the possible connection between drug use and suicide. The hope was that this would stimulate closer monitoring of the effects of these antidepressants. What made this bold move different from past actions is that the FDA request was not preceded by very clear evidence from clinical research about the connection between the actual medications and harm. Reactions of providers and others to the FDA action (see, e.g., Elias, 2004, 2005; "FDA Seeks Warning," 2004; Sood, 2005) have ranged from relief (from those who have long thought the use of psychiatric medications among children had become too casual) to anger (from those who described it as an overreaction and completely unwarranted) to worry about the chilling effect it may have on getting treatment to children who may benefit.

Misuse by Consumers

First noticed in the mid-1990s, little is empirically known about the misuse, diversion, or illegal trading or selling of psychiatric medications among youth. Methylphenidate (Ritalin), known by such street names as "vitamin R" and "Skippy," is especially suspect. One study several years ago examined 116 students in Wisconsin with ADHD and found that 16% reported having been approached at least once to sell, trade, or give away their stimulant medication in the past 5 years (Musser, Ahmann, Mundt, Broste, & Mueller-Rizner, 1998). Reports from those in the field, including social workers, school administrators, and law enforcement authorities, suggest the problem may be much broader and more widespread. Middle school, high school, and college students, who may be trying to balance employment and academics, use medications to become hyperalert or to give them an extra energy boost to stay up all night studying or even partying. Finally, there are reports that some youth use their medications in combination with other medications or alcohol to make "cocktails" so that they can get better effects from getting stoned or high. This abuse has led to students with ADHD selling or trading their much-needed medications to other students.

In a review, Klein-Schwartz (2002) noted disagreement about the extent of abuse and diversion. Although the drug is pharmacologically similar to cocaine, some experts note lower than expected misuse of Ritalin in comparison with other drugs. However, Kollins, MacDonald, and Rush (2001) concluded that it is "not benign with respect to abuse potential" (p. 624) and called on school administrators and parents to be aware of the potential for its diversion and misuse. Importantly, they added: "This caution should, of course, be weighed against the well-documented clinical benefits of the drug for many children, adolescents, and adults" (p. 624). Likewise, Musser and colleagues (1998) sensibly called for "monitoring prescription usage, periodic reassessment of efficacy, and continuing education of family and teaching staff."

What We Can Do

Typical Rationales for Physician Referral

School social workers and other school counselors will be in the position to suggest that parents seek a psychopharmacological assessment for their child, as well as to explain to students or parents why others may have suggested following-through with such a referral. In either case, there seem to be two overarching reasons for referral: first, that teachers or others are seeing the kind of difficulties in a student's behavior or mood that is thought to respond to medications, or second, that the problematic issues or symptoms in the student that have been of concern have not changed with some sort of intervention by teachers or school care providers (psychologists, social workers). Whether or not medication is conceptualized as a last resort, if a referral is being considered, there is an implication that the problems are of such severity that outside medical/psychiatric attention is warranted and likely to be helpful to all of the stakeholders in the situation.

What to Expect From a Pharmacological Evaluation
(Processes and Outcomes)

A solid, comprehensive psychopharmacological assessment in children and adolescents is thought to be a bit more complicated than for adults because of the need for family input, the wide developmental differences in the age group, diagnostic ambiguities, and ethical issues around decision making and the rights of minors (Bentley & Walsh, 2006). Although great variability exists in the processes and procedures used, certain common elements can be expected. The goal is to obtain the most complete, accurate, and rich information possible so that decisions about diagnosis and, if relevant, specific medication type and dosage can be made with appropriate confidence. However, it is likely that conclusions by the physician will be presented as tentative, with disclaimers about how adjustments in diagnosis and treatment may be made in the future.

It may go without saying that the process done right will involve one or more face-to-face interviews with the student and parents. A "quick and dirty" 10- or 15-minute evaluation by a single provider should be considered inadequate. The interviewer(s) may be a stranger to the student and her family, or a family may choose to use its primary care physician. Interviews should consist of one or more long sessions where a series of related questions is asked, often seeking quite detailed information on developmental history (parents) or past and current patterns of behavior, thinking, and feeling (student). Interviewers may also seek information/documentation related to the student's situation from a referral source in the school system. For example, the interviewer may want medical records from the primary care physician. Sessions where psychological tests or checklists are administered may be anticipated. Importantly, anticipating a range of emotional responses to the interview by both parents and student will be helpful. Certainly, a comprehensive psychopharmacological assessment is likely to be anxiety producing for the student and his family, even if it is associated with great hope for positive change in the future. Disclosures by students or parents, if they become known, may shock each other. Students may welcome the opportunity for help with their difficulties, or they may respond by denying problems, attempting to diminish their severity, blaming others, or expressing fears of being different or not good enough. Questions may abound, or silence may rule the day.

Helping Students and Parents to Manage and Monitor Medications

Assessing and Maximizing Therapeutic Effects and Side Effects

School social workers and other school-based professionals are not called on to medically evaluate the impact of medications, as might be the case for physicians or nurses. We do not make final decisions about medication adjustments. Instead, our concern is to collaborate with others to help keep track of the whole picture in terms of effects and side effects, both positive and negative. *Therapeutic effects* are those that are desired and represent the positive effects of medications. This could certainly mean a reduction of behavioral problems or psychiatric symptoms or an increase in normal activity, enhanced mood, or a sense of being "more like me," with greater investment in personal interests. Negative or adverse effects, referred to as *side effects* because they are, by definition, unwanted, can be physical (such as drowsiness, weight gain, tremors), psychological (such as feeling controlled or "sick"), or social (such as being rejected by a friend). Some specific challenges in monitoring medications with children and adolescents, summarized in Bentley and Walsh (2006), include the fact that they may experience more marked side effects, like sedation or extrapyramidal symptoms (e.g., neuromuscular slowness, rigidity) with antipsy-chotics, but talk about them less. Hormonal changes may make measuring the effectiveness of antidepressants more problematic, as is the fact that the placebo effect is so prominent in children. Indeed, causal attributions for clinical improve-ment should be made with care. While children seem to tolerate long-term treatment with lithium well, there are concerns about the long-term build-up of lithium in the body. More concern is expressed over the possible precipitation of agitation or mania with Tegretol (carbamazepine) or the less common but still serious lowered seizure threshold with antihistamine use in the treatment of anxiety.

A number of authors have summarized lists of existing measurement devices that social workers and school-based mental health counselors could use to help track, for example, the positive and negative symptoms of schizophrenia, dyski-nesia, or akathesia; the extent of Parkinsonism symptoms; or the levels of anxiety or depression, mania or impulsivity (e.g., Bentley & Walsh, 2006; Bond & Lader, 1996). It is, however, unclear whether social workers in the field regularly use this type of assessment tool. Instead, social workers and school counselors may rely on simple graphs or checklists generated from their idiosyncratic knowledge of clients' responses or rely on charting simple, brief, descriptive statements, like a mini-mental status exam, and comparing them over time.

Direct observation and candid, open dialogue are the methods for assessing effects and side effects. Helping students to manage both kinds of effects calls for a range of techniques, including simple exercises (stretching), more educa-tion (around time lags, need for patience), concrete changes in behavior (using sunscreen, dieting), problem-solving or skills training (around what to tell people at school, how to talk to the school psychologist), or reflective discussion on meaning or stigma. Obviously, tracking the effectiveness, or lack thereof, of psy-chiatric medications may also call for additional consultation with the physician for possible reevaluation of dosing or medication type.

Addressing Adherence Issues

Bentley and Walsh (2006) argue that to protect against inappropriately simplis-tic or unidimensional explanations of medication nonadherence, social workers should be equipped with a comprehensive explanatory model of adherence. They argue that *adherence* is best understood as a complex interplay of factors that relate to the *characteristics of clients* (such as health beliefs, the desire to self-regulate, the meaning of medication, and locus of control), *aspects of treatment* (such as regimen complexity, cost, timing of effects, negative side effects, and friendliness of the aftercare environment), *aspects of the social environment* (such as family beliefs and support, and messages from the media and popular culture), and *aspects of the illness or symptoms* (denial, paranoia, depression, hostility, cognitive impairment). A good grasp of the risk and protective factors associated with nonadherence is helpful. For example, we know that bothersome side effects, a history of substance abuse, ambivalence, anger, therapeutic delays, and a poor relationship with helpers all put people at higher risk for nonadherence. Accepting or believing that one has a mental illness, having adequate preparation for and education about medication, and feeling empathy from others are, on the other hand, protective factors. Although the research that undergirds this admittedly partial list is drawn from adult samples, applying developmental theories of adolescence might help us to hypothesize that students are going to be less concerned, for example, with the impact of medication on later life than they are on the current larger meaning and symbolism (to themselves or others) of having to take a psychiatric medication for personal difficulties. It might tell us that issues of authority and trust may have a powerful impact on nonadherence, as will the parental attitudes and beliefs (Brown & Sammons, 2002).

Categories of interventions to directly affect adherence would seem to be the same for adults as for children and adolescents, in that they are likely to rely on education, cognitive and behavioral strategies, and the assessment and management of meaning. However, opportunities to creatively tailor interventions to students can and should be exploited. For example, in getting children and adolescents to express meaning, that is, the perceived impact of taking medication on their sense of self and identity, school social workers and mental health counselors could encourage storytelling, puppet play, drawing and painting and, with older students, using existing or original contemporary music and poetry. An overarching consideration is that issues of adherence are more complicated with children and adolescents in light of their limited decision-making powers. This issue may be likely to regularly rear its head in work with students.

Maximizing the Power of Collaboration

If school social workers and other school counselors are going to fully embrace their role of being a meaningful resource to students, their families, and others in the school community, close and mutually satisfying relationships with physicians, teachers, and other school-related providers is, obviously, crucial. Some philosophical foundations that may be key include the following:

- Embrace a client-centered "partnership" perspective around the range of medication-related dilemmas and issues that emerge in real-world practice. This suggests working toward a nonthreatening alliance, a demystification of the helping process, and a mutual sharing of respective expertise.
- Maintain a balanced perspective about psychiatric medication in the face of admittedly complex issues related to human rights and professional roles and the very real costs and benefits of psychiatric medication use.

- Work toward the successful integration of psychosocial interventions, therapeutic services, and psychopharmacology, and recognize the intrinsic power of combined treatments.
- Work toward interdisciplinary relationships characterized by equality, flexibility, decreased professional control, mutual understanding, and shared goals, but also appreciate the ideological and practical challenges that emerge, especially in managing parallel treatments.
- Genuinely appreciate both the strengths and the limitations of students and their families. Work should center on students' and families' unique strengths and aspirations and away from pathology, symptoms, or weaknesses. Yet real limitations (barriers to progress), such as a lack of skills or inadequate resources, have to be appreciated. (list adapted from Bentley & Walsh, 2002)

A balanced perspective acknowledges the positive impact that medications have on the lives of many, yet is not blind to the sociopolitical dimensions of prescribing, the very real dangers involved, or the negative experiences of some. It also seems to call for a rejection of any professional arrogance that would suggest that we are the only ones who embrace a "holistic perspective," are the only ones to have the "best interest" of the client at heart, or that we alone "get it."

Instead, while social workers should recognize the potential for ideological conflict, rivalry, or awkwardness when working with those who were trained and socialized very differently, we should still strive for greater understanding of the legitimate roles and expertise of others. Indeed, a recent survey of practicing social workers concluded that most social workers get their knowledge about psychiatric medications not from books or school, but from everyday interactions with physicians and clients (Bentley, Walsh, & Farmer, in press). Thus, school social workers and other school-based professionals working with physicians and others around medication issues should reject building a professional life around keeping insulated or second-guessing the decisions of others, and instead build one around inquiring exchanges and reciprocity of respect. This is so important because we know that off-label practices, the greater acceptability of polypharmacy (the use of multiple medications at one time), and even the use of dosages beyond what the desk references allow for are not uncommon. To automatically conclude malpractice would represent naiveté. That is not to say that seeking greater understanding of others, whether clients or other providers, means being passive or not asking the tough questions when needed: *Tell me more about how you came to choose that one first? Why are you prescribing that medication in addition? What is the purpose of different doses for different times? What are you hoping for with that unusual schedule? What would the signs of overmedication look like? Isn't that drug usually used with someone with different symptoms or diagnoses? Is that more than is typically prescribed? What is your thinking on this?* These questions are consistent with the professional mandate, not only to understand the entire service plan of any case, but to be advocates for clients and be an approachable, consumer-friendly translator of information for students and their families. Thus, social workers' efforts to maximize collaboration and increase our confidence in carrying out these roles may center on maximizing our learning about what others do as well as increasing time spent in interaction (Bentley et al., in press). Further suggestions for discussing medications are provided in the next section.

Tools and Practice Examples

Table 12.1 provides a summary of common mental disorders that are frequently treated with medication and some case examples. Table 12.2 provides a summary of medications that are frequently provided to children.

Table 12.1 Case Vignettes of Common Mental Disorders

Category of Disorder:
Anxiety

Common Symptomatology:
Excessive fear, worry, or uneasiness; social withdrawal, poor concentration, irritability; terror of certain objects or situations; anxiety and/or panic at being separated from parent or guardian; nightmares, continuous memories of traumatic events

Vignette:
Jana is 8 years old and has extreme separation anxiety. On the days her mother is able to get her to go to school, Jana has bouts of hyperventilating, crying spells, trembling hands, and wanting to sit by herself in the corner of the room. She states she is afraid that something bad will happen to her mother if she is not with her.

Category of Disorder:
Depression

Common Symptomatology:
Feelings of sadness, hopelessness, worthlessness, and/or suicide; irritability, somatic complaints, poor concentration; loss of interest in friends and/or play; deterioration of school work; poor sleep and appetite, lack of motivation

Vignette:
Ten-year-old Colin's grades went from A's and B's to failing over the course of 6 weeks. He has lost interest in going to recess and spends most of his time alone. Colin told his school counselor that he was really sad and felt like he would never be good enough to pass fifth grade. His parents state that when he comes home from school, he is irritable and usually just wants to go to bed and doesn't even want to eat with the family.

(continued)

Table 12.1 *(Continued)*

Category of Disorder:
Oppositional defiant/ conduct

Common Symptomatology:
Violates rights of others by lying, theft, aggression, truancy, the setting of fires, and vandalism; low self-esteem, depression; running away from home

Vignette:
Sonya is in tenth grade. She had to go to juvenile court twice for truancy this school year. Sonya told the judge she would never amount to anything and didn't care that her parents had to pay fines for school truancy. Recently, Sonya also confided to her friend that she has been stealing her teachers' money over the past year so that she can buy a house for herself. Her friend said that Sonya stated that if she told anyone about what she was doing, she would hurt her friend's little brother.

Category of Disorder:
ADD/ ADHD

Common Symptomatology:
Inattentive, hyperactive, aggressive and/or defiant, impulsive, easily distracted; difficulty completing tasks, fidgets, cannot sit still; interrupts often, cannot wait turn

Vignette:
Jaime's teacher has noticed that she is constantly out of her chair and walking around the room, talking to the other children. Jaime's parents report that they have difficulty calming her down so that she can focus on her homework. They also say she has been teasing and hitting her younger sister.

Category of Disorder:
Learning and communication

Common Symptomatology:
Problems with spoken and written language, coordination, attention, or self-control; struggles to explain feelings and thoughts; difficulty with math, technology, and scientific information; delayed in grade-level progress

Vignette:
Alex's counselor describes him as a bright and articulate 12-year-old. If he hears a story, he can tell it back to his teacher and parents verbatim. Yet, he has difficulty answering questions about the significance of characters or actions of characters in the stories. Alex's written work is poor. He cannot create simple sentences, and because he cannot comprehend short stories, he cannot complete his homework assignments without his parents reading to him. His teacher states that his written work is at a third-grade level instead of a sixth-grade level.

(continued)

Table 12.1 *(Continued)*

Category of Disorder:
Autism spectrum (pervasive developmental)

Common Symptomatology:
Range of mild to severe problems with interpersonal interactions and communication; difficulty with cognition or thinking; struggles with understanding the feelings of others; becomes attached to one object or situation; poor eye contact, tunes people out, does not react to others (such as saying hello or waving goodbye); prefers to play alone and seems independent for stated age; general difficulty with interpreting the world

Vignette:
Tia just started kindergarten. She has very poor eye contact and does not smile when her teacher smiles at her or praises her. Tia's parents told her teacher that they often have to continuously repeat steps of tasks to her and that she seems "to be in her own world" and "does not hear them." During the first week of school, the teacher noticed that Tia constantly echoes what other children say in class and when she is asked to stop, she begins screaming and then has a tantrum.

Category of Disorder:
Schizophrenia

Common Symptomatology:
Delusions, hallucinations; withdrawal from others; loss of contact with reality; catatonic or other bizarre motor behaviors, hyperactive without an apparent stimulus; flat affect, does not show emotion

Vignette:
Brian is 17 years old. He had a flat affect when he told the school social worker that sometimes he feels confused because he hears voices telling him to steal things and to hurt himself. He relayed that the only time he can concentrate is after praying late at night in front of the news correspondent on television. Brian believes that the correspondent is the only person who can hear him and understand what he is going through in his life. He asks the social worker if she believes him.

Category of Disorder:
Tic

Common Symptomatology:
Involuntary twitches or movements of muscle groups, such as eye blinking, sneezing, shoulder shrugging; involuntary vocalizations, such as humming, grunting, or actual words that are expressed in a spastic or explosive manner; partial control can be obtained for short periods of time; tic behaviors fluctuate in intensity and frequency

(continued)

Table 12.1 (*Continued*)

Vignette:
Sam was sitting on his hands and holding his face very rigid when he visited his principal for disrupting the class. The principal told Sam that he could relax, that he just wanted to talk to him. Sam said, "I can't or I will be in trouble again." Promptly, Sam took a deep breath and started holding his breath. After a few moments, he let out his breath and his shoulders began jerking up and down a few times. The principal continued talking to Sam about his school behavior and noticed Sam's rapid eye blinking. Throughout their talk, Sam also grunted and then would hold his breath until the next grunt. The principal realized that Sam was trying to stop his motor and vocal tics due to embarrassment.

Table 12.2 Common Psychiatric Medications for Children and Adolescents

Trade Name of Drug (generic name): Abilify (aripiprazole)
Type/Class of Medication: Antipsychotic (atypical)
Common Psychiatric Uses: Schizophrenia, bipolar, aggression
Common Side Effects: Dry mouth, weight gain, drowsiness
Approved for Children? No

Trade Name of Drug (generic name): Adderall (amphetamine mixed salts)
Type/Class of Medication: Stimulant
Common Psychiatric Uses: ADHD
Common Side Effects: High blood pressure, rapid heart rate, gastrointestinal complaints, somnolence, weight gain, middle-ear infection
Approved for Children? Age 3 and older

Trade Name of Drug (generic name): Anafranil (clomipramine)
Type/Class of Medication: Antidepressant
Common Psychiatric Uses: OCD
Common Side Effects: —
Approved for Children? Age 10 and older for OCD

Trade Name of Drug (generic name): BuSpar (buspirone)
Type/Class of Medication: Anti-anxiety
Common Psychiatric Uses: Anxiety, phobias
Common Side Effects: Drowsiness or fatigue, dry mouth, increase in nightmares or dreams
Approved for Children? No

Trade Name of Drug (generic name): Catapres (clonidine)
Type/Class of Medication: Alpha-adrenergic
Common Psychiatric Uses: Impulsivity, hyperactivity
Common Side Effects: Dry mouth, sedation, hypotension
Approved for Children?

(continued)

Table 12.2 (*Continued*)

Trade Name of Drug (generic name): Cibalith-S (lithium citrate)
Type/Class of Medication: Mood stabilizer
Common Psychiatric Uses: Mania, bipolar
Common Side Effects: Diarrhea, drowsiness, lack of coordination, loss of appetite, muscle weakness, nausea or vomiting, slurred speech, trembling
Approved for Children? Age 12 and older

Trade Name of Drug (generic name): Clozaril (clozapine)
Type/Class of Medication: Antipsychotic (atypical)
Common Psychiatric Uses: Schizophrenia
Common Side Effects: Fast or irregular heart beat, dizziness, constipation
Approved for Children? No

Trade Name of Drug (generic name): Concerta (methylphenidate)
Type/Class of Medication: Stimulant
Common Psychiatric Uses: ADHD
Common Side Effects: Headache, stomach pain, insomnia
Approved for Children? Age 6 and older

Trade Name of Drug (generic name): Cylert (pemoline)
Type/Class of Medication: Stimulant
Common Psychiatric Uses: ADHD
Common Side Effects: Potential for serious side effects affecting the liver
Approved for Children? Age 6 and older

Trade Name of Drug (generic name): Depakote (sodium valproate)
Type/Class of Medication: Antiseizure, mood stablizer
Common Psychiatric Uses: Bipolar, mania
Common Side Effects: Headache, nausea, drowsiness, liver and white cell abnormalities
Approved for Children? Not for this use. Age 12 and older for seizures

Trade Name of Drug (generic name): Dexedrine (dextroamphetamine sulfate)
Type/Class of Medication: Stimulant
Common Psychiatric Uses: ADHD
Common Side Effects: Headache, restlessness, diarrhea, drowsiness, weight loss
Approved for Children? Age 3 and older

Trade Name of Drug (generic name): Dextrostat (dextroampheta-mine)
Type/Class of Medication: Stimulant
Common Psychiatric Uses: ADHD
Common Side Effects: Headache, restlessness, diarrhea, drowsiness, weight loss
Approved for Children? Age 3 and older

(*continued*)

Table 12.2 (*Continued*)

Trade Name of Drug (generic name): Effexor (venlafaxine)
Type/Class of Medication: Antidepressant (SSRI)
Common Psychiatric Uses: Depression
Common Side Effects: Reduced appetite, nausea, constipation
Approved for Children? No

Trade Name of Drug (generic name): Eskalith (lithium)
Type/Class of Medication: Mood stabilizer
Common Psychiatric Uses: Bipolar, mania, bulimia
Common Side Effects: Nausea, frequent urination, hand tremor, mild thirst
Approved for Children? Age 12 and older

Trade Name of Drug (generic name): Haldol (haloperidol)
Type/Class of Medication: Antipsychotic
Common Psychiatric Uses: Schizophrenia, Tourette's syndrome, aggression, hyperactivity
Common Side Effects: Dry mouth, drowsiness, dizziness, confusion, tardive dyskinesia
Approved for Children? Age 3 and older

Trade Name of Drug (generic name): Klonopin (clonazepam)
Type/Class of Medication: Anti-anxiety (benzodiazepine)
Common Psychiatric Uses: Anxiety, eating disorders, Tourette's
Common Side Effects: Drowsiness
Approved for Children? No

Trade Name of Drug (generic name): Lexapro (escitalopram)
Type/Class of Medication: Antidepressant (SSRI)
Common Psychiatric Uses: Depression, anxiety
Common Side Effects: Nausea
Approved for Children? No

Trade Name of Drug (generic name): Lithium
Type/Class of Medication: Mood stabilizer
Common Psychiatric Uses: Bipolar, mania
Common Side Effects: Reduced appetite, hand tremors
Approved for Children? No

Trade Name of Drug (generic name): Lithobid (lithium carbonate)
Type/Class of Medication: Mood stabilizer
Common Psychiatric Uses: Bipolar, mania
Common Side Effects: Reduced appetite, hand tremors, blurred vision, constipation, decreased appetite, gastrointestinal problems, nausea
Approved for Children? Age 12 and older

(*continued*)

Table 12.2 *(Continued)*

Trade Name of Drug (generic name): Luvox (fluvoxamine)
Type/Class of Medication: Antidepressant (SSRI)
Common Psychiatric Uses: OCD
Common Side Effects: —
Approved for Children? Age 8 and older for OCD

Trade Name of Drug (generic name): Mellaril (thioridazine)
Type/Class of Medication: Antipsychotic
Common Psychiatric Uses: Schizophrenia
Common Side Effects: Nausea, gastrointestinal problems, drowsiness, tardive dyskinesia
Approved for Children? Age 2 and older

Talking with students, parents, and teachers about medication can be challenging. Following are some guidelines on how to talk to students, parents, and teachers about medication:

1. Healthy skepticism about the use of psychiatric medication is appropriate.
2. Offer chances for folks to talk about their doubts, fears, hopes, and dreams with respect to psychiatric medication.
3. Acknowledge the multiple forces influencing the use of medication with children and adolescents today.
4. Explain off-label use as both common and legal.
5. Welcome conversation on the public controversies around kids and psychiatric medication.
6. Encourage the reporting of trading or selling of medication.
7. Provide examples of the typical rationale underlying referrals to a prescriber for medication assessment.
8. Explain the usual relationship among diagnoses, symptoms, and prescriber choices of drug type and dosage.
9. Anticipate a range of emotional reactions to a referral to a prescriber and the medication assessment process itself.
10. Ask about both the positive and negative effects of medication.
11. Explain the complexity of adherence.
12. Develop easy-to-understand (noncommercial) written psychoeducational materials.
13. Offer to be a resource for information, support, and problem solving around medication-related dilemmas.

14. Give folks a chance to talk about the impact of taking medication in general but especially on their sense of self and personal identity.

Key Points to Remember

Sood (2004) noted that, after looking at all of the scientific data, a case could be made for either the overprescribing or the underprescribing of medications to children and adolescents. Certainly, data show staggering increases in the number of prescriptions written and the number of children taking medications. Other data show that many children who suffer are not getting the pharmacological and other treatments that may be helpful. Sood urges us to consider the implications of our own beliefs about mental illness in children (does it exist? where does it come from?) on our attitudes toward medication and strive to deliver evidence-based practices to those in need. For school social workers and others, our goals are to help facilitate access to care, participate in multimodal approaches to service delivery, and provide much-needed supports to students, parents, teachers, and health care providers. Summarized above are the "how to's" of reaching these goals, that is, how to help students, parents, and teachers make sense of the controversy and ambiguity in child and adolescent psychopharmacotherapy, understand mental disorders and the medications used to treat them, negotiate referral processes and pharmacological assessment, and manage and monitor medication in the short and long term.

References

Chapter I

Alexander, J. F., & Parsons, B. V. (1973). Short-term behavioral intervention with delinquents: Impact on family process and recidivism. *Journal of Abnormal Psychology, 81*, 219–225.

American Psychiatric Association. (2000). *Diagnostic and statistical manual of mental disorders (4th ed., text revision)*. Washington, DC: Author.

Baer, R. A., & Nietzel, M. T. (1991). Cognitive and behavioral treatment of impulsivity in children: A meta analytic review of the outcome literature. *Journal of Clinical Child Psychology.*

Bank, L., Marlowe, J. H., Reid, J. B., Patterson, G. R., & Weinrott, M. R. (1991). A comparative evaluation of parent training interventions for families of chronic delinquents. *Journal of Abnormal Child Psychology, 19*, 15–33.

Barkley, R. A. (1987). *Defiant children: A clinician's manual for parent training.* New York: Guilford.

Barkley, R., Edwards, G., Laneri, M., Fletcher, K., & Metevia, L. (2001). The efficacy of problem-solving communication training alone, behavior management training alone, and their combination for parent–adolescent conflict in teenagers with ADHD and ODD. *Journal of Consulting & Clinical Psychology, 69*, 926–941.

Barkley, R. A., Guevremont, D. C., Anastopoulos, A. D., & Fletcher, K. E. (1992). A comparison of three family therapy programs for treating family conflicts in adolescents with attention-deficit hyperactivity disorder. *Journal of Consulting and Clinical Psychology, 60*, 450–462.

Bernal, M. E., Klinnert, M. D., & Schultz, L. A. (1980). Outcome evaluation of behavioral parent training and client-centered parent counseling for children with conduct problems. *Journal of Applied Behavior Analysis, 13*, 677–691.

Block, J. (1978). Effects of a rational-emotive mental health program on poorly achieving disruptive high school students. *Journal of Counseling Psychology, 25*, 61–65.

Bloomquist, M. L., & Schnell, S. V. (2002). *Helping children with aggression and conduct problems: Best practices for intervention.* New York: Guilford.

Borduin, C. M., Mann, B. J., Cone, L. T., Henggeler, S. W., Fucci, B. R., Blaske, D. M., & Williams, R. A. (1995). Multisystemic treatment of serious juvenile offenders: Long-term prevention of criminality and violence. *Journal of Consulting and Clinical Psychology, 63*, 569–578.

Brestan, E. V., & Eyberg, S. M. (1998). Effective psychosocial treatments of conduct-disordered children and adolescents: 29 years, 82 studies, and 5,272 kids. *Journal of Clinical Child Psychology, 27*(2), 180–189.

Cavell, T. A. (2000). *Working with parents of aggressive children: A practitioner's guide.* Washington, DC: American Psychological Association.

Dishion, T. J., & Patterson, G. R. (1992). Age effects in parent training outcomes. *Behavior Therapy, 23,* 719–729.

Durlak, J., Fuhrman, T., & Lampman, C. (1991). Effectiveness of cognitive-behavior therapy for maladapting children: A meta-analysis. *Psychological Bulletin, 110,* 204–214.

D'Zurilla, T., & Nezu, A. (2001). Problem-solving therapies. In K. Dobson & S. Keith (Eds.), *Handbook of cognitive-behavioral therapies* (2nd ed., pp. 211–245). New York: Guilford.

Eyberg, S. (1988). Parent–child interaction therapy: Integration of traditional and behavioral concerns. *Child and Family Behavior Therapy, 10,* 33–45.

Eyberg, S. M., Boggs, S., & Algina, J. (1995). Parent–child interaction therapy: A psychosocial model for the treatment of young children with conduct problem behavior and their families. *Psychopharmacology Bulletin, 110,* 204–214.

Feindler, D. L., Marriott, S. A. A., & Iwata, M. (1984). Group anger control training for junior high school delinquents. *Cognitive Therapy and Research, 8,* 299–311.

Fonagy, P., & Kurtz, A. (2002). Disturbance of conduct. In P. Fonagy, M. Target, D. Cottrell, J. Phillips, & Z. Kurtz (Eds.), *What works for whom? A critical review of treatments for children and adolescents* (pp. 106–192). New York: Guilford.

Forehand, R. L., & McMahon, R. J. (1981). *Helping the noncompliant child: A clinician's guide to present training.* New York: Guilford.

Hamilton, S. B., & MacQuiddy, S. L. (1984). Self-administered behavioral parent training: Enhancement of treatment efficacy using a time-out signal seat. *Journal of Clinical Child Psychology, 13,* 61–69.

Henggeler, S. W., Melton, G. B., & Smith, L. A. (1992). Family preservation using multisystemic therapy: An effective alternative to incarcerating serious juvenile offenders. *Journal of Consulting and Clinical Psychology, 60,* 953–961.

Henggeler, S. W., Rodick, J. D., Bourdin, C. M., Hanson, C. L., Watson, S. M., & Urey, J. R. (1986). Multisystemic treatment of juvenile offenders: Effects on adolescent behavior and family interaction. *Developmental Psychology, 22,* 132–141.

Huey, W. C., & Rank, R. C. (1984). Effects of counselor and peer-led group assertiveness training on black adolescent aggression. *Journal of Counseling Psychology, 31,* 95–98.

Kazdin, A. E. (1994). Psychotherapy for children and adolescents. In A. E. Bergin, & S. L. Garfield (Eds.), *Handbook of psychotherapy and behavior change* (4th ed., pp. 543–594). New York: Wiley.

Kazdin, A. E. (2000). *Psychotherapy for children and adolescents: Directions for research and practice.* New York: Oxford University Press.

Kazdin, A. E. (2002). Psychosocial treatments for conduct disorder in children and adolescents. In P. E. Nathan & J. M. Gorman (Eds.), *A guide to treatments that work* (2nd ed., pp. 57–85). New York: Oxford University Press.

Kazdin, A. E. (2003). Problem-solving skills training and parent management training for conduct disorder. In A. E. Kazdin & J. R. Weisz (Eds.), *Evidence-based psychotherapies for children and adolescents* (pp. 241–262). New York: Guilford.

Kazdin, A. E. (2004). Psychotherapy for children and adolescents. In M. J. Lambert (Ed.), *Bergin and Garfield's handbook of psychotherapy and behavior change* (5th ed., pp. 543–589). New York: Wiley.

Kazdin, A. E., Esveldt-Dawson, K., French, N. H., & Unis, A. S. (1987a). Effect of parent management training and problem-solving skills training combined in the treatment of antisocial child behavior. *Journal of the American Academy of Child and Adolescent Psychiatry, 26*, 416–424.

Kazdin, A. E., Esveldt-Dawson, K., French, N. H., & Unis, A. S. (1987b). Problem-solving skills training and relationship therapy in the treatment of antisocial child behavior. *Journal of Consulting and Clinical Psychology, 55*, 76–85.

Kazdin, A. E., Siegel, T. C., & Bass, D. (1992). Cognitive problem-solving skills training and parent management training in the treatment of antisocial behavior in children. *Journal of Consulting and Clinical Psychology, 60*, 733–747.

Kronenberger, W. S., & Meyer, R. G. (2001). *The child clinician's handbook* (2nd ed.). Needham Heights, MA: Allyn & Bacon.

Little, E., & Hudson, A. (1998). Conduct problems and treatment across home and school: A review of the literature. *Behavior Change, 15*, 213–227.

Lochman, J. E., Burch, P. R., Curry, J. F., & Lampron, L. B. (1984). Treatment and generalization effects of cognitive-behavioral and goal-setting interventions with aggressive boys. *Journal of Consulting and Clinical Psychology, 52*, 915–916.

Lochman, J. E., Lampron, L. B., Gemmer, T. C., & Harris, S. R. (1989). Teacher consultation and cognitive-behavioral interventions with aggressive boys. *Psychology in the Schools, 26*, 179–188.

Loeber, R., Farrington, D. P., & Waschbusch, D. A. (1998). Serious and violent juvenile offenders. In R. Loeber & D. P. Farrington (Eds.), *Serious and violent juvenile offenders: Risk factors and successful interventions* (pp. 13–29). Thousand Oaks, CA: Sage.

McNeil, C. B., Eyberg, S., Eisenstadt, T. H., Newcomb, K., & Funderburk, B. W. (1991). Parent-child interaction therapy with behavior problem children: Generalization of treatment effects to the school setting. *Journal of Clinical Child Psychology, 20*, 140–151.

Moffitt, T. E., Caspi, A., Dickson, N., Silva, P., & Stanton, W. (1996). Childhood-onset versus adolescent-onset antisocial problems in males: Natural history from ages 3 to 18 years. *Developmental Psychopathology, 9*, 399–424.

Mortimore, P. (1995). The positive effects of schooling. In M. Rutter (Ed.), *Psychosocial disturbances in young people: Challenges for prevention* (pp. 333–363). Cambridge: Cambridge University Press.

Patterson, G. R., & Gullion, M. E. (1968). *Living with children: New methods for parents and teachers.* Champaign, IL: Research Press.

Patterson, G. R., Reid, J. B., Jones, R. R., & Conger, R. E. (1975). *A social learning approach to family intervention: Vol. 1. Families with aggressive children.* Eugene, OR: Castalia.

Peed, S., Roberts, M., & Forehand, R. (1977). Evaluation of the effectiveness of a standardized parent training program in altering the interaction of mothers and their noncompliant children. *Behavior Modification, 1*, 323–350.

Pullis, M. (1991). Practical considerations of excluding conduct disordered students: An empirical analysis. *Behavioral Disorders, 17*(1), 9–22.

Reid, M. J., Webster-Stratton, C., & Baydar, N. (2004). Halting the development of conduct problems in Head Start children: The effects of parent training. *Journal of Clinical Child and Adolescent Psychology, 33*(2), 279–291.

Reid, M. J., Webster-Stratton, C., & Hammond, M. (2003). Follow-up of children who received the incredible years intervention for oppositional defiant disorder: Maintenance and prediction of 2-year outcome. *Behavior Therapy, 34*(4), 471–491.

Reynolds, D., Sammons, P., Stoll, L., Barber, M., & Hillman, J. (1996). School effectiveness and school improvement in the United Kingdom. *School Effectiveness and School Improvement, 7,* 133–158.

Rosen, A., & Proctor, E. K. (2002). Standards for evidence-based social work practice: The role of replicable and appropriate interventions, outcomes, and practice guidelines. In A. R. Roberts & G. J. Greene (Eds.), *Social workers' desk reference* (pp. 743–747). New York: Oxford University Press.

Schlichter, K. J., & Horan, J. J. (1981). Effects of stress inoculation on the anger and aggression management skills of institutionalized juvenile delinquents. *Cognitive Therapy and Research, 5,* 359–365.

Sells, S. P. (1998). *Treating the tough adolescent: A family-based, step-by-step guide.* New York: Guilford.

Serketich, W. J., & Dumas, J. E. (1996). The effectiveness of behavioral parent training to modify antisocial behavior in children: A meta analysis. *Behavior Therapy, 27,* 171–186.

Spaccarelli, S., Cotler, S., & Penman, D. (1992). Problem-solving skills training as a supplement to behavioral parent training. *Cognitive Therapy and Research, 16,* 1–18.

Springer, D. W. (2002). Assessment protocols and rapid assessment instruments with troubled adolescents. In A. R. Roberts & G. J. Greene (Eds.), *Social workers' desk reference* (pp. 217–221). New York: Oxford University Press.

Tremblay, R. E., Pagani-Kurtz, L., Masse, L. C., Vitaro, F., & Phil, R. (1995). A bimodal preventive intervention for disruptive kindergarten boys: Its impact through mid-adolescence. *Journal of Consulting and Clinical Psychology, 63,* 560–568.

U.S. Department of Health and Human Services. (2001). *Youth violence: A report of the Surgeon General.* Rockville, MD: Author.

Vitaro, F., & Tremblay, R. E. (1994). Impact of a prevention program on aggressive children's friendships and social adjustment. *Journal of Abnormal Child Psychology, 22,* 457–475.

Webster-Stratton, C. (1984). Randomized trial of two parent-training programs for families with conduct-disordered children. *Journal of Consulting and Clinical Psychology, 52,* 666–678.

Webster-Stratton, C. (1990). Enhancing the effectiveness of self-administered videotape parent training for families with conduct-problem children. *Journal of Abnormal Child Psychology, 18,* 479–492.

Webster-Stratton, C. (1994). Advancing videotape parent training: A comparison study. *Journal of Consulting and Clinical Psychology, 62,* 583–593.

Webster-Stratton, C. (1998). Preventing conduct problems in Head Start children: Strengthening parenting competencies. *Journal of Consulting and Clinical Psychology, 66*(5), 715–730.

Webster-Stratton, C., & Hammond, M. (1997). Treating children with early-onset conduct problems: A comparison of child and parent training interventions. *Journal of Consulting and Clinical Psychology, 65*(1), 93–109.

Webster-Stratton, C., Kolpacoff, M., & Hollinsworth, T. (1988). Self-administered videotape therapy for families with conduct-problem children: Comparison with two cost effective treatments and a control group. *Journal of Consulting and Clinical Psychology, 56,* 558–566.

Webster-Stratton, C., & Reid, M. J. (2003a). Treating conduct problems and strengthening social emotional competence in young children (ages 4–8 years): The Dina Dinosaur treatment program. *Journal of Emotional and Behavioral Disorders, 11*(3), 130–143.

Webster-Stratton, C., & Reid, M. J. (2003b). The incredible years parents, teachers, and children training series: A multifaceted treatment approach for young children with conduct problems. In A. E. Kazdin & J. R. Weisz (Eds.), *Evidence-based psychotherapies for children and adolescents* (pp. 224–240). New York: Guilford.

Webster-Stratton, C., Reid, M. J., & Hammond, M. (2001a). Preventing conduct problems, promoting social competence: A parent and teacher training partnership in Head Start. *Journal of Clinical Child Psychology, 30*(3), 283–302.

Webster-Stratton, C., Reid, M. J., & Hammond, M. (2001b). Social skills and problem solving training for children with early-onset conduct problems: Who benefits? *Journal of Child Psychology and Psychiatry, 42*(7), 943–952.

Webster-Stratton, C., Reid, M. J., & Hammond, M. (2004). Treating children with early onset conduct problems: Intervention outcomes for parent, child, and teacher training. *Journal of Clinical Child and Adolescent Psychology, 33*(1), 105–124.

Wells, K. C., & Egan, J. (1988). Social learning and systems family therapy for childhood oppositional disorder: Comparative treatment outcome. *Comprehensive Psychiatry, 29*, 138–146.

Wiltz, N. A., & Patterson, G. R. (1974). An evaluation of parent training procedures designed to alter inappropriate aggressive behavior of boys. *Behavior Therapy, 5*, 215–221.

Zangwill, W. M. (1983). An evaluation of a parent training program. *Child and Family Behavior Therapy, 5*, 1–6.

Chapter 2

American Psychiatric Association. (2000). *Diagnostic and statistical manual of mental disorders (4th ed., text revision)*. Washington, DC: Author.

Bentley, K., & Collins, K. (in press). Psychopharmacological treatments for children & adolescents. In C. F. Franklin et al., *Social workers and mental health workers training and resource manual.* New York: Oxford University Press.

DuPaul, G. J., & Eckert, T. L. (1997). The effects of school-based interventions for attention deficit hyperactivity disorder: A meta-analysis. *School Psychology Review, 26*(3), 2–27.

DuPaul, G. J., Eckert, T. L., & McGoey, K. E. (1997). Interventions for students with attention-deficit/hyperactivity disorder: One size dose not fit all. *School Psychology Review, 26*(3), 369–381.

Erk, R. R. (1995). A diagnosis of attention deficit disorder: What does it mean for school counselors? *School Counselor, 42*, 292–299.

Erk, R. R (2000). Five frameworks for increasing understanding and effective treatment of attention deficit/hyperactivity disorder: Predominately inattentive type. *Journal of Counseling and Development, 78*(4), 389–399.

Hoagwood, K., Kelleher, K. J., Feil, M., & Comer, D. (2000). Treatment services for children with ADHD: A national perspective. *Journal of the American Academy of Child and Adolescent Psychiatry, 38*(7), 797–804.

Jensen, P. S. (2000). The National Institutes of Health attention-deficit/hyperactivity disorder consensus statement: Implications for practitioners and scientists. *CNS Spectrums, 5*(6), 29–33.

Jensen, P. S., Kettle, L., Roper, M. T., Sloan, M. T., Dulcan, M. K., Hoven, C., Bird, H., Bauermeister, J., & Panye, J. (1999). Are stimulants overprescribed? Treatment of ADHD in four U.S. communities. *Journal of the American Academy of Child and Adolescent Psychiatry, 38*(7), 797–804.

LeFever, G. B., Villers, M. S., Morrow, A. L., & Vaughn, E. S. (2002). Parental perceptions of adverse educational outcomes among children diagnosed and treated for ADHD: A call for improved school/provider collaboration. *Psychology in the Schools, 39*(1), 63–71.

Litner, B. (2003). Teens with ADHD: The challenge of high school. *Children and Youth Care Forum, 32*(3), 137–158.

McGoey, K., Eckert, T. L., & DuPaul, G. J. (2002). Early intervention for preschool-age children with ADHD: A literature review. *Journal of Emotional and Behavioral Disorders, 10*(1), 14–28.

Olfson, M., Gameroff, M. J., Marcus, S. C., & Jensen, P. S. (2003). National trends in the treatment of attention deficit hyperactivity disorder. *American Journal of Psychiatry, 160*(6), 1071–1077.

Perrin, J. M., Stein, M. T., Amler, R. W., Blondis, T. A., Feldman, H. M., Meyer, B. P., Shaywitz, A. B., & Wolraich, M. L. (2001). Clinical practice guideline: Treatment of the school-aged child with attention-deficit/hyperactivity disorder. *Pediatrics, 108*(4), 1033–1042.

Richters, J. E., Arnold, L. E., Jensen, P. S., Abikoff, H., Conners, C. K., Greenhill, L. L., Laurence, L., Hechtman, L., Hinshaw, S. P., Pelham, W. E., & Swanson, J. M. (1995). NIMH collaborative multisite multimodal treatment study of children with ADHD: I. Background and rationale. *Journal of the American Academy of Child and Adolescent Psychiatry, 34*(8), 987–1000.

Smith, B. H., Waschbusch, D. A., Willoughby, M. T., & Evans, S. (2000). The efficacy, safety, and practicality of treatments for adolescents with attention-deficit/hyperactivity disorder. *Clinical Child and Family Psychology Review, 3*(4), 2243–2266.

Thomas, C., & Corcoran, J. (2000). Family approaches to attention deficit hyperactivity disorder: Review of guide school social work practice. *Children & Schools, 25*(1), 19–34.

Chapter 3

Abolt, T., & Thyer, B. A. (2002). Social work assessment of children with oppositional defiant disorder: Reliability and validity of the Child Behavior Checklist. *Social Work in Mental Health, 1*, 73–84.

American Psychiatric Association. (2000). *Diagnostic and statistical manual of mental disorders (4th ed., text revision).* Washington, DC: Author.

Barker, P. (1999). *Talking cures: An introduction to the psychotherapies for health care professionals.* London: NT Books.

Bierman, K. L., Miller, C. M., & Stabb, S. (1987). Improving the social behavior and peer acceptance of rejected boys: Effects of social skill training with instructions and prohibitions. *Journal of Consulting and Clinical Psychology, 55*, 194–200.

Block, J. (1978). Effects of a rational emotive mental health program on poorly achieving, disrupting high school students. *Journal of Counseling Psychology, 25*, 61–65.

Brinkmeyer, M., & Eyberg, S. M. (2003). Parent–child interaction therapy for oppositional children. In A. E. Kazdin & J. R. Weisz (Eds.), *Evidence-based psychotherapies for children and adolescents* (pp. 204– 223). New York: Guilford.

Burns, G., & Patterson, D. (2001). Normative data on the Eyberg Child Behavior Inventory and Sutter-Eyberg Student Behavior Inventory: Parent and teacher rating scales of disruptive behavior problems in children and adolescents. *Child and Family Behavior Therapy, 23*, 15–28.

Coie, J., Lochman, J., Terry, R., & Hyman, C. (1992). Predicting early adolescent disorder from childhood aggression and peer rejection. *Journal of Consulting and Clinical Psychology, 60*, 783–792.

Dodge, K. A., & Price, J. M. (1994). On the relation between social information processing and socially competent behavior in early school-aged children. *Child Development, 65*, 1385–1397.

Eamon, M. K., & Altshuler, S. J. (2004). Can we predict disruptive school behavior? *Children & Schools, 26*, 23–37.

Feindler, E. L., Marriott, S., & Iwata, M. (1984). Group anger-control training for junior high school delinquents. *Cognitive Therapy and Research, 8*, 299–311.

Fisher, P. A., & Fagot, B. I. (1996). Development of consensus about child oppositional behavior: Increased convergence with entry into school. *Journal of Applied Developmental Psychology, 17*, 519–534.

Freeman, E. M., Franklin, C. G., Fong, R., Shaffer, G. L., and Timberlake, E. M. (Eds.). (1998). *Multisystem skills and interventions in school social work practice.* Washington, DC: NASW Press.

Frey, K. S., Hirschstein, M. K., & Guzzo, B. A. (2000). Second step: Preventing aggression by promoting social competence. *Journal of Emotional and Behavioral Disorders, 8*(2), 102–112.

Garbarino, J. (1999). *Lost boys.* New York: Free Press.

Hamlet, C., Axelrod, S., & Kuerschner, S. (1984). Eye contact as an antecedent to compliant behavior. *Journal of Applied Behavior Analysis, 17*, 553–557.

Harris, V. W., & Sherman, J. A. (1973). Use and analysis of the "good behavior game" to reduce disruptive classroom behavior. *Journal of Applied Behavior Analysis, 6*, 405–417.

Hemphill, S., & Littlefield, L. (2001). Evaluation of a community-based group therapy program for children with behavior problems and their parents. *Behaviour Research and Therapy, 39*, 823–841.

Hoagwood, K., Burns, B., Kiser, L., Ringeisen, H., & Schoenwald, S. (2001). Evidence-based practice in child and adolescent mental health services. *Psychiatric Services, 52*(9), 1179–1189.

Huey, W. C., & Rank, R. C. (1984). Effects of counselor- and peer-led group assertive training on black adolescent aggression. *Journal of Counseling Psychology, 31*(1), 95–98.

Kazdin, A. E. (1997). Practitioner review: Psychosocial treatments for conduct disorder in children. *Journal of Child Psychology and Psychiatry, 38*, 161–178.

Kehle, T. J., Madaus, M. R., Baratta, V. S., & Bray, M. A. (1998). Employing self-modeling with children with selective mutism. *Journal of School Psychology, 36*, 247–260.

Kupersmidt, J. B., & Coie, J. D. (1990). Preadolescent peer status, aggression, and school adjustment as predictors of externalizing problems in adolescence. *Child Development, 61*, 1350–1362.

Kupersmidt, J. B., & Patterson, C. J. (1991). Childhood peer rejection, aggression, withdrawal, and perceived competence as predictors of self-reported behavior problems in preadolescence. *Journal of Abnormal Child Psychology, 19*, 427–503.

Lochman, J., Coie, J., Underwood, M., & Terry, R. (1993). Effectiveness of a social relations intervention program for aggressive and nonaggressive, rejected children. *Journal of Consulting and Clinical Psychology, 61*, 1053–1058.

Loeber, R. (1990). Development and risk factors of juvenile antisocial behavior and delinquency. *Clinical Psychology Review, 10*, 1–42.

Mader, C. (2000). Child-centered play therapy with disruptive school students. In H. G. Kaduson & C. E. Schaffer (Eds.), *Short-term play therapy for children* (pp. 53–68). New York: Guilford.

Markward, M. J., & Bride, B. E. (2001). Oppositional defiant disorder and the need for family-centered practice in schools. *Children & Schools, 23*(2), 73–83.

Meichenbaum, D. H. (1977). *Cognitive-behavior modification: An integrative approach.* New York: Plenum.

Musser, E. H., Bray, M. A., Kehle, T. J., & Jenson, W. R. (2001). Reducing disruptive behaviors in students with serious emotional disturbance. *School Psychology Review, 30*, 294–305.

O'Leary, K. D., Kaufman, K. F., Kass, R., & Drabman, R. (1970). The effects of loud and soft reprimands on the behavior of disruptive students. *Exceptional Children 37*(2), 145–155.

Osenton, T., & Chang, J. (1999). Solution-oriented classroom management: Application with young children. *Journal of Systemic Therapies, 18*(2), 65–76.

Rhode, G., Jenson, W. R., & Reavis, H. K. (1993). *The tough kid book: Practical classroom management strategies.* Longmont, CO: Sopris West.

Rosenberg, M. S. (1986). Maximizing the effectiveness of structured classroom management programs: Implementing rule-review procedures with disruptive and distractible students. *Behavioral Disorders, 11*, 239–248.

Sprague, A., & Thyer, B. A. (2002). Psychosocial treatment of oppositional defiant disorder: A review of empirical outcome studies. *Social Work in Mental Health, 1*, 63–72.

Van Houten, R., Nau, P., MacKenzie-Keating, S., Sameoto, D., & Colavecchia, B. (1982). An analysis of some variables influencing the effectiveness of reprimands. *Journal of Applied Behavior Analysis, 15*, 65–83.

Chapter 4

Achenbach, T. (1991). *Manual for the teacher's report form and 1991 profile.* Burlington: University of Vermont, Department of Psychiatry.

Albano, A. M. (2003). Treatment of social anxiety disorder. In M. A. Reinecke & F. M. Dattilio (Eds.), *Cognitive therapy with children and adolescents: A casebook for clinical practice* (2nd ed., pp. 128–161). New York: Guilford.

Albano, A. M., & Kendall, P. C. (2002). Cognitive behavioral therapy for children and adolescents with anxiety disorders: Clinical research advances. *International Review of Psychiatry, 14*(2), 129–134.

American Psychiatric Association. (2000). *Diagnostic and statistical manual of mental disorders (4th ed., text revision)*. Washington, DC: Author.

Angold, A., & Costello, E. J. (2000). The Child and Adolescent Psychiatric Assessment (CAPA). *Journal of the American Academy of Child & Adolescent Psychiatry, 39*(1), 39–48.

Barrett, P. M. (1998). Evaluation of cognitive-behavioral group treatments for childhood anxiety disorders. *Journal of Clinical Child Psychology, 27*(4), 459–468.

Barrett, P. M., Dadds, M. R., & Rapee, R. M. (1996). Family treatment of childhood anxiety: A controlled trial. *Journal of Consulting & Clinical Psychology, 64*(2), 333–342.

Birmaher, B., Khetarpal, S., Brent, D., Cully, M., Balach, L., Kaufman, J., & Neer, S. M. (1997). The Screen for Child Anxiety Related Emotional Disorders (SCARED): Scale construction and psychometric characteristics. *Journal of the American Academy of Child & Adolescent Psychiatry, 36*(4), 545–553.

Carruth, S. G. (2000). Separation anxiety disorder: Planning treatment. *Pediatrics in Review, 21*(7), 248.

Cobham, V. E., Dadds, M. R., & Spence, S. H. (1998). The role of parental anxiety in the treatment of childhood anxiety. *Journal of Consulting & Clinical Psychology, 66*(6), 893–905.

Compton, S. N., Nelson, A. H., & March, J. S. (2000). Social phobia and separation anxiety symptoms in community and clinical samples of children and adolescents. *Journal of the American Academy of Child & Adolescent Psychiatry, 39*(8), 1040–1046.

Fischer, D. J., Himle, J. A., & Thyer, B. A. (1999). Separation anxiety disorder. In R. T. Ammerman, M. Hersen, & C. G. Last (Eds.), *Handbook of prescriptive treatments for children and adolescents* (2nd ed., pp. 141–154). Needham Heights, MA: Allyn & Bacon.

Flannery-Schroeder, E. C., & Kendall, P. C. (2000). Group and individual cognitive-behavioral treatments for youth with anxiety disorders: A randomized clinical trial. *Cognitive Therapy & Research, 24*(3), 251–278.

Francis, G., Last, C. G., & Strauss, C. C. (1987). Expression of separation anxiety disorder: The roles of age and gender. *Child Psychiatry & Human Development, 18*(2), 82–89.

Gittelman, R., & Klein, D. F. (1984). Relationship between separation anxiety and panic and agoraphobic disorders. *Psychopathology, 17*(Suppl. 1), 56–65.

Hagopian, L. P., & Slifer, K. J. (1993). Treatment of separation anxiety disorder with graduated exposure and reinforcement targeting school attendance: A controlled case study. *Journal of Anxiety Disorders, 7*(3), 271–280.

James, E. M., Reynolds, C. R., & Dunbar, J. (1994). Self-report instruments. In T. H. Ollendick, N. J. King, & W. Yule (Eds.), *International handbook of phobic and anxiety disorders in children and adolescents* (pp. 317–329). New York: Plenum.

Kearney, C. A., & Silverman, W. K. (1993). Measuring the function of school refusal behavior: The School Assessment Scale. *Journal of Clinical Child Psychology, 22*(1), 85–96.

Kearney, C. A., & Silverman, W. K. (1998). A critical review of pharmacotherapy for youth with anxiety disorders: Things are not as they seem. *Journal of Anxiety Disorders, 12*(2), 83–102.

Kendall, P. C. (1992). *Coping Cat workbook*. Ardmore, PA: Workbook Publishing.

Kendall, P. C. (1994). Treating anxiety disorders in children: Results of a randomized clinical trial. *Journal of Consulting & Clinical Psychology, 62*(1), 100–110.

Kendall, P. C. (2000a). *Cognitive-behavioral therapy for anxious children: Therapist manual* (2nd ed.). Ardmore, PA: Workbook Publishing.

Kendall, P. C. (2000b). Guiding theory for therapy with children and adolescents. In P. C. Kendall (Ed.), *Child and adolescent therapy: Cognitive-behavioral procedures* (2nd ed., pp. 3–27). New York: Guilford.

Kendall, P. C., Aschenbrand, S. G., & Hudson, J. L. (2003). Child-focused treatment of anxiety. In A. E. Kazdin & J. R. Weisz (Eds.), *Evidence-based psychotherapies for children and adolescents* (pp. 81–100). New York: Guilford.

Kendall, P. C., Choudhury, M., Hudson, J., & Webb, A. (2002a). *The C.A.T. project therapist manual.* Ardmore, PA: Workbook Publishing.

Kendall, P. C., Choudhury, M., Hudson, J., & Webb, A. (2002b). *The C.A.T. project workbook for the cognitive-behavioral treatment of anxious adolescents.* Ardmore, PA: Workbook Publishing.

Kendall, P. C., & Chu, B. C. (2000). Retrospective self-reports of therapist flexibility in a manual-based treatment for youths with anxiety disorders. *Journal of Clinical Child Psychology, 29*(2), 209–220.

Kendall, P. C., Flannery-Schroeder, E., Panichelli-Mindel, S. M., Southam-Gerow, M., Henin, A., & Warman, M. (1997). Therapy for youths with anxiety disorders: A second randomized clinical trial. *Journal of Consulting & Clinical Psychology, 65*(3), 366–380.

Kendall, P. C., & Gosch, E. A. (1994). Cognitive-behavioral interventions In T. H. Ollendick, N. J. King, & W. Yule (Eds.), *International handbook of phobic and anxiety disorders in children and adolescents* (pp. 415–438). New York: Plenum.

Kendall, P. C., Kane, M., Howard, B., & Siqueland, L. (1990). *Cognitive-behavioral treatment of anxious children: Treatment manual.* (Available from P. C. Kendall, Department of Psychology, Temple University, Philadelphia, PA 19122)

Kendall, P. C., & Southam-Gerow, M. A. (1995). Issues in the transportability of treatment: The case of anxiety disorders in youths. *Journal of Consulting & Clinical Psychology, 63*(5), 702–708.

Kendall, P. C., & Southam-Gerow, M. A. (1996). Long-term follow-up of a cognitive-behavioral therapy for anxiety-disordered youth. *Journal of Consulting & Clinical Psychology, 64*(4), 724–730.

Langley, A. K., Bergman, R. L., & Piacentini, J. C. (2002). Assessment of childhood anxiety. *International Review of Psychiatry, 14*(2), 102–113.

Last, C. G., Hersen, M., Kazdin, A. E., Finkelstein, R., & Strauss, C. C. (1987). Comparison of DSM-III separation anxiety and overanxious disorders: Demographic characteristics and patterns of comorbidity. *Journal of the American Academy of Child & Adolescent Psychiatry, 26*(4), 527–531.

March, J. S., Parker, J. D. A., Sullivan, K., Stallings, P., & Conners, C. K. (1997). The Multidimensional Anxiety Scale for Children (MASC): Factor structure, reliability, and validity. *Journal of the American Academy of Child & Adolescent Psychiatry, 36*(4), 554–565.

Mendlowitz, S. L., Manassis, K., Bradley, S., Scapillato, D., Miezitis, S., & Shaw, B. F. (1999). Cognitive-behavioral group treatments in childhood anxiety disorders: The role of parental involvement. *Journal of the American Academy of Child & Adolescent Psychiatry, 38*(10), 1223–1229.

Miller, S. J., & Binder, J. L. (2002). The effects of manual-based training on treatment fidelity and outcome: A review of the literature on adult individual psychotherapy. *Psychotherapy: Theory, Research, Practice, Training, 39*(2), 184–198.

Ollendick, T. H., Hagopian, L. P., & Huntzinger, R. M. (1991). Cognitive-behavior therapy with nighttime fearful children. *Journal of Behavior Therapy & Experimental Psychiatry, 22*(2), 113–121.

Perwien, A. R., & Berstein, G. A. (2004). Separation anxiety disorder. In T. H. Ollendick & J. S. March (Eds.), *Phobic and anxiety disorders in children and adolescents* (pp. 272–305). New York: Oxford University Press.

Reich, W. (2000). Diagnostic interview for children and adolescents (DICA). *Journal of the American Academy of Child & Adolescent Psychiatry, 39*(1), 59–66.

Saavedra, L. M., & Silverman, W. K. (2002). Classification of anxiety disorders in children: What a difference two decades make. *International Review of Psychiatry, 14*(2), 87–101.

Shaffer, D., Fisher, P., Lucas, C. P., Dulcan, M. K., & Schwab-Stone, M. E. (2000). NIMH diagnostic interview schedule for children version IV (NIMH DISC-IV): Description, differences from previous versions, and reliability of some common diagnoses. *Journal of the American Academy of Child & Adolescent Psychiatry, 39*(1), 28–38.

Silverman, W. K., & Dick-Niederhauser, A. (2004). Separation anxiety disorder. In T. L. Morris & J. S. March (Eds.), *Anxiety disorders in children and adolescents* (2nd ed., pp. 164–188). New York: Guilford.

Silverman, W. K., Kurtines, W. M., Ginsburg, G. S., Weems, C. F., Lumpkin, P. W., & Carmichael, D. H. (1999). Treating anxiety disorders in children with group cognitive-behavioral therapy: A randomized clinical trial. *Journal of Consulting & Clinical Psychology, 67*(6), 995–1003.

Silverman, W. K., & Nelles, W. B. (1988). The anxiety disorders interview schedule for children. *Journal of the American Academy of Child & Adolescent Psychiatry, 27*(6), 772–778.

Spence, S. H. (1997). A measure of anxiety symptoms among children. *Behaviour Research & Therapy, 36*(5), 545–566.

Thyer, B. A., & Sowers-Hoag, K. M. (1988). Behavior therapy for separation anxiety disorder. *Behavior Modification, 12*(2), 205–233.

Tonge, B. (1994). Separation anxiety disorder. In T. H. Ollendick, N. J. King, & W. Yule (Eds.), *International handbook of phobic and anxiety disorders in children and adolescents* (pp. 145–167). New York: Plenum.

Treadwell, K. R. H., Flannery-Schroeder, E. C., & Kendall, P. C. (1995). Ethnicity and gender in relation to adaptive functioning, diagnostic status, and treatment outcome in children from an anxiety clinic. *Journal of Anxiety Disorders, 9*(5), 373–384.

Velting, O. N., Setzer, N. J., & Albano, A. M. (2004). Update on and advances in assessment and cognitive-behavioral treatment of anxiety disorders in children and adolescents. *Professional Psychology: Research & Practice, 35*(1), 42–54.

Walkup, J. T., & Ginsburg, G. S. (2002). Anxiety disorders in children and adolescents. *International Review of Psychiatry, 14*(2), 85–86.

Walkup, J. T., Labellarte, M. J., & Ginsburg, G. S. (2002). The pharmacological treatment of childhood anxiety disorders. *International Review of Psychiatry, 14*(2), 135–142.

Weller, E. B., Weller, R. A., Fristad, M. A., Rooney, M. T., & Schecter, J. (2000). Children's interview for psychiatric syndromes (ChIPS). *Journal of the American Academy of Child & Adolescent Psychiatry, 39*(1), 76–84.

Chapter 5

Abramowitz, J. S. (1998). Does cognitive-behavioral therapy cure obsessive-compulsive disorder? A meta-analytic evaluation of clinical significance. *Behavior Therapy, 29*(2), 339–355.

Adams, G. B., Waas, G. A., March, J. S., & Smith, M. C. (1994). Obsessive-compulsive disorder in children and adolescents: The role of the school psychologist in identification, assessment, and treatment. *School Psychology Quarterly, 9*(4), 274–294.

Albano, A. M., & Kendall, P. C. (2002). Cognitive behavioural therapy for children and adolescents with anxiety disorders: Clinical research advances. *International Review of Psychiatry, 14*, 129–134.

American Academy of Child and Adolescent Psychiatry. (1998). Practice parameters for the assessment and treatment of children and adolescents with obsessive-compulsive disorder. *Journal of the American Academy of Child and Adolescent Psychiatry, 37*, 27S–45S.

American Psychiatric Association. (2000). *Diagnostic and statistical manual of mental disorders (4th ed., text revision)*. Washington, DC: Author.

Berg, C. Z., Whitaker, A., Davies, M., Flament, M. F., & Rapoport, J. L. (1988). The survey form of the Leyton Obsessional Inventory–child version: Norms from an epidemiological study. *Journal of the American Academy of Child and Adolescent Psychiatry, 27*(6), 759–763.

Clark, D. A. (2000). Cognitive behavior therapy for obsessions and compulsions: New applications and emerging trends. *Journal of Contemporary Psychotherapy, 30*(2), 129–147.

Foa, E. B., Franklin, M. E., & Kozak, M. J. (1998). Psychosocial treatments for obsessive-compulsive disorder. In R. P. Swinson, M. M. Antony, et al. (Eds.), *Obsessive-compulsive disorder: Theory, research, and treatment* (pp. 258–276). New York: Guilford.

Foster, P. S., & Eisler, R. M. (2001). An integrative approach to the treatment of obsessive-compulsive disorder. *Comprehensive Psychiatry, 42*(1), 24–31.

Franklin, M. E., Abramowitz, J. S., Bux, Jr., D. A., Zoellner, L. A., & Feeny, N. C. (2002). Cognitive-behavioral therapy with and without medication in the treatment of obsessive-compulsive disorder. *Professional Psychology, 33*(2), 162–168.

Franklin, M. E., Foa, E., & March, J. S. (2003). The pediatric obsessive-compulsive disorder treatment study: Rationale, design, and methods. *Journal of Child and Adolescent Psychopharmacology, 13*(1), S39–S51.

Franklin, M. E., Kozak, M. J., Cashman, L. A., Coles, M. E., Rheingold, A. A., & Foa, E. B. (1998). Cognitive-behavioral treatment of pediatric obsessive-compulsive disorder: An open clinical trial. *Journal of the American Academy of Child and Adolescent Psychiatry, 37*(4), 412–419.

Franklin, M. E., Rynn, M., Foa, E. B., & March, J. S. (2003). Treatment of obsessive-compulsive disorder. In M. A. Reinecke, M. F. Dattilio, et al. (Eds.), *Cognitive therapy with children and adolescents: A casebook for clinical practice* (2nd ed., pp. 162–184). New York: Guilford.

Geller, D. A., Biederman, J., Faraone, S., Agranat, A., Cradock, K., Hagermoser, L., Kim, G., Frazier, J., & Coffey, B. J. (2001). Developmental aspects of obsessive-compulsive disorder: Findings in children, adolescents, and adults. *Journal of Nervous and Mental Disease, 189*(7), 471–477.

Geller, D. A., Hoog, S. L., Heiligenstein, J. H., Ricardi, R. K., Tamura, R., Kluszynski, S., Jacobson, J. G., & Fluoxetine Pediatric OCD Study Team. (2001). Fluoxetine treatment for obsessive-compulsive disorder in children and adolescents: A placebo-controlled clinical trial. *Journal of the American Academy of Child and Adolescent Psychiatry, 40*(7), 773–779.

Goodman, W., Price, L., Rasmussen, S., Mazure, C., Delgado, P., Heninger, G. R., & Charney, D. S. (1989a). The Yale-Brown Obsessive Compulsive Scale: II. Validity. *Archives of General Psychiatry, 46*(11), 1012–1016.

Goodman, W., Price, L., Rasmussen, S., Mazure, C., Fleischmann, R. L., Hill, C. L., Heninger, G. R., & Charney, D. S. (1989b). The Yale-Brown Obsessive Compulsive Scale: I. Development, use, and reliability. *Archives of General Psychiatry, 46*(11), 1006–1011.

Kampman, M., Keijsers, G. P. J., Hoogduin, C. A. L., & Verbraak, M. J. P. M. (2002). Addition of cognitive-behaviour therapy for obsessive-compulsive disorder patients non-responding to fluoxetine. *Acta Psychiatrica Scandinavica, 106*, 314–319.

Kazdin, A. E., & Weisz, J. R. (1998). Identifying and developing empirically supported child and adolescent treatments. *Journal of Consulting & Clinical Psychology, 66*(1), 19–36.

Kendall, P. C., & Chu, B. C. (2000). Retrospective self-reports of therapist flexibility in a manual-based treatment for youth with anxiety disorders. *Journal of Clinical Child Psychology, 29*(2), 209–220.

March, J. S., Biederman, J., Wolkow, R., Safferman, A., Mardekian, J., Cook, E. H., Cutler, N. R., Dominguez, R., Ferguson, J., Muller, B., Riesenberg, R., Rosenthal, M., Sallee, F. R., & Wagner, K. D. (1998). Sertraline in children and adolescents with obsessive-compulsive disorder: A multicenter randomized controlled trial. *Journal of the American Medical Association, 280*(20), 1752–1757.

March, J., Frances, A., Kahn, D., & Carpenter, D. (1997). The expert consensus guidelines series: Treatment of obsessive-compulsive disorder. *Journal of Clinical Psychiatry, 58*(Suppl. 4), 1–72.

March, J. S., Franklin, M., Nelson, A., & Foa, E. (2001). Cognitive-behavioral psychotherapy for pediatric obsessive-compulsive disorder. *Journal of Clinical Child Psychology, 30*(1), 8–18.

March, J. S., & Mulle, K. (1998). *OCD in children and adolescents: A cognitive-behavioral treatment manual.* New York: Guilford.

March, J. S., Mulle, K., & Herbel, B. (1994). Behavioral psychotherapy for children and adolescents with obsessive-compulsive disorder: An open trial of a new protocol-driven treatment package. *Journal of the American Academy of Child & Adolescent Psychiatry, 33*(3), 333–341.

March, J. S., Parker, J.D.A., Sullivan, K., Stallings, P., & Conners, C. K. (1997). The Multidimensional Anxiety Scale for Children (MASC): Factor structure, reliability, and validity. *Journal of the American Academy of Child & Adolescent Psychiatry, 36*(4), 554–565.

Ollendick, T. H., & King, N. J. (1998). Empirically supported treatments for children with phobic and anxiety disorders: Current status. *Journal of Clinical Child Psychology, 27*(2), 156–167.

Piacentini, J., Bergman, L., Keller, M., & McCracken, J. (2003). Functional impairment in children and adolescents with obsessive-compulsive disorder. *Journal of Child and Adolescent Psychopharmacology, 13*(1), S61–S69.

Rowa, K., Antony, M. M., & Swinson, R. P. (2000). Behavioral treatment of obsessive-compulsive disorder. *Behavioural and Cognitive Psychotherapy, 28*, 353–360.

Silverman, W. K., & Nelles, W. B. (1988). The Anxiety Disorders Interview Schedule for Children. *Journal of the American Academy of Child & Adolescent Psychiatry, 27*(6), 772–778.

Southam-Gerow, M. A., & Kendall, P. C. (2000). Cognitive-behavioral therapy with youth: Advances, challenges, and future directions. *Clinical Psychology and Psychotherapy, 7*, 343–366.

Stanley, M. A., & Turner, S. M. (1995). Current status of pharmacological and behavioral treatment of obsessive-compulsive disorder. *Behavior Therapy, 26*(1), 163–186.

Thomsen, P. H. (1998). Obsessive-compulsive disorder in children and adolescent: Clinical guidelines. *European Child and Adolescent Psychiatry, 7*, 1–11.

Velting, O. N., Setzer, N. J., & Albano, A. M. (2004). Update on and advances in assessment and cognitive-behavioral treatment of anxiety disorders in children and adolescents. *Professional Psychology, 35*(1), 42–54.

Wagner, A. P. (2002). *What to do when your child has obsessive-compulsive disorder: Strategies and solutions.* Rochester, NY: Lighthouse Press.

Wagner, A. P. (2003a). Cognitive-behavioral therapy for children and adolescents with obsessive-compulsive disorder. *Brief Treatment and Crisis Intervention, 3*(3), 291–306.

Wagner, A. P. (2003b). *Treatment of OCD in children and adolescents: A cognitive-behavioral therapy manual.* Rochester, NY: Lighthouse Press.

Warren, R., & Thomas, J. C. (2001). Cognitive-behavior therapy of obsessive-compulsive disorder in private practice: An effectiveness study. *Anxiety Disorders, 15*, 277–285.

Chapter 6

Atkins, M. S., Graczyk, P. A., Frazier, S. L., & Abdul-Adil, J. (2003). Toward a new model for promoting urban children's mental health: accessible, effective, and sustainable school-based mental health services. *School Psychology Review, 35*, 525–529.

Beck, A. T., Brown, G., & Steer, R. A. (1996). *Beck Depression Inventory II manual.* San Antonio, TX: Psychological Corporation.

Birmaher, B., Ryan, N., Williamson, D., Brent, D., Kaufman, J., & Dahl, R. (1996). Childhood and adolescent depression: A review of the past 10 years, part I. *Journal of the American Academy of Child & Adolescent Psychiatry, 35*, 1427–1439.

Clarke, G., Hawkins, W., Murphy, M., Sheeber, L., Lewinsohn, P., & Seeley, J. (1995). Targeted prevention of unipolar depressive disorder in an at-risk sample of high school adolescents: A randomized trial of a group cognitive intervention. *Journal of the American Academy of Child and Adolescent Psychiatry, 34,* 312–321.

Clarke, G., Lewinsohn, P., & Hops, H. (1990). *The adolescent coping with depression course.* Available: http://www.kpchr.org/public/acwd/acwd.html.

Cohen, J. (1988). *Statistical power analysis for the behavioral sciences* (2nd ed.). Hillsdale, NJ: Earlbaum.

Cottrell, D., Fonagy, P., Kurtz, Z., Phillips, J., & Target, M. (2002). What works for whom? A critical review of treatments for children and adolescents. In P. Fonagy, M. Target, D. Cottrell, J. Phillips, & Z. Kurtz (Eds.), *Depressive disorders* (pp. 89–105). New York: Guilford.

Cuijpers, P. (1998). A psychoeducational approach to the treatment of depression: A meta-analysis of Lewinsohn's "Coping with Depression" course. *Behavior Therapy, 29,* 521–533.

Diamond, G. S., Reis, B. F., Diamond, G. M., Siqueland, L., & Isaacs, L. (2002). Attachment-based family therapy for depressed adolescents: A treatment development study. *Journal of the American Academy of Child and Adolescent Psychiatry, 41*(10), 1190–1197.

Hazell, P., O'Connell, D., Heathcote, D., & Henryk D. (2003). Tricyclic drugs for depression in children and adolescents (Cochrane Review). In *The Cochrane Library,* Issue 1. Oxford: Update Software.

Kaslow, N., & Thompson, M. (1998). Applying the criteria for empirically supported treatment to studies of psychosocial interventions for child and adolescent depression. *Journal of Clinical Child Psychology, 27,* 146–155.

Klein, D., Dougherty, L., & Olino, T. (2005). Toward guidelines for evidence-based assessment of depression in children and adolescents. *Journal of Clinical Child and Adolescent Psychology, 34,* 412–432.

Kovacs, M. (1992). *Children's Depression Inventory manual.* (Available from Multi-Health Systems, 908 Niagara Falls Blvd., North Tonawanda, NY 14120-2060; (800) 456-3003; www.mhs.com)

Lewinsohn, P., Clarke, G., Hops, H., & Andrews, J. (1990). Cognitive-behavioral treatment for depressed adolescents. *Behavior Therapy, 21,* 385–401.

Lewinsohn, P., Clarke, G., Rhode, P., Hops, H., & Seeley, J. (1996). A course in coping: A cognitive-behavioral approach to the treatment of adolescent depression. In E. D. Hibbs & P. S. Jensen (Eds.), *Psychosocial treatments for child and adolescent disorders: Empirically based strategies for clinical practice* (pp. 109–135). Washington, DC: American Psychological Association.

Lewinsohn, P., & Essau, C. (2002). Depression in adolescents. In I. H. Gotlib & C. Hammen (Eds.), *Handbook of depression* (pp. 541–559). New York: Guilford.

McCarthy, A.M., Kelly, M. W., & Reed, D. (2000). Medication administration practices of school nurses. *Journal of School Health, 70*(9), 371–376.

Mufson, L., & Moreau, D. (1997). Depressive disorders. In R. T. Ammerman & M. Hersen (Eds.), *Handbook of prevention and treatment with children and adolescents: Intervention in the real world context* (pp. 403–430). New York: John Wiley.

Myers, K., & Winters, N.C. (2002). Ten-year review of rating scales: II. Scales for internalizing disorders. *Journal of the American Academy of Child and Adolescent Psychiatry, 41,* 634–660.

Reinecke, M., Ryan, N., & Dubois, D. (1998). Cognitive-behavioral therapy of depression and depressive symptoms during adolescence: A review and meta-analysis. *Journal of the American Academy of Child and Adolescent Psychiatry, 37,* 26–34.

Reynolds, W. (1987). *Reynolds Adolescent Depression Scale (RADS).* Odessa, FL: Psychological Assessment Resources.

Satcher, D. (2004). School-based mental health services (policy statement). *Pediatrics, 113,* 1839–1845.

Stark, K., Reynolds, W., & Kaslow, N. (1987). A comparison of the relative efficacy of self-control therapy and a behavioral problem-solving therapy for depression in children. *Journal of Abnormal Child Psychology, 15,* 91–113.

Stark, K., Rouse, L., & Livingston, R. (1991). Treatment of depression during childhood and adolescence: Cognitive-behavioral procedures for the individual and family. In P. Kendall (Ed.), *Child and adolescent therapy* (pp. 165–206). New York: Guilford.

Treatment for Adolescents With Depression Study Team. (2004). Fluoxetine, cognitive-behavioral therapy, and their combination for adolescents with depression: Treatment for adolescents with depression study (tads) randomized controlled trial. *Journal of the American Medical Association, 292,* 807–820.

Waslick, B. D., Kandel, B. A., & Kakouros, B. S. (2002). Depression in children and adolescents: An overview. In D. Shaffer & B. D. Waslick (Eds.), *The many faces of depression in children and adolescents* (pp. 1–36). Washington, DC: American Psychiatric Association Publishing.

Chapter 7

American Academy of Child and Adolescent Psychiatry. (1997). Practice parameters for the assessment and treatment of children and adolescents with bipolar disorder. *Journal of the American Academy of Child and Adolescent Psychiatry, 36*(1), 138–157.

American Psychiatric Association. (1994). *Diagnostic and statistical manual of mental disorders (4th ed.).* Washington, DC: Author.

Anglada, T. (2002). *The student with bipolar disorder: An educator's guide.* Murdock, FL: Child and Adolescent Bipolar Foundation.

Badner, J. (2003). The genetics of bipolar disorder. In B. Geller & M. DelBello (Eds.), *Bipolar disorder in childhood and early adolescence* (pp. 247–254). New York: Guilford.

Biederman, J., Mick, E., Faraone, S., Spencer, T., Wilens, T., & Wozniak, J. (2000). Pediatric mania: A developmental subtype of bipolar disorder? *Biological Psychiatry, 48,* 458–466.

Carlson, G., Bromet, E., & Sievers, S. (2000). Phenomenology and outcomes of subjects with early and adult-onset psychotic mania. *American Journal of Psychiatry, 157,* 213–219.

Craddock, N., & Jones, I. (1999). Genetics of bipolar disorder. *Journal of Medical Genetics, 36*(8), 585–594.

DelBello, M., & Kowatch, R. (2003). Neuroimaging in pediatric bipolar disorder. In B. Geller & M. DelBello (Eds.), *Bipolar disorder in childhood and early adolescence* (pp. 158–174). New York: Guilford.

DelBello, M., Schwiers, M., Rosenberg, H., & Strakowski, S. (2002). A double-blind, randomized, placebo-controlled study of quetiapine adjunctive treatment for adolescent mania. *Journal of the American Academy of Child and Adolescent Psychiatry, 41*(10), 1216–1223.

Findling, R., Gracious, B., & McNamara, N. (2001). Rapid, continuous cycling and psychiatric comorbidity in pediatric bipolar I disorder. *Bipolar Disorder, 3*, 202–210.

Findling, R., Kowatch, R., & Post, R. (2003). *Pediatric bipolar disorder: A handbook for clinicians.* London: Cromwell.

Fristad, M., & Goldberg Arnold, J. (2003). Family interventions for early onset bipolar disorder. In B. Geller & M. DelBello (Eds.), *Bipolar disorder in childhood and early adolescence* (pp. 295–313). New York: Guilford.

Fristad, M., & Goldberg Arnold, J. (2004). *Raising a moody child: How to cope with depression and bipolar disorder.* New York: Guilford.

Geller, B., Bolhofner, K., Craney, J., Williams, M., DelBello, M., & Gunderson, K. (2000). Psychosocial functioning in prepubertal and early adolescent bipolar disorder phenotype. *Journal of the American Academy of Child and Adolescent Psychiatry, 39*(12), 1486–1493.

Geller, B., Craney, J., Bolhofner, K., DelBello, M., Axelson, D., & Luby, J. (2003). Phenomenology and longitudinal course of children with a prepubertal and early adolescent phenotype. In B. Geller & M. DelBello (Eds.), *Bipolar disorder in childhood and early adolescence* (pp. 25–50). New York: Guilford.

Geller, B., Williams, M., Zimmerman, B., Frazier, J., Beringer, L., & Warner, K. (1998). Prepubertal and early adolescent bipolarity differentiate from ADHD by manic symptoms, grandiose delusion, ultra-rapid or ultradian cycling. *Journal of Affective Disorders, 51*, 81–91.

Geller, B., Zimmerman, B., Williams, M., DelBello, M., Frazier, J., & Beringer, L. (2002). Phenomenology of prepubertal and early adolescent bipolar disorder: Examples of elated mood, grandiose behaviors, decreased need for sleep, racing thoughts and hypersexuality. *Journal of Child and Adolescent Psychopharmacology, 12*(1), 3–9.

Johnson, S., & Miller, I. (1997). Negative life events and time to recovery from episodes of bipolar disorder. *Journal of Abnormal Psychology, 106*(3), 449–457.

Kafantaris, V., Coletti, D., Dicker, R., Padula, G., & Kane, J. (2003). Lithium treatment of acute mania in adolescents: A large open trial. *Journal of the Academy of Child and Adolescent Psychiatry, 42*, 1038–1045.

Keck, P., & McElroy, S. (2002). Pharmacological treatments for bipolar disorder. In J. Nathan & J. Gorman (Eds.), *A guide to treatments that work* (2nd ed., pp. 277–299). Oxford: Oxford University Press.

Kinscherff, R. (1999). Empirically supported treatments: What to do until the data arrive (or now that they have)? *Clinical Child Psychology Newsletter, 14*, 4–6.

Kowatch, R., Sethuraman, G., Hume, J., Kromelis, M., & Weinberg, W. (2003). Combination pharmacotherapy in children and adolescents with bipolar disorder. *Biological Psychiatry, 53*(11), 978–984.

Leibenluft, E., Charney, D., Towbin, K., Bhangoo, R., & Pine, D. (2003). Defining clinical phenotypes of juvenile mania. *American Journal of Psychology, 160*(3), 430–437.

Lewinsohn, P., Klein, D., & Seeley, J. (2000). Bipolar disorder during adolescence and young childhood in a community sample. *Bipolar Disorders, 2*, 281–293.

Lewinsohn, P., Klein, J., & Klein, D. (1995). Bipolar disorder in a community sample of older adolescents: Prevalence, co-morbidity, and course. *Journal of the American Academy of Child and Adolescent Psychiatry, 34,* 454–463.

Lofthouse, N., & Fristad, M. (2004). Psychosocial interventions for children with early onset bipolar spectrum disorder. *Clinical Child and Family Psychological Review, 7*(2), 71–88.

Malkoff-Schwartz, S., Frank, E., Anderson, B., Sherill, J., Siegel, L., & Patterson, D. (1998). Stressful life events and social rhythm disruption in the onset of mania and depressive bipolar episodes. *Archives of General Psychiatry, 55*(8), 702–707.

McClure, E., Kubiszyn, T., & Kaslow, N. (2002). Advances in the diagnosis and treatment of childhood mood disorders. *Professional Psychology: Research and Practice, 23*(2), 125–134.

Miklowitz, D., & Goldstein, M. (1997). *Bipolar disorder: A family focused approach.* New York: Guilford Press.

National Institute of Mental Health. (2001). National Institute of Mental Health roundtable on prepubertal bipolar disorder. *Journal of the American Academy of Child and Adolescent Psychiatry, 40*(8), 871–878.

Oldroyd, J. (1997). Paroxetine-induced mania. *Journal of the American Academy of Child and Adolescent Psychiatry, 36*(6), 721–722.

Ollendick, T. (2003) Advances towards evidence-based practice with children and adolescents. *Clinical Child and Adolescent Psychology Newsletter, 18*(1), 1–3.

Pavuluri, M., Naylor, M., & Janicak, P. (2002). Recognition and treatment of pediatric bipolar disorder. *Contemporary Psychiatry, 1*(1), 1–10.

Rivas-Vasquez, R., Johnson, S., Rey, G., & Blais, M. (2002). Current treatments for bipolar disorder: A review and update for psychologists. *Professional Psychology: Research and Practice, 33*(2), 212–223.

Simmoneau, T., Miklowitz, D., & Saleem, R. (1998). Expressed emotion and interactional patterns in the family of bipolar patients. *Journal of Abnormal Psychology, 107*(3), 497–507.

Wozniak, J., Biederman, J., Kiely, K., Ablon, J., Faraone, S., & Mundy, E. (1995). Mania-like symptoms suggestive of childhood-onset bipolar disorder in clinically referred children. *Journal of the American Academy of Child and Adolescent Psychiatry, 34*(7), 867–876.

Chapter 8

Cantor, S., & Kestenbaum, C. (1986). Psychotherapy with schizophrenic children. *Journal of the American Academy of Child and Adolescent Psychiatry, 25,* 623–630.

Caplan, R. (1994). Thought disorder in childhood. *Journal of the Academy of Child and Adolescent Psychiatry, 33,* 605–615.

Frazier J., Gordon C., McKenna, K., et al. (1994). An open trial of clozapine in 11 adolescents with childhood-onset schizophrenia. *Journal of the American Adolescent Psychiatry, 33*(5), 658–663.

Gage, A. (2003). Atypical antipsychotics in children and adolescents. *Case Management, 9*(1).

Kaplan, H., Sadock, B., & Grebb, J. (1994). *Kaplan and Sadock's synopsis of psychiatry* (7th ed.). Baltimore, MD: Williams and Wilkins.

Kumra S., Frazier, J., Jacobsen L., et al. (1996). Childhood-onset schizophrenia: A double-blind clozapine-haloperidol comparison. *Archives of General Psychiatry, 53*(12), 1090–1097.

Lewis, M. (2002). *Child and adolescent psychiatry: A comprehensive textbook* (3rd ed.). Hagerstown, MD: Lippincott/Williams and Wilkins.

McClellan, J., McCurry, C., Snell, J., & DuBose, A. (1999). Early onset psychotic disorders: Course and outcome over a 2-year period. *Journal of the American Academy of Child and Adolescent Psychiatry, 38*(11), 1380–1388.

National Institute of Mental Health. (2003). *Childhood-onset schizophrenia: An update from the National Institute of Mental Health.* Bethesda, MD: Author.

Policy Leadership Cadre for Mental Health in Schools. (2001). *Mental health in schools: Guidelines, models, resources and policy considerations.* Los Angeles: University of California, Center for Mental Health in Schools.

Remschmidt, H., Schulz, E., & Martin, P. (1994). An open trial of clozapine in thirty-six adolescents with schizophrenia. *Journal of Child and Adolescent Psychopharmacology, 4*(1), 31–41.

Schur, S., Sikich, L., Findling, R., Malone, R., Crismon, M., Derivan, A., Macintyre, I., Pappadopulos, E., Greenhill, L., Schooler, N., Van Orden, K., & Jensen, P. (2003). *Treatment recommendations for the use of antipsychotics for aggressive youth (TRAAY), part I: A review.* New York: Center for the Advancement of Children's Mental Health, Columbia University/ New York State Psychiatric Institute.

Turetz, M., Mozes, T., Toren, P., et al. (1997). An open trial of clozapine in neuroleptic resistant childhood-onset schizophrenia. *British Journal of Psychiatry, 170,* 507–510.

Volkmar, F. (1996). Childhood and adolescent psychosis: A review of the past 10 years. *Journal of the American Academy of Child and Adolescent Psychiatry, 35*(7), 843–851.

Werry, J. S. (1992). Child and early adolescent schizophrenia: A review in light of the DSM III-R. *Journal of Autism Developmental Disorder, 22,* 610–614.

Chapter 9

Aman, M. G., Collier-Crespin, A., & Lindsay, R. L. (2000). Pharmacotherapy of disorders in mental retardation. *European Child and Adolescent Psychiatry, 9,* 98–107.

American Psychiatric Association. (2000). *Diagnostic and statistical manual of mental disorders (4th ed., text revision).* Washington, DC: Author.

Anderson, S. R., & Romanczyk, R. G. (1999). Early intervention for young children with autism: Continuum-based behavioral models. *Journal of the Association for Persons With Severe Handicaps, 24*(3), 162–173.

Anderson, S. R., Taras, M., & Cannon, B. O. (1996). Teaching new skills to young children with autism. In C. Maurice, G. Green, & S. C. Luce (Eds.), *Behavioral intervention for young children with autism: A manual for parents and professionals* (pp. 181–194). Austin, TX: Pro-Ed.

Arick, J. R., Krug, D. A., Fullerton, A., Loos, L., & Falco, R. (2005). School-based programs. In D. J. Cohen & F. R. Volkmar (Eds.), *Handbook of autism and pervasive developmental disorders*: Vol. 2, *Assessment, interventions, and policy* (3rd ed., 1003–1028). New York: Wiley.

Baer, D., Wolf, M., & Risley, R. (1968). Some current dimensions of applied behavior analysis. *Journal of Applied Behavior Analysis, 1,* 91–97.

Baker, L. J., & Welkowitz, L. A. (Eds.). (2005). *Asperger's syndrome: Intervening in schools, clinics and communities.* Mahwah, NJ: Earlbaum.

Bregman, J. (2005). Definitions and characteristics of the spectrum. In D. Zager (Ed.), *Autism spectrum disorders: Identification, education and treatment* (3rd ed., pp. 3–46). Mahwah, NJ: Erlbaum.

Bregman, J., Zager, D., & Gerdtz, J. (2005). Behavioral interventions. In F. R. Volkmar, R. Paul, A. Klin, & D. Cohen (Eds.), *Handbook of autism and pervasive developmental disorders: Vol. 2. Assessment, interventions and policy* (3rd ed., pp. 897–924). Hoboken, NJ: Wiley.

Bryson, S., & Smith, I. M. (1998). Epidemiology of autism: Prevalence, associated characteristics, and implications for research and service delivery. *Mental Retardation and Developmental Disabilities Research Reviews, 4*(2), 97–103.

Campbell, J. M. (2005). Diagnostic assessment of Asperger's disorder: A review of five third-party rating scales. *Journal of Autism and Developmental Disorders, 35*(1), 25–35.

Charman, T., & Baird, G. (2002). Practitioner review: Diagnosis of autism spectrum disorder in 2- and 3-year-old children. *Journal of Child Psychology and Psychiatry and Allied Disciplines, 43*(3), 289–305.

Chez, M. G., Buchanan, T., Becker, M., Kessler, J., Aimonovitch, M. C., & Mrazek, S. R. (2003). Donepezil hydrochloride: A double-blind study in autistic children. *Journal of Pediatric Neurology, 1*(2), 83–88.

Constantino, J. N. (2002). *The social-responsiveness scale.* Los Angeles: Western Psychological Services.

Cooper, J. O., Heron, T., & Heward, W. (1987). *Applied behavior analysis.* Columbus, OH: Merrill.

Courchesne, E. (2002). Abnormal early brain development in autism. *Molecular Psychiatry, 7*(Suppl. 2), S21–23.

Cummings, A. R., & Williams, W. L. (2000). Visual identity matching and vocal imitation training with children with autism: A surprising finding. *Journal on Developmental Disabilities, 7*(2), 109–122.

Dawson, G., & Osterling, J. (1997). Early intervention in autism. In M. Guralnick (Ed.), *The effectiveness of early intervention* (pp. 307–326). Baltimore: Brookes.

Delquadri, J. C., Greenwood, C. R., Stretton, K., & Hall, R. V. (1983). The peer tutoring spelling game: A classroom procedure for increasing opportunity to respond and spelling performance. *Education and Treatment of Children, 6*(3), 225–239.

DuCharme, R. W., & McGrady, K. A. (2003). What is Asperger syndrome? In R. W. DuCharme & T. P. Gullotta (Eds.), *Asperger syndrome: A guide for professionals and families* (pp. 1–20). New York: Kluwer Academic/Plenum.

Dunlap, G. (1984). The influence of task variation and maintenance tasks on the learning and affect of autistic children. *Journal of Experimental Child Psychology, 31,* 41–64.

Ehlers, S., Gillberg, C., & Wing, L. (1999). A screening questionnaire for Asperger syndrome and other high-functioning autism spectrum disorders in school-age children. *Journal of Autism and Developmental Disabilities, 29*(2), 129–141.

Filipek, P. A., Accardo, P. J., Ashwal, S., Baranek, G. T., Cook, E. H., Dawson G., et al. (2000). Practice parameter: Screening and diagnosis of autism. *Neurology, 55,* 468–479.

Filipek, P. A., Accardo, P. J., Baranek, G. T., Cook, E. H., Jr., Dawson, G., Gordon B., et al. (1999). The screening and diagnosis of autism spectrum disorders. *Journal of Autism and Developmental Disorders, 29*(6), 439–484.

Fombonne, E. (1999). The epidemiology of autism: A review. *Psychological Medicine, 29*, 769–786.

Fombonne, E. (2005). Epidemiological studies of pervasive developmental disorders. In F. R. Volkmar, R. Paul, A. Klin, & D. Cohen (Eds.), *Handbook of autism and pervasive developmental disorders: Vol. 1. Diagnosis, development, neurobiology and behavior* (3rd ed., pp. 42–69). Hoboken, NJ: Wiley.

Fombonne, E., Du Mazaubrun, C., Cans, C., & Grandjean, H. (1997). Autism and associated medical disorders in a French survey. *Journal of the American Academy of Child and Adolescent Psychiatry, 36*(11), 1561–1569.

Fombonne, E., Simmons, H., Ford, T., Meltzer, H., & Goodman, R. (2001). Prevalence of pervasive developmental disorders in the British Nationwide Survey of Child Mental Health. *Journal of the American Academy of Child and Adolescent Psychiatry, 40*(7), 820–827.

Ghaziuddin, M., Tsai, L., & Ghaziuddin, N. (1992). Brief report: A comparison of the diagnostic criteria for Asperger's syndrome. *Journal of Autism and Developmental Disorders, 22*(4), 643–649.

Goldstein, H. (2002). Communication intervention for children with autism: A review of treatment efficacy. *Journal of Autism and Developmental Disorders, 35*(2), 373–396.

Green, G. (1996). Early behavioral intervention for autism: What does research tell us? In C. Maurice, G. Green, & S. C. Luce (Eds.), *Behavioral intervention for young children with autism* (pp. 29–44). Austin, TX: Pro-Ed.

Gresham, F. M., Beebe-Frankenberger, M. E., & MacMillan, D. L. (1999). A selective review of treatments for children with autism: Description and methodological considerations. *School Psychology Review, 28*(4), 559–575.

Harris, S. L., & Handleman, J. S. (1994). *Preschool education programs for children with autism.* Austin, TX: Pro-Ed.

Harris, S. L., Handleman, J. S., Gordon, R., Kristoff, B., & Fuentes, F. (1991). Changes in cognitive and language functioning of preschool children with autism. *Journal of Autism and Developmental Disorders, 21*, 281–290.

Hollander, E., & Nowinski, C. V. (2003). Core symptoms, related disorders and course of autism. In E. Hollander (Ed.), *Autism spectrum disorders* (pp. 15–38). New York: Dekker.

Hollander, E., Phillips, A., Chaplin, W., Zagursky, K., Novotny, S., Wasserman, S., et al. (2005). A placebo controlled crossover trial of liquid fluoxetine on repetitive behaviors in childhood and adolescent autism. *Neuropsychopharmacology, 30*(3), 582–589.

Howlin, P. (1998). *Children with autism and Asperger syndrome: A guide for practitioners and carers.* Chichester, UK: Wiley.

Idol, L. (1988). A rationale and guidelines for establishing special education consultation programs. *Remedial and Special Education, 9*(6), 48–58.

Idol, L., Paolucci-Whitcomb, P., & Nevin, A. (1986). *Collaboration consultation.* Austin, TX: Pro-Ed.

Jacobson, J. W., Foxx, R. M., & Mulick, J. A. (Eds.). (2005). *Controversial therapies for developmental disabilities: Fad, fashion and science in professional practice.* Mahwah, NJ: Erlbaum.

Jacobson, J. W., Mulick, J. A., & Green, G. (1998). Cost-benefit estimates for early intensive behavioral intervention for young children with autism: General model and single state case. *Behavioral Interventions, 13,* 201–206.

King, B. H., Wright, D. M., Handen, B. L., Sikich, L., Zimmerman, A., McMahon, W., et al. (2001). Double-blind, placebo-controlled study of amantadine hydrochloride in the treatment of children with autistic disorder. *Journal of the American Academy of Child and Adolescent Psychiatry, 40*(6), 658–665.

Klin, A., McPartland, J., & Volkmar, F. R. (2005). Asperger syndrome. In F. R. Volkmar, R. Paul, A. Klin, & D. Cohen (Eds.), *Handbook of autism and pervasive developmental disorders: Vol. 1. Diagnosis, development, neurobiology and behavior* (3rd ed., pp. 88–125). Hoboken, NJ: Wiley.

Klin, A., & Volkmar, F. R. (1997). The pervasive developmental disorders: Nosology and profiles of development. In S. Luthar, J. Burack, D. Cicchetti, & J. Weisz (Eds.), *Developmental psychopathology: Perspectives on adjustment, risk, and disorder* (pp. 208–226). New York: Cambridge University Press.

Koegel, L. K., Koegel, R. L., Harrower, J. K., & Carter, C. M. (1999). Pivotal response intervention I: Overview of approach. *Journal of the Association for Persons With Severe Handicaps, 24*(3), 174–185.

Koegel, L. K., Koegel, R. L., Shoshan, Y., & McNerney, E. (1999). Pivotal response intervention II: Preliminary long-term outcome data. *Journal of the Association for Persons with Severe Handicaps, 24*(3), 186–198.

Koegel, R. L., O'Dell, M., & Dunlap, G. (1988). Producing speech use in nonverbal autistic children by reinforcing attempts. *Journal of Autism and Developmental Disorders, 18,* 525–538.

Koegel, R. L., & Frea, W. D. (1993). Treatment of social behavior in autism through the modification of pivotal social skills. *Journal of Applied Behavior Analysis, 26*(3), 369–377.

Koegel, R. L., & Koegel, L. K. (Eds.). (1995). *Teaching children with autism: Strategies for initiating positive interactions and improving learning opportunities.* Baltimore: Brookes.

Koegel, R. L., Schreffirnan, L., Good, A., Cerniglia, L., Murphy, C., & Koegel, L. K. (n.d.). *How to teach pivotal behaviors to children with autism: A training manual.* Available: http://www.users.qwest.net/~tbharris/prt. htm.

Koegel, R. L., & Williams, J. A. (1980). Direct versus indirect response-reinforcer relationships in teaching autistic children. *Journal of Abnormal Child Psychology, 8,* 537–547.

Krug, D. A., & Arick, J. R. (2003). *Krug Asperger's Disorder Index.* Austin, TX: Pro-Ed.

Leekam, S. R., Libby, S. J., Wing, L., Gould, J., & Gillberg, C. (2000). Comparison of ICD-10 and Gillberg's criteria for Asperger syndrome. *Autism, 4*(1), 11–28.

Lord, C., & Cosello, C. (2005). Diagnostic instruments in autistic spectrum disorders. In F. R. Volkmar, R. Paul, A. Klin, & D. Cohen (Eds.), *Handbook of autism and pervasive developmental disorders: Vol. 2. Assessment, interventions and policy* (3rd ed., pp. 730–771). Hoboken, NJ: Wiley.

Lord, C., & Paul, R. (1997). Language and communication in autism. In D. J. Cohen & F. R. Volkmar (Eds.), *Handbook of autism and pervasive developmental disorders* (2nd ed., pp. 460–483). New York: Wiley.

Lord, C., Rutter, M. L., DiLavore, P. C., & Risi, S. (1999). *Autism Diagnostic Observation Schedule-WPS* (WPS ed.). Los Angeles: Western Psychological Services.

Lord, C., Rutter, M. L., & Le Couteur, A. (1994). The Autism Diagnostic Interview-Revised: A revised version of the diagnostic interview for caregivers of individuals with possible pervasive developmental disorders. *Journal of Autism and Developmental Disorders, 24*(5), 659–685.

Lovaas, O. (1993). The development of a treatment-research project for developmentally disabled and autistic children. *Journal of Applied Behavior Analysis, 26*(4), 617–630.

Lovaas, O. I. (1981). *Teaching developmentally disabled children: The me book.* Austin, TX: Pro-Ed.

Lovaas, O. I. (1987). Behavioral treatment and normal educational and intellectual functioning in young autistic children. *Journal of Consulting and Clinical Psychology, 55,* 3–9.

Lovaas, O. I., & Smith, T. (1989). A comprehensive behavioral theory of autistic children: Paradigm for research and treatment. *Journal of Behavior Therapy and Experimental Psychology, 20,* 17–29.

Loveland, K. A., & Tunali-Kotoski, B. (2005). The school-age child with an autistic spectrum disorder. In F. R. Volkmar, R. Paul, A. Klin, & D. Cohen (Eds.), *Handbook of autism and pervasive developmental disorders: Vol. I. Diagnosis, development, neurobiology and behavior* (3rd ed., pp. 247–287). Hoboken, NJ: Wiley.

Martin, A., Scahill, L., Klin, A., & Volkmar, F. R. (1999). Higher functioning pervasive developmental disorders: Rates and patterns of psychotropic drug use. *Journal of the American Academy of Child and Adolescent Psychiatry, 38*(7), 923–931.

Matson, J. L., Benavidez, D. A., Compton, L. S., Paclawskyj, T., & Baglio, C. (1996). Behavioral treatment of autistic persons: A review of research from 1980 to the present. *Research in Developmental Disabilities, 17,* 433–465.

Maurice, C., Green, G., & Luce, S. C. (Eds.). (1996). *Behavioral intervention for young children with autism: A manual for parents and professionals.* Austin, TX: Pro-Ed.

McCarton, C. (2003). Assessment and diagnosis of pervasive developmental disorder. In E. Hollander (Ed.), *Autism spectrum disorders* (pp. 101–132). New York: Dekker.

McClannahan, L. E., & Krantz, P. J. (2004). Selecting behavioral intervention programs for children with autism. In H. E. Briggs & T. L. Rzepnicki (Eds.), *Using evidence in social work practice: Behavioral perspectives.* Chicago: Lyceum.

McDougle, C. J., Scahill, L., McCracken, J. T., Aman, M. G., Tierney, E., Arnold, L. E., et al. (2000). Research units on pediatric psychopharmacology (RUPP) autism network: Background and rationale for an initial controlled study of risperidone. *Child and Adolescent Psychiatric Clinics of North America, 9,* 201–224.

McEachin, J. J., Smith, T., & Lovaas, O. I. (1993). Long-term outcome for children with autism who received early intensive behavioral treatment. *American Journal of Mental Retardation, 4,* 359–372.

Miranda-Linne, F., & Melin, L. (1992). Acquisition, generalization and spontaneous use of color adjectives: A comparison of incidental teaching and traditional discrete-trial procedures for children with autism. *Research in Developmental Disabilities, 13,* 191–210.

National Research Council. (2001). *Educating children with autism.* Washington, DC: National Academy Press.

Newsome, C. B. (1998). Autistic disorder. In E. J. Mash & R. A. Barkley (Eds.), *Treatment of childhood disorders* (2nd ed., pp. 416–467). New York: Guilford.

New York State Department of Health, Early Intervention Program. (1999a). *Clinical practice guideline: Guideline technical report: Autism/pervasive developmental disorders, assessment and intervention for young children (ages 0–3 years)* (No. 4217). Albany, NY: Author.

New York State Department of Health, Early Intervention Program. (1999b). *Clinical practice guideline: Report of the recommendations: Autism/PDD, assessment and intervention in young children (age 0–3 years)* (No. 4215). Albany, NY: Author.

Odom, S. L., Brown, W. H., Frey, T., Karasu, N., Smith-Canter, L. L., & Strain, P. S. (2003). Evidence-based practices for young children with autism: Contributions for single-subject design research. *Focus on Autism and Other Developmental Disabilities, 18*(3), 166–175.

Paul, R., & Sutherland, D. (2005). Enhancing early language in children with autism spectrum disorders. In F. R. Volkmar, R. Paul, A. Klin, & D. Cohen (Eds.), *Handbook of autism and pervasive developmental disorders: Vol. 2. Assessment, interventions and policy* (3rd ed., pp. 946–976). Hoboken, NJ: Wiley.

Prizant, B. M., & Wetherby, A. (1998). Understanding the continuum of discrete-trial traditional behavioral to social-pragmatic developmental approaches in communication enhancement for young children with autism/PDD. *Seminars in Speech and Language, 19,* 329–353.

Pryor, C. B., Kent, C., McGunn, C., & LeRoy, B. (1996). Redesigning social work in inclusive schools. *Social Work, 41,* 668–676.

Research Units on Pediatric Psychopharmacology Autism Network. (2002). Risperidone in children with autism and serious behavioral problems. *New England Journal of Medicine, 347,* 314–321.

Robins, D. L., Fein, D., Barton, M. L., & Green, J. A. (2001). The Modified Checklist for Autism in Toddlers: An initial study investigating the early detection of autism and pervasive developmental disorders. *Journal of Autism and Developmental Disorders, 31*(2), 131–145.

Rogers, S. (1998). Empirically supported comprehensive treatments for young children with autism. *Journal of Clinical Child Psychology, 27,* 168–179.

Sackett, D. L., Straus, S. E., Richardson, W. C., Rosenberg, W., & Haynes, R. M. (2000). *Evidence-based medicine: How to practice and teach EBM* (2nd ed.). New York: Churchill Livingstone.

Safran, S. P. (2005). Diagnosis. In L. J. Baker & L. A. Welkowitz (Eds.), *Asperger's syndrome: Intervening in schools, clinics and communities* (pp. 43–61). Mahwah, NJ: Erlbaum.

Scahill, L., & Martin, A. (2005). Psychopharmacology. In F. R. Volkmar, R. Paul, A. Klin, & D. Cohen (Eds.), *Handbook of autism and pervasive developmental disorders: Vol. 2. Assessment, interventions and policy* (3rd ed., pp. 1102–1117). Hoboken, NJ: Wiley.

Schopler, E., Reichler, R. J., & Renner, B. R. (1986). *The Childhood Autism Rating Scale (CARS) for diagnostic screening and classification of autism.* New York: Irvington.

Schreibman, L., Charlop, M. H., & Milstein, J. P. (1993). Autism: Behavioral treatment. In V. P. VanHasselt & M. Hersen (Eds.), *Handbook of behavior therapy and pharmacotherapy of children: A comparative analysis* (pp. 149–170). Needham Heights, MA: Allyn & Bacon.

Schreibman, L., Kaneko, W. M., & Koegel, R. L. (1991). Positive affect of parents of autistic children: Comparison across two teaching techniques. *Behavior Therapy, 22*, 479–490.

Scott, J., Clark, C., & Brady, M. P. (2000). *Students with autism: Characteristics and instructional programming for special educators.* San Diego, CA: Singular.

Shea, S., Turgay, A., Carroll, A., Schulz, M., Orlik, H., Smith, I., et al. (2004). Risperidone in the treatment of disruptive behavioral symptoms in children with autistic and other pervasive developmental disorders. *Pediatrics, 114*(5), 634–641.

Simpson, R. L., de Boer-Ott, S. R., Griswold, D. E., Myles, B. S., Byrd, S. E., Ganz, J. B., et al. (2004). *Autism spectrum disorders: Interventions and treatments for children and youth.* Thousand Oaks, CA: Corwin.

Smith, T. (1996). Are other treatments effective? In C. Maurice, G. Green, & S. C. Luce (Eds.), *Behavioral intervention for young children with autism* (pp. 45–59). Austin, TX: Pro-Ed.

Smith, T. (2001). Discrete trial training in the treatment of autism. *Focus on Autism and Other Developmental Disabilities, 16*(2), 86–92.

Smith, T., Groen, A. D., & Wynn, J. W. (2000). Randomized trial of intensive early intervention for children with pervasive developmental disorder. *American Journal on Mental Retardation, 105*(4), 269–285.

Stahmer, A. C. (1995). Teaching symbolic play skills to children with autism using pivotal response training. *Journal of Autism and Developmental Disorders, 25*, 123–141.

Stahmer, A. C. (1999). Using pivotal response training to facilitate appropriate play in children with autistic spectrum disorders. *Child Language Teaching and Therapy, 15*(1), 29–40.

Stahmer, A. C., Ingersoll, B., & Carter, C. (2003). Behavioral approaches to promoting play. *Autism, 7*(4), 401–413.

Stone, W. L., Coonrod, E. E., & Ousley, O. Y. (2000). Brief report: Screening tool for autism in two-year-olds (STAT): Development and preliminary data. *Journal of Autism and Developmental Disorders, 30*(6), 607–612.

Stone, W. L., Coonrod, E. E., Turner, L. M., & Pozdol, S. L. (2004). Psychometric properties of the STAT for early autism screening. *Journal of Autism and Developmental Disorders, 34*(6), 691–701.

Strock, M. (2004). *Autism spectrum disorders (pervasive developmental disorders)* (NIH Publication No. 04–5511, pp. 1–40). Bethesda, MD: U.S. Department of Health and Human Services.

Sulzer-Azaroff, B., & Mayer, R. (1991). *Behavior analysis for lasting change.* Fort Worth, TX: Holt, Rinehart & Winston.

Szatmari, P., Bryson, S. E., Boyle, M. H., Streiner, D. L., & Duku, E. (2003). Predictors of outcome among high functioning children with autism and Asperger syndrome. *Journal of Child Psychology and Psychiatry, 44*(4), 520–528.

Thorpe, D. M., Stahmer, A. C., & Schreibman, L. (1995). Effects of sociodramatic play training on children with autism. *Journal of Autism and Developmental Disorders, 25*, 265–281.

U.S. Department of Health and Human Services. (1999). *Mental health: A report of the surgeon general.* Rockville, MD: Author.

Volkmar, F. R. (2000). Medical problems, treatments, and professionals. In M. D. Powers (Ed.), *Children with autism: A parent's guide* (2nd ed., pp. 67–90). Bethesda, MD: Woodbine House.

Volkmar, F. R., Koenig, K., & McCarthy, M. (2003). Autism: Diagnosis and epidemiology. In E. Hollander (Ed.), *Autism spectrum disorders* (pp. 1–14). New York: Dekker.

Wagner, A., & McGrady, K. A. (2003). Counseling and other therapeutic strategies for children with Asperger syndrome and their families. In R. W. DuCharme & T. P. Gullotta (Eds.), *Asperger syndrome: A guide for professionals and families* (pp. 83–134). New York: Kluwer Academic/Plenum.

Whalen, C., & Schreibman, L. (2003). Joint attention training for children with autism using behavior modification procedures. *Journal of Child Psychology and Psychiatry, 44*, 456–468.

World Health Organization. (1992). *International classification of diseases: Diagnostic criteria for research* (10th ed.). Geneva, Switzerland: Author.

Yeargin-Allsopp, M., Rice, C., Karapurkar, T., Doernberg, N., Boyle, C., & Murphy, C. (2003). Prevalence of autism in a U.S. metropolitan area [comment]. *Journal of the American Medical Association, 289*(1), 49–55.

Chapter 10

American Psychiatric Association Steering Committee on Practice Guidelines. (2003). *Practice guideline for the assessment and treatment of patients with suicidal behavior.* Washington, DC: Author.

Beck, A. T., Brown, G., & Steer, R. (1997). Psychometric characteristics of the scale for suicide ideation with psychiatric outpatients. *Behavior Research and Therapy, 11*, 1039–1046.

Beck, A. T., Brown, G., Steer, R., Dahlsgaard, K., & Grisham, J. (1999). Suicide ideation at its worst point: A predictor of eventual suicide in psychiatric outpatients. *Suicide and Life-Threatening Behavior, 29*(1), 1–9.

Beck, A. T., & Lester, D. (1976). Components of suicidal intent in completed and attempted suicides. *Journal of Psychology: Interdisciplinary & Applied, 92*(1), 35–38.

Berman, A. L. (1975). Self-destructive behavior and suicide: Epidemiology and taxonomy. In A. Roberts (Ed.), *Self-destructive behavior* (pp. 5–21). Springfield, IL: Thomas.

Berman, A. L., & Jobes, D. A. (1991). *Adolescent suicide assessment and intervention.* Washington, DC: American Psychological Association.

Eaton, Y. M. (2005). The comprehensive crisis intervention model of Safe Harbor Behavioral Health Crisis Services. In A. R. Roberts (Ed.), *Crisis intervention handbook: Assessment, treatment and research* (3rd ed., pp. 619–631). New York: Oxford University Press.

Eaton, Y., & Roberts, A. R. (2002). Frontline crisis intervention: Step-by-step practice guidelines with case applications. In A. R. Roberts and G. J. Greene (Eds.), *Social workers' desk reference* (pp. 89–96). New York: Oxford University Press.

Jobes, D. A., Berman, A. L., & Martin, C. (2005). Adolescent suicidality and crisis intervention. In A. R. Roberts (Ed.), *Crisis intervention handbook* (3rd ed., pp. 395–415). New York: Oxford University Press.

Kovacs, M., Beck, A. T., & Weissman, A. (1976). The communication of suicidal intent: A reexamination. *Archives of General Psychiatry, 33*(2), 198–201.

Maris, R. W., Berman, A. L., Maltsberger, J. T., & Yufit, R. I. (Eds.). (1992). *Assessment and prediction of suicide.* New York: Guilford.

Roberts, A. R. (1975). Self-destruction by one's own hand. In A. Roberts (Ed.), *Self-destructive behavior* (pp. 21–77). Springfield, IL: Thomas.

Roberts, A. R. (1991). *Contemporary perspectives on crisis intervention and prevention.* Englewood Cliffs, NJ: Prentice-Hall.

Roberts, A. R. (2000). Glossary. In A. R. Roberts (Ed.), *Crisis intervention handbook: Assessment, treatment and research* (2nd ed., pp. 513–529). New York: Oxford University Press.

Roberts, A. R. (2002). Assessment, crisis intervention and trauma treatment: The Integrative ACT Intervention Model. *Brief Treatment and Crisis Intervention, 2*(1), 1–21.

Roberts, A. R., & Yeager, K. R. (2005). Lethality assessments and crisis intervention with persons presenting with suicidal ideation. In A. R. Roberts (Ed.), *Crisis intervention handbook: Assessment, treatment and research* (3rd ed., pp. 35–63). New York: Oxford University Press.

Roberts, A. R., Yeager, K. R., & Streiner, D. L. (2004). Evidence-based practice with comorbid substance abuse, mental illness and suicidality: Can the evidence be found? *Brief Treatment and Crisis Intervention, 4*(2), 123–136.

Rudd, M., & Joiner, T. (1998). The assessment, management, and treatment of suicidality: Toward clinically informed and balanced standards of care. *Clinical Psychology: Science and Practice, 5,* 135–150.

Simon, R. I. (1992). *Psychiatry and law for clinicians.* Washington, DC: American Psychiatric Press.

U.S. Department of Health and Human Services. (2001). *National strategy for suicide prevention: Goals and objectives for action.* Rockville, MD: Author.

Weishaar, M. E. (2004). A cognitive-behavioral approach to suicide risk reduction in crisis intervention. In A. R. Roberts and K. Yeager (Eds.), *Evidence-based practice manual: Research and outcome measures in health and human services* (pp. 749–757). New York: Oxford University Press.

Yeager, K. R., & Gregoire, T. K. (2000). Crisis intervention application of brief solution-focused therapy in addictions. In A. R. Roberts (Ed.), *Crisis intervention handbook: Assessment, treatment and research* (2nd ed., pp. 275–306). New York: Oxford University Press.

Chapter 11

Chatlos, J. C. (1994). Dual diagnosis in adolescent populations. In N. S. Miller (Ed.), *Treating coexisting psychiatric and addictive disorders* (pp. 85–110). Center City, MN: Hazelden.

DeLeon, G. (2000). *The therapeutic community.* New York: Springer.

Evans, K., & Sullivan, M. (2001). *Dual diagnosis: Counseling the mentally ill substance abuser.* New York: Guilford.

Greenstein, D. D., Franklin, M. E., & McGuffin, P. (1999). Measuring motivation to change: An examination of the University of Rhode Island change assessment questionnaire (URICA) in an adolescent sample. *Psychotherapy, 36*(1), 47–55.

Henggeler, S. (1999). Multisystemic therapy: An overview of clinical procedures, outcomes, and policy implications. *Child Psychology and Psychiatric Review, 4*(1), 1–10.

Kaminer, Y., Tarter, R., & Buckstein, O. (1999). Psychotherapies for adolescent substance abusers: 15-month follow-up of a pilot study. *Journal of the American Academy of Child and Adolescent Psychiatry, 31*(6), 1046–1049.

Keys, S. (1999). School counselor's role in facilitating multisystemic change. *Professional School Counseling, 3*(2), 101–108.

Manwani, S., & Weiss, R. (2003). 5 keys to improve counseling for dual diagnosis patients: An empathic approach can be effective when treating psychiatric patients with substance use disorders. Retrieved July 14, 2004, from http://www.currentpsychiatry.com/ 2003_09/0903_counseling.asp.

Matson, J., & Bamberg, J. (1998). Reliability of assessment of dual diagnosis. *Research in Developmental Disabilities, 19*(1), 89–95.

Mee-Lee, D., Shulman, G., Fishman, M., Gastfriend, D., & Griffith, J. (2001). *ASAM patient placement criteria for the treatment of substance related disorders* (2nd ed.). Chevy Chase, MD: American Society of Addiction Medicine.

Osher, F. C., & Kofoed, L. L. (1989). Treatment of patients with psychiatric and psychoactive substance abuse disorders. *Hospital and Community Psychiatry, 40,* 1025–1030.

Rahdert, E. R. (1991). *The adolescent assessment/referral system manual* (DHHS Publication No. ADM 91–1735). Rockville, MD: National Institute on Drug Abuse.

Riggs, P. D. (2003). Treating adolescents for substance abuse and comorbid psychiatric disorders. *Science and Practice Perspectives, 2*(1), 18–32.

Roget, N. A., Fisher, G. L., & Johnson, M. L. (1998). A protocol for reducing juvenile recidivism through relapse prevention. *Journal of Addiction & Offender Counseling, 19*(1), 33–34.

Schoenwald, S., Brown, T., & Henggeler, S. (2000). Inside multisystemic therapy: Therapist, supervisor, and program practices. *Journal of Emotional and Behavioral Disorders, 8*(2), 83–104.

Substance Abuse and Mental Health Services Administration. (2002a). *Evidence-based practices for co-occurring disorders: Interventions for children and adolescents with co-occurring disorders.* Rockville, MD: U.S. Department of Health and Human Services.

Substance Abuse and Mental Health Services Administration. (2002b). *Prevention of co-occurring disorders: Prevention for children and adolescents.* Rockville, MD: U.S. Department of Health and Human Services.

Tarter, R. (1990). Evaluation and treatment of adolescent substance abuse: A decision tree method. *American Journal of Drug and Alcohol Abuse, 16,* 1–46.

U.S. Department of Health and Human Services. (1993). *Screening and assessment of alcohol- and other drug-abusing adolescents* (DHHS Publication No. ADM93–2009). Rockville, MD: Center for Substance Abuse Treatment.

Wise, B., Cuffe, S., & Fischer, D. O. (2001). Dual diagnosis and successful participation of adolescents in substance abuse treatment. *Journal of Substance Abuse Treatment, 21*(3), 161–165.

Zweben, J. E. (1994). Working with the family. In N. S. Miller (Ed.), *Treating coexisting psychiatric and addictive disorders* (pp. 213–230). Center City, MN: Hazelden.

Chapter 12

Allen-Meares, P. (1991). The contribution of social workers to schooling. In R. Constable, J. P. Flynn, & S. McDonald (Eds.), *School social work.* Chicago: Lyceum.

American Psychiatric Association. (2000). *Diagnostic and statistical manual of mental disorders (4th ed., text revision).* Washington, DC: Author.

Bentley, K. J., & Walsh, J. (2002). Social workers' roles in psychopharmacotherapy. In A. R. Roberts and G. J. Greene (Eds.), *Social workers' desk reference* (pp. 643–645). New York: Oxford University Press.

Bentley, K. J., & Walsh, J. (2006). *The social worker & psychotropic medication: Toward effective collaboration with mental health clients, families and providers* (3rd ed.). Pacific Grove, CA: Brooks/Cole-Wadsworth.

Bentley, K. J., Walsh, J., & Farmer, R. (in press). Roles and activities of clinical social workers in psychopharmacotherapy: Results of a national survey. *Social Work.*

Bond, A. L., & Lader, M. H. (1996). *Understanding drug treatment in mental health care.* West Sussex, England: John Wiley.

Brown, R., & Sammons, M. (2002). Pediatric psychopharmacology: A review of recent developments and recent research. *Professional Psychology, 33*(2), 135–147.

Center for Mental Health in Schools at UCLA. (2003). *A resource aid packet on students and psychotropic medication: The school's role.* Los Angeles: Author.

Elias, M. (2004, January 22). Antidepressants and suicide. *USA Today,* p. 7D.

Elias, M. (2005, February 5). Suicide alert has parents rethinking antidepressants. *USA Today,* p. 1A.

FDA seeks warning for depression drugs. (2004, March 22). *Richmond Times Dispatch,* p. A1.

Floersch, J. (2003). The subjective experience of youth psychotropic treatment. *Social Work in Mental Health, 1*(4), 51–69.

Greenhill, L. L., & Setterberg, S. (1993). Pharmacotherapy of disorders of adolescents. *Psychiatric Clinics of North America, 16*(4), 793–814.

Klein-Schwartz, W. (2002). Abuse and toxicity of methylphenidate. *Current Opinions in Pediatrics, 14*(2), 219–223.

Kollins, S. H., MacDonald, E. K., & Rush, C. R. (2001). Assessing abuse potential of methylphenidate in human and non-human subjects. *Pharmacology, Biochemistry and Behavior, 68*(3), 611–627.

Magno-Zito, J., Safer, D. J., DosReis, S., Gardner, J. F., Soeken, K., Boles, M., & Lynch, F. (2002). Rising prevalence of antidepressants among US youth. *Pediatrics, 108*(5), 721–727.

Musser, C. J., Ahmann, F. W., Mundt, P., Broste, S. K., & Mueller-Rizner, N. (1998). Stimulant use and the potential for abuse in Wisconsin. *Journal of Developmental and Behavioral Pediatrics, 19*(3), 187–192.

National Institute of Mental Health. (2004, June 3). *Treatment of children with mental disorders.* (NIH Publication No. NIH-04–4702). Available: http://www. nimh.nih. gov/publicat/childqa.cfm#link3.

Olfson, M., Marcus, S. C., Weissman, M. M., & Jensen, J. S. (2002). National trends in the use of psychotropic medications by children. *Journal of the American Academy of Child & Adolescent Psychiatry, 41*(5), 514–521.

Popper, C. W. (2002). Child and adolescent psychopharmacology at the turn of the millennium In S. Kutcher (Ed.), *Practical child and child psychopharmacology* (p. 137). Cambridge: Cambridge University Press.

Rutter, M. (2000). Psychosocial influences: critiques, findings, and research needs. *Developmental Psychopathology, 12*(3), 375–405.

Rutter, M. (2002). The interplay of nature, nurture, and developmental influences. *Archives of General Psychiatry, 59*(11), 996–1000.

Sood, A. B. (2004, May 14). *Controversy of the millennium: Drugging of America's children or catalysts for healthy minds.* Keynote address, 42nd Annual Child Psychiatry Spring Forum, Virginia Commonwealth University, Richmond, VA.

Thomson Healthcare. (2003). *PDR health.* Available: http://www.pdrhealth.com/index.html.

U.S. Department of Health and Human Services. (1999). *Mental health: A report of the surgeon general.* Rockville, MD: Author.

Why give kids drugs without pediatric testing. (2002, April 8). *USA Today,* p. 12A.

Wilens, T. E. (1999). *Straight talk about psychiatric medication for kids.* New York: Guilford.

Wilens, T. E., & Wozniak, J. (2003). Bipolar disorder in children and adolescents: Diagnostic and therapeutic issues, *Psychiatric Times, 20*(8). Accessed through http://www.psychiatrictimes.com/p030855.html

Index

Note: Page numbers in *italics* refer to boxes, figures, and tables

CPSIA information can be obtained
at www.ICGtesting.com
Printed in the USA
BVHW04s2348080918
526945BV00003B/9/P

9 780195 370584